"An elegant synthesis of ancient wisdom [...] f
powerful insights and practical tools, this [...]
not just for acceptance and commitment [...] r
anyone with an interest in compassion. Highly recommended!"

—**Russ Harris**, author of *The Happiness Trap* and *ACT Made Simple*

"*The ACT Practitioner's Guide to the Science of Compassion* by Tirch, Schoendorff, and Silberstein is an excellent integration of acceptance and commitment therapy (ACT) and compassion-focused therapy (CFT). User-friendly and filled with insights and clinical examples, this book will open new possibilities in therapy. Highly recommended."

—**Robert Leahy, PhD**, director of the American Institute for
Cognitive Therapy

"This is a truly unique book that examines the points of intersection between acceptance and commitment therapy (ACT) and other approaches to mindfulness and self-compassion. While having a remarkable level of detail and theoretical sophistication, the book also provides case examples and easy, practical techniques to help therapists integrate compassion practice into their work with clients in a meaningful way."

—**Kristin Neff, PhD**, associate professor in educational psychology
at the University of Texas at Austin, TX, pioneering researcher
into the mental health benefits of self-compassion, and author of
Self-Compassion

"This is the book I've waited for—a guide that melds acceptance and commitment therapy (ACT) processes with the transformative power of compassion. Values, defusion, committed action, self-as-context—every component of ACT is strengthened as we learn to access and use compassion."

—**Matthew McKay, PhD**, coauthor of *Your Life on Purpose*

"Compassion is a defining aspect of humanity that contributed to the survival of our species. In addition, compassion is one of the common elements of all world religions and at the heart of clinical practice. In this remarkable volume, Tirch, Schoendorff, and Silberstein examine the many aspects of compassion within the context of modern cognitive behavioral therapy (CBT). Highly accessible, this remarkable book provides clinicians with concrete recommendations to cultivate compassion and implement it into clinical practice. This book is a must-read."

—**Stefan G. Hofmann, PhD**, professor of psychology at Boston University, MA, and author of *An Introduction to Modern CBT: Psychological Solutions to Mental Health Problems*

"Evolutionary science is providing us with a deeper understanding of the centrality of connection in human well-being. As result, the science of compassion is growing dramatically and compassion is taking a critical place in the study and practice of empirical clinical psychology. Tirch, Schoendorff, and Silberstein provide welcome guidance for clinicians interested in a more explicit focus on compassion in their work."

—**Kelly G. Wilson, PhD**, associate professor of psychology at the University of Mississippi, MS, and coauthor of *Acceptance and Commitment Therapy*

"This comprehensive compendium on compassion will satisfy practitioners who hunger for theory and conceptual analysis, as well as those who want innovative and step-by-step treatment tools. This book belongs in the library of any clinician who wants to deepen the impact of their therapeutic relationships using not only their intellect, but their heart."

—**Mavis Tsai, PhD**, coauthor of *Functional Analytic Psychotherapy: Creating Intensive and Curative Therapeutic Relationships* and senior research scientist and director of the FAP Specialty Clinic in the Psychological Services and Training Center at the University of Washington, WA

"Compassion is one of—if not the most—powerful antidotes to human suffering. More than 2,600 years of collective wisdom and a decade of psychological research teaches us why that is so. But why is compassion so elusive? How do we harness the power of compassion to alleviate forms of human suffering and to promote psychological health? This intriguing, insightful, and immensely practical book offers answers to these and other questions, and will show you how to put compassion into action. Though written with acceptance and commitment therapy (ACT) practitioners in mind, this book goes into territory that can be readily adapted within any form of mental health practice. I am grateful to the authors for giving us this clinically rich book. It is a gift and a must-read for all mental health professionals."

—**John P. Forsyth, PhD**, professor of psychology and director of the Anxiety Disorders Research Program at the University at Albany, NY, and coauthor of *Acceptance and Commitment Therapy for Anxiety Disorders, The Mindfulness and Acceptance Workbook for Anxiety, ACT on Life Not on Anger*, and *Your Life on Purpose*

"From my first encounter with acceptance and commitment therapy (ACT) to my romps with functional analytic psychotherapy (FAP) and compassion-focused therapy (CFT), I have felt an inherent pulse of compassion in the processes and interventions that are built into these psychotherapeutic approaches. In *The ACT Practitioner's Guide to the Science of Compassion*, the authors bring together theory, science, and application in a way that easily guides the clinician to understanding compassion and its place in the contextual behavioral therapies, while also weaving the cloth of engagement and flexibility into deepening the sense of connection to others and what it means to be human. An essential read for all those determined to create a more compassionate world!"

—**Robyn D. Walser, PhD**, associate clinical professor at the University of California, Berkeley, CA, and associate director for the National Center for PTSD, Dissemination and Training Division

"A growing body of research shows that cultivating compassion is good for us, and an increasing number of therapists are looking to bring compassion work into their practice. Tirch, Schoendorff, and Silberstein skillfully teach us how to do this. Filled with solid science and pragmatic clinical instruction, this book gives clinicians a powerful repertoire of clinical strategies reflecting a skillful integration of compassion-focused therapy (CFT) and acceptance and commitment therapy (ACT). Highly recommended for the ACT practitioner, the CFT practitioner, or any mental health professional looking to bring compassion into the therapy room."

—**Russell Kolts, PhD,** professor of psychology at Eastern Washington University and author of several books, including *The Compassionate-Mind Guide to Managing Your Anger*

The ACT Practitioner's Guide

to the

Science *of* Compassion

Tools for Fostering Psychological Flexibility

DENNIS TIRCH, PhD

BENJAMIN SCHOENDORFF, MA, MSc

LAURA R. SILBERSTEIN, PsyD

New Harbinger Publications, Inc.

Publisher's Note

This publication is designed to provide accurate and authoritative information in regard to the subject matter covered. It is sold with the understanding that the publisher is not engaged in rendering psychological, financial, legal, or other professional services. If expert assistance or counseling is needed, the services of a competent professional should be sought.

Distributed in Canada by Raincoast Books

Copyright © 2014 by Dennis Tirch, Benjamin Schoendorff, and Laura Silberstein
      New Harbinger Publications, Inc.
      5674 Shattuck Avenue
      Oakland, CA 94609
      www.newharbinger.com

Cover design by Amy Shoup
Acquired by Tesilya Hanauer
Edited by Jasmine Star

Library of Congress Cataloging-in-Publication Data

Tirch, Dennis D., 1968- , author.
  The ACT practitioner's guide to the science of compassion : tools for fostering psychological flexibility / Dennis Tirch, Benjamin Schoendorff, and Laura R. Silberstein.
     p. ; cm.
  Includes bibliographical references and index.
  Summary: "An important addition to any ACT professional's library, The ACT Practitioner's Guide to the Science of Compassion explores the emotionally healing benefits of compassion-based practices when applied to traditional acceptance and commitment therapy (ACT). This book offers case conceptualization, assessments, and direct clinical applications that integrate ACT, functional analytic psychotherapy (FAP), and the science of compassion to enhance therapists' processes. The book also explores how these modalities work in harmony, ultimately making ACT more effective in increasing client psychological flexibility"--Provided by publisher.
  ISBN 978-1-62625-055-0 (paperback : alk. paper) -- ISBN 978-1-62625-056-7 (PDF e-book) -- ISBN 978-1-62625-057-4 (ePub)
  I. Schoendorff, Benjamin, author. II. Silberstein, Laura R., author. III. Title.
  [DNLM: 1. Acceptance and Commitment Therapy--methods. 2. Empathy. WM 425.5.C6]
  RC489.A32
  616.89'1425--dc23
                  2014033244

Printed in the United States of America

22   21   20

10   9   8   7   6   5   4   3

For a true friend and mentor, Professor Paul Gilbert, PhD, OBE.

—Dennis Tirch

To my infinitely beloved wife, Marie-France, son, Thomas, and stepdaughters, Ariane and Camille, for so patiently and consistently coaching me to practice the walk behind the talk.

—Benjamin Schoendorff

Dedicated to two women who personified compassion and lived love: Marge and Esta.

—Laura Silberstein

Contents

Foreword

The last ten years have seen a proliferation of interest in the scientific study of compassion. Given that Buddhism argued that the cultivation of compassion is central to the well-being of self and others over 2,500 years ago, some would say "about time"! Yet when William Tuke established one of the first therapeutic communities at the York Retreat in 1796, he purposely tried to create a compassionate, supportive environment. The medical historian Roy Porter (2002) says "Tuke's grandson Samuel noted that medical therapies had initially been tried there with little success; the Retreat had then abandoned 'medical' for 'moral' means, kindness, mildness, reason, and humanity, all within a family atmosphere—with excellent results" (p. 104).

However, until recently, compassion has not fared well as a scientific focus in psychotherapy. Although Carl Rogers identified core ingredients of the therapeutic relationship based on empathy and positive regard, the idea of the "compassionate therapeutic relationship" was always rather vague, while the deliberate cultivation of compassion for self and others in our clients as a therapeutic aim is entirely new (Gilbert, 2009a, 2010). The early psychodynamic formulations of Freudians focused on the darker side of humanity—sexuality and violence— and compassion was but a sublimation of these (Kriegman 1990, 2000). Behaviorists were interested in exposure to what we fear, and cognitive therapies were keen to help us our address our irrational thinking.

Today, however, psychotherapists are beginning to look anew at the concept of compassion and its therapeutic potential. Part of this is because compassion has gained scientific acceptability. This was especially inspired by neuroscientists working with the Dalai Lama and studying what happens in the brain when people practice compassion (Lutz, Brefczynski-Lewis, Johnstone, & Davidson, 2008). A second major impetus for the integration of compassion in therapy has come from the increasing recognition of the evolved nature and importance of attachment, which is rooted in competencies for parents to be sensitive to the distress of their infants and have the ability to respond to that stress, and for infants to be responsive to that care (Mikulincer & Shaver, 2007b). A third influence is the growing evidence that prosocial behavior, affection, affiliation, and a sense of belonging and connectedness with others all have major impacts on mental well-being (Cacioppo & Patrick, 2008) and on many physiological processes (Cozolino, 2007), including genetic expression (Slavich & Cole, 2013). In fact, there is good evidence now to suggest that humans function at their best when they feel valued, loved, and cared for, and when they in turn can be valuing and caring of others (Gilbert & Choden, 2013). So affiliative relationships are the center of well-being, and it's rather surprising that psychotherapists have been so slow in looking at the processes by which affiliative emotion is created, is shared, and heals.

Against this growing research interest in affiliative, prosocial, and compassionate behavior, many therapies now are beginning to think about the nature and therapeutic potential of compassion. It is therefore timely that acceptance and commitment therapy (ACT), as one of the major new schools of psychotherapy, is also beginning to consider the nature and value of compassion within its own context. ACT has always seen the therapeutic relationship as central to the therapeutic journey (Pierson & Hayes, 2007), but it is comparatively recently that compassion itself has become a focus of interest. So, what better guides to have for the ACT therapist to begin the journey into compassion than Drs. Dennis Tirch, Laura Silberstein, and Benjamin Schoendorff? Dr. Tirch not only is an experienced and world-recognized ACT therapist, he has trained in compassion-focused therapy (CFT; Gilbert 2009a, 2010) and been involved with Buddhist practice for many, many years. He has established The Compassionate Mind Foundation USA (http://www.compassionfocusedtherapy .com) and The Center for Mindfulness and CFT (http://www.mindfulcompas sion.com), both of which seek to further training, research, and development of CFT in North America. Dr. Schoendorff is an internationally known expert in and trainer of ACT and functional analytic psychotherapy (FAP) who emphasizes training self-compassion in the psychotherapeutic relationship. Dr.

Silberstein is an expert in the role of emotions in psychological flexibility and has been researching, practicing, and writing about the integration of CFT, Buddhist psychology, and ACT throughout her career. These authors bring unique scholarship and wisdom to offer important insights into the different models of ACT, FAP, CFT, and more, with rich and innovative ideas on how these approaches can be integrated in bringing compassion into therapeutic focus.

Compassion is easily misunderstood and confused with love and kindness. In fact, the hardest but most powerful forms of compassion are for things we neither love nor like, and this includes such things in ourselves. In the Mahayana Buddhist tradition, for which the Dalai Lama is one of the most powerful advocates, the core of compassion is motivation—the motivation to be of benefit to others—called *bodhicitta*. This motivation is to cultivate one's ability to be sensitive and attentionally and emotionally attuned to the suffering in self and others, able to see into its causes and to acquire the wisdom and commitment to try to alleviate and prevent it. Captured here is obviously the motivation to turn toward suffering, into its wind, rather than away from it; to cultivate a willingness to engage with suffering and its causes. Here we see an immediate resonance with ACT, which since its inception has focused so elegantly on the issue of emotional avoidance and on creating a willingness to experience things as they are. More importantly, however, in both CFT and ACT, compassion is made a therapeutic focus not just for the relief of suffering but for the promotion of well-being. This is partly why CFT pays a lot of attention to the underlying dynamics of attachment and affiliative behavior. Compassion as a therapeutic focus must be about *promoting* well-being, not just reducing suffering.

While CFT has sought to illuminate some of the key constituents of compassion—such as care-focused motivation, attentional sensitivity, sympathy, distress tolerance, empathy, and nonjudgment—and to help people cultivate these attributes, ACT has focused more on principles of liberating people from the tangles the mind can weave. These tangles arise because in addition to basic motives and emotions that we share with other animals, about 2 million years ago humans evolved capacities for imagination, rumination, a sense of self, and self-monitoring. The way these newly evolved cognitive competencies integrate and *fuse* with older emotion motivational systems is a central concern for ACT. Essential to helping people disengage from aversive self-monitoring and self-labeling that have become *fused* with painful emotions is the cultivation of what ACT calls *psychological flexibility*. Like compassion, this concept is not a straightforward one; it is really an outcome of a number of sub-processes such as defusion, values, self-as-context, acceptance, committed action, and mindfulness.

So Tirch, Schoendorff, and Silberstein set themselves the task of considering how the different processes of compassion and psychological flexibility relate to each other and how each can be considered from the other's perspective. The aim is not to collapse one model into another but to illuminate how ACT can address the phenomenology of compassion in its own terms. The result is an innovative and thought-provoking narrative on new ways of cultivating compassion, or at least creating the conditions for it to arise. So if ACT practitioners want to think about how they can bring compassion center ground in ACT terms, here is a way of doing so.

CFT suggests that the healing qualities of compassion are rooted in particular states of mind that recruit core physiological systems that evolved in part alongside attachment, altruism, and caring behavior (Gilbert, 2009a)—oxytocin and the myelinated vagus nerve of the parasympathetic nervous system being two such systems. So CFT involves breath training, mindfulness, imagery, and body-focusing work. CFT also uses method acting techniques to practice *acting as if...*, and *imagining oneself to be* a compassionate person (Gilbert, 2010), which help clients to build a self-identity around the core attributes of compassion. This sense of self then becomes the focus—the secure base and safe haven, to use attachment terms—from which we can engage with suffering.

ACT derives its theoretical nutrients from behavioral research, and it does not call on attachment theory or focus on any specific underlying physiological mechanisms that may create a calmer, wiser, more affiliative mind. Although ACT also sees compassion as rooted in ancient evolved systems of mind, it places its evolutionary emphasis on cooperation, rather than caring. For ACT, the advantages of cooperation created evolutionary pressures that enhanced human beings' abilities to cooperate. Obvious ones were verbal communication and languages open to the use of symbols as representations of the world. So, words and symbols became signifiers that allowed people to share knowledge, concepts, and learning. But none of that could arise without people having a fundamental interest in each other and a desire to share, as well as to take some joy in the sharing. In ACT it was the evolution of human language and the symbolic and verbal representations it enabled that opened the door to fusion; that is to say, symbolic and verbal representations could become fused with a person's sense of self. By contrast, a monkey that experienced threat from a dominant and responded submissively would not have the linguistic or symbolic capacity to begin to think of *itself* as inferior and subordinate or consider the consequences of that experience for its life and relationships with other monkeys—indeed, it wouldn't have a sense of self in this sense. So as you will see, this book has a lot of focus on the concept of verbal labeling, since that is an ability unique to humans.

This is not unimportant in CFT, but less important, because CFT is more focused on direct experience and would be interested in the "emotional scenes in the mind" and the emotional memories associated with feelings of inferiority, rather than their verbal labeling. For instance, in the case of shame: If a parent is angry with a child, the child lays down memories of self (*conditioned emotional learning*) as stimulating anger in others. This is coded as an "emotional scene," and such emotional scenes become the basis for subsequent self-definition. So an individual who has experienced anger from a parent (and may also have verbally labeled them as inadequate or bad) may talk about feeling inadequate or vulnerable to criticism. But actually the key is they are indicating that "In my emotional memory, I have experienced myself as inadequate and as the target of others' anger" (Gilbert, 2009c). In CFT, it is trying to illuminate these powerful emotional experiences, which can be seen in classical conditioning learning terms, that is central, rather than exploring verbal labels to experience. So a CFT practitioner would inquire when that individual first thought of herself like that and what early scenes come to mind when she talks about herself in that way.

Importantly, however, ACT is the most prominent therapy exploring the way our newly evolved cognitive competencies for symbolization, mentalizing, developing a self-identity, and having the self-as-context play significant roles in determining our vulnerability to mental health difficulties. The way ACT choreographs these important evolutionary adaptations in the human line in a story of compassion is innovative, and again, Tirch, Schoendorff, and Silberstein provide excellent guidance.

These authors offer many clinical examples which helpfully guide the ACT therapist and also offer important points of contrast between ACT and CFT. For example, in CFT, shame and self-criticism are seen to be at the root of many psychological difficulties, but they in turn are rooted in real and feared experiences of social loss and rejection. Behind self-criticism are the fears of the abused, marginalized, and forgotten, and fueling them are painful emotional memories. Indeed, CFT was partly born out of efforts to work with these ways of thinking and feeling about oneself. CFT notes that Freud had two basic theories of self-criticism. One was that self-criticism arose from the internalization of the critical voice of the parent, sometimes referred to as superego prohibition. The other was that it was anger turned inward, whereby people became critical of themselves rather than directing anger towards others whom they needed in some way. The treatment of these may be quite different, with the latter requiring some engagement with repressed and avoided rage (Busch, 2009); but for each case, the fear of giving up self-criticism is central (Tierney & Fox, 2010). Indeed, many therapies now have their ways of working with self-criticism because it's potentially so disruptive to well-being (Kannan & Levitt, 2013). In CFT we develop compassion to develop the courage to engage with the difficult stuff, which includes some of the darker aspects of our minds. Indeed, CFT suggests that the emotions that don't turn up in the therapy can be ones the client is frightened of, and the ones that require the most work. For example, a depressed person might be quite confident in talking about his sadness and sense of loss but not about the rage he feels for the parent who failed to protect him or love him as he needed or wanted. Similarly, the angry person may be quite happy to rage about the world but entirely out of touch with the sense of loss and loneliness that hides real grief and pain. ACT therapists will be very familiar with experiential avoidance and the idea that one emotion can be a safety strategy to hide another emotion. The ACT therapist treating the angry person might ask "I see you are angry right now, but if I was to peel back the anger, what might I see behind it?" (Robyn Walser, personal communication, 2012).

However, when exploring self-criticism, ACT also places a central focus on the verbal construction of experience. Time and again in the clinical anecdotes we see this focusing on verbal representations. As the authors of this book write, "Understanding the verbal processes that lie at the root of self-hatred and reinforce it can help clinicians devise targeted interventions that can gradually undermine self-critical behavior and foster a more compassionate approach to how hard it is to live in this world" (p. 91). This makes it clear how ACT sees "verbal experience" and labeling as being at the root of self-hatred. In ACT, we verbally create representations of ourselves out of the experiences that we have had; ACT focuses on the words people use to describe their experience.

Meanwhile, CFT would focus on in-the-body experience, the actual memories that created this experience, and fear of changing an identity of being a shameful, self-critical person. In some of the later clinical chapters, the authors draw heavily from the CFT approach, offering ACT practitioners many new ways of creating compassion and utilizing its therapeutic potential. Central there is the fact that the "compassionate self" CFT encourages individuals to build helps them access the inner courage and wisdom necessary to begin to work with difficult aspects of the mind, be they anger, anxiety, or trauma.

This book shows how ACT practitioners can bring their own unique version of compassion into the therapeutic process, even to the degree that it can become a core value. At some point, of course, we will need to do further research to see how different models of compassion and their therapeutic strategies compare. But for the moment, endeavors to understand and cultivate compassion are vitally important. This is not just because we desperately need better ways to understand and help those seeking our support but because compassion is crucial to the creation of a better world. The more deeply we understand compassion and how to cultivate it in our schools, businesses, and politics, the greater the chance is that those yet to be born will arrive in a fairer, more just, and caring world. Tirch, Schoendorff, and Silberstein offer us a fascinating and remarkable book to help us on that journey. They've written the book in a spirit of real encouragement and enthusiasm for the potential of improving our therapies. As such, it makes a significant contribution to the ongoing journey to understand and find ways to better help patients.

—Paul Gilbert, PhD, FBPsS, OBE

Building a Cooperative, Caring, and Productive Relationship: ACT and CFT as a Test Case

There is an interesting juxtaposition between the human issues of acceptance and compassion on the one hand and the scientific relationship between acceptance and commitment therapy (ACT) and compassion-focused therapy (CFT) on the other. In order to build quality human relationships, it is important that these relationships be based on understanding and caring. We have to be able to see the world through the eyes of the other person, with genuineness and openness take the time to feel what it might feel like to be that other person, and then not run away—perhaps even step forward—when what we see is painful or difficult.

The skills needed to do these things are essential to the construction of cooperative, caring, and productive human relationships. And success in these processes predicts the degrees to which people enjoy being with each other and avoid the objectification and dehumanization of others. Finally, when challenges to that success are overcome, each party to the relationship is changed by it.

It is relatively easy to care about and take the perspectives of people who are just like us; it is harder with people who seem to be different. Both the challenge and the importance of compassion are greatest when the divisions between people are greatest.

In a parallel way, when dealing with the relationship between two scientific traditions, productive relationships are based on the ability to take the perspective of the other tradition and to take the time to understand what it is that's being said, even when this is hard. As in human relationships more generally, that is most important precisely when differences in background and assumptions exist.

It seems to me that this book reveals how profoundly these two different scientific perspectives, ACT and CFT, have taken the time to understand each other over the last several years. When we look at ACT and CFT side-by-side, we are looking at two perspectives with fairly different scientific backgrounds. ACT developed inside the functional contextual wing of behavioral psychology. CFT, conversely, grew out of developmental psychology, affective neuroscience, Buddhist practical philosophy, and evolutionary theory. Despite that fact, ACT and CFT have an overlap that is so great now that it is almost impossible for contemporary practitioners of either to avoid the other. The issue of compassion is now crucial to ACT and the issue of psychological flexibility is increasingly relevant to CFT. And each party to this scientific relationship is being changed by it.

This book presents the issue of compassion for ACT practitioners, but not just that. It also presents the importance of psychological flexibility processes for CFT practitioners. Careful and comprehensive, this book is a kind of extended exercise that demonstrates the mutual benefit each tradition can have for the other.

The issue the book addresses is critical. At the level of psychological process, it turns out that compassion is integral to psychological flexibility. Indeed, it is arguably essential.

In the earlier days of ACT development, this was not obvious, but it has been for several years now. A person with good perspective-taking abilities and empathy will feel pain when seeing the pain of others. This means that in order for me to reject care and concern toward you when you are in pain, I would have to reject my own feelings; to be non-compassionate, I have to be non-accepting. Compassion and acceptance are two faces of the same issue. It is not possible for me to be truly accepting of myself as a human being if I'm rejecting of you as a human being. In a similar way, it is not possible for me to be truly compassionate toward you if I show no compassion toward myself. We have an essential bond in our common humanity which projects into our very consciousness and verbal abilities.

Just as in a profoundly intimate and caring human relationship each party is changed, so too, in the handful of years in which topics of this kind have been central, have ACT and CFT moved closer and closer to each other. The linkage of each perspective to evolutionary thinking has increased a working alliance between ACT and CFT. CFT emphasizes the importance of cooperation and social inclusion to the fundamental neurobiology of stress. In contextual behavioral science, it's been argued that concern for others and cooperation were fundamental to the development of basic relational-framing skills—that verbal meaning is a cooperative act of perspective taking.

You can see this process of the two traditions moving closer to each other in the present volume. As I read this book, at times it was hard to say where ACT left off and CFT began, and vice versa. At the level of issues, technology, and focus, these therapeutic perspectives are now fellow travelers embarked on a common journey, and likely with a common fate.

This book will profoundly change ACT practitioners who have not already come to view compassion as a central topic in their work. And those ACT practitioners who do know that compassion is key will be empowered by detailed, step-by-step knowledge of how to integrate the two. I think the same can be said for CFT practitioners who are not necessarily clear about the value of psychological flexibility.

Given the deep interconnections that are developing between these perspectives, what is the likely end of this process? At this point we cannot say. But we can say that compassion work is now central to ACT practice, and that ACT practitioners look to CFT to help them apply evidence-based methods in this area. That sense of coming together is not very different than that which manifests in profound human relationships in general. When human beings meet each other with openness, cooperation, and caring, life moves in new directions. Where it will go we do not know—but it promises to be both exciting and productive. This scientific relationship is much the same.

The reader can test the value of the emerging relationship of ACT and CFT easily enough. This book will provide you with a test case: you. Your work. Your clients' progress.

As I just said: It promises to be both exciting and productive.

—Steven C. Hayes, PhD

Acknowledgments

Firstly, my deep gratitude and appreciation goes out to my coauthors. Benji, you are a true spiritual brother. Laura, you will always be my one true and most beloved partner in our shared life's work. Freelance copyeditor Jasmine Star and Tesilya Hanauer, our editor at New Harbinger, were remarkable allies and collaborators in this work, and they have my ongoing gratitude. I would like to acknowledge the intellectual and spiritual mentors whom I have been blessed to know, including Paul Gilbert, Robert Fripp, Robert Leahy, Kelly Wilson, Steven C. Hayes, Robyn Walser, Richard Amodio, Lillian Firestone, Paul Genki Kahn, Michael Hughes, Jim Campilongo, and Stephen K. Hayes. My gratitude goes out to all of my trusted colleagues, especially Russell Kolts, Chris Irons, Martin Brock, Laura Oliff, Poonam Melwani, Louise McHugh, M. Joann Wright, Aisling Curtain, Nanni Presti, Josh Pritchard, Louise Hayes, Christine Braehler, Mia Sage, Victoria Taylor, Nikki Rubin, Jennifer Taitz, Yotam Heineberg, Kristin Neff, Meredith Rayner, Margherita Gurrieri, Sonja Batten, Mark Sisti, Tara Deliberto, Chris Germer, Brian Pilecki, Jason Luoma, Ross White, Stanislaw Malicki, Mike Femenella, Trent Codd III, James Bennett Levy, and Christian Chan. Laura's family, the Silbersteins, was also a great source of strength during our work. I would like to thank my wonderful mother and family, especially my brother, John, and his miraculously supportive wife and children. I would like to acknowledge the help and support of our friends as we prepared this book, particularly Jean Gilbert, Philip Inwood, Nicholas Colavito, and Torrey Kleinman. Also, I want to send good wishes to all of the clients who have walked this compassionate path with us over the years. Finally, I would like to express my gratitude to our spiritual ancestors, who are innumerable and represent the evolution that we hold so dear. For our purposes today, I would like to acknowledge, with deep love and respect, Shakyamuni Buddha and George Ivanovich Gurdjieff.

—Dennis Tirch

I would like to acknowledge Dennis Tirch for codreaming this book with Laura and me, and for doing most of the hard work of manifesting this beautiful dream. Dennis, you're a star. I wrote to you, as a joke, that a fair acknowledgment for this book might run to fifty pages. Compassion is a lifelong project, and when I look at my path on its road, I can see many significant faces—those of countless allies, whether we met in sympathy or hostility. To all those I have ever met, chances are you played a part in my becoming interested in and imperfectly walking the compassionate path. Gratitude to Sharon Salzberg for introducing me to loving-kindness; Steven Hayes for putting compassion at the heart of ACT; Kelly Wilson for that deepest of ongoing conversations; Rachel Collis, Michaele Saban, and Jonathan Kanter for showing it; and Mavis Tsai and Monica Valentim for being it. I acknowledge the deep influence of every one of my clients, supervisees, and ACT training colleagues, with special mention to Kevin Polk, Jerold Hambright, and Mark Webster for dreaming up the ACT matrix. Gratitude to the clients who allowed extracts of our sessions to be used in this book, for their courage and generosity. Gratitude to Tesilya Hanauer, freelancer Jasmine Star, and all at New Harbinger. Finally, gratitude to my wife, Marie-France, for her unwavering support through diverse writing projects, and to my son, Thomas, for being such an inexhaustible fount of joy, wonder, and gratitude.

—Benjamin Schoendorff

I am delighted to have the opportunity to express my warmest appreciation to coauthors Dennis and Benji. Dennis, your talent, patience, and capacity for caring know no bounds. Thank you for your unwavering partnership and our shared enthusiasm, and for reminding me to take time. Benji, I am truly grateful for the opportunity to work with you and to learn from your profound kindness and warmth. My heartfelt gratitude goes out to those who have taught me the nuance and skill involved in giving and receiving compassion: Paul Gilbert, Thomas Bein, James Cardinale, Robert Woolfolk, Leslie Allen, Shara Sand, Kelly Wilson, Steven Hayes, Jack Kornfield, Sharon Salzberg, Robert Leahy, and Lata McGinn. I want to thank my friends and fellow travelers for their encouragement and contributions to the science of compassion: Russell Kolts, Christine Braehler, Wendy Wood, Chris Irons, Chris Germer, Kristin Neff, Tom Borkovec, M. Joann Wright, Aisling Curtain, Louise McHugh, Josh Pritchard, Louise Hayes, Nanni Presti, Meredith Rayner, Margherita Gurrieri, Sonja Batten, David Gillanders, Mike Femenella, Mark Sisti, Brian Pilecki, Jennifer Egert, Jennifer Lerner, Lauren Whitelaw, and Sara Reichenbach. I would also like to acknowledge my parents and sister. Mom, you have shown me what true grace, warmth, and unconditional love look and feel like. Dad, your wisdom, strength, and courage are a constant source of awe and inspiration. Erica Beth, your sensitivity, brilliance, and wit are my compass home. Finally, I want to thank my family of families, especially the Young, Fritz, Kondo, Tirch, Ewig, Mann, Samuels, Flax, and ACBS families. Your support came in many forms over the years, and I thank you for all your encouragement, time, acceptance, insight, laughter, and love.

—Laura Silberstein

Introduction

Our human compassion binds us the one to the other, not in pity or patronizingly, but as human beings who have learnt how to turn our common suffering into hope for the future.

—Nelson Mandela

We're all going to die, all of us, what a circus! That alone should make us love each other but it doesn't. We are terrorized and flattened by trivialities, we are eaten up by nothing.

—Charles Bukowski

The education of a psychotherapist begins when he or she is a toddler and is first able to recognize the difference between "I" and "you." It continues as we learn how the pain of others may cause us to feel pain. And it goes on (through the pain of graduate school) to become a lifelong journey of cultivating knowledge, compassion, and even some wisdom. For many of us, intensive, workshop-based training is one of the more engaging aspects of our continuing education in cognitive and behavioral therapies, such as acceptance and commitment therapy (ACT; Hayes, Strosahl, & Wilson, 1999), compassion-focused therapy (CFT; Gilbert, 2009a), and functional analytic psychotherapy (FAP; Kohlenberg & Tsai, 1991). Participants ask a lot of themselves in these trainings, engaging with a considerable amount of conceptual material and, more importantly, working with their own emotions and personal history of suffering. Our work as psychotherapists asks us to step into difficult emotional spaces with our fellow human beings. Total strangers are willing to come to us, with courage or perhaps in desperation, looking for some way to alleviate or prevent the suffering they experience. They want to stop putting their lives on hold and start engaging more deeply with the world. Importantly, they are suffering, and they wish to find some relief.

At the beginning of a weekend workshop in CFT, we often pause and invite our fellow clinicians to rest in the breath, drop into the present moment, and gently move into a space of mindful awareness. From that collected and kind attentional space, we reflect and remember that whenever we are referring to a "case," we are speaking about an *actual person*. Each clinical example emanates from a real human being, who, just like us, has known ambition and loss, joy and regret—a person who wishes to be happy. We'd like to pause in the same way now, as we begin this book. Together, let us all remember our connection to our clients and to each other. The essence of compassion in ACT, and in life, resides in this sensitivity to and awareness of the suffering we all carry, and a deep motivation to take action to alleviate and prevent the suffering we encounter in the world. This definition of compassion has ancient origins and current relevance; found in pre-Buddhist wisdom traditions, it has been carried through the Western intellectual tradition and is now emerging in twenty-first-century CFT.

Throughout this book, we will cover technical and philosophical ground that may be challenging. We will encounter and reflect upon clinical applications and exchanges that require bringing the best version of ourselves into the consultation room. By reading this book, you will engage in committed action to further develop your abilities in your role as a healer, teacher, or guide. We have committed our time and care to bringing the best of ourselves to this book and the work herein. Together, let us all honor the work we are engaging in as therapists, writers, readers, and clients—roles we have probably all held at one point or another—as we begin to approach a compassion-focused ACT.

Those acquainted with the evolution of psychotherapy in the early twenty-first century may know ACT as a popular form of mindfulness-oriented, evidence-based therapy. Perhaps it is even a "third wave behavioral therapy," as is sometimes said. However, for those who have been involved with the emergence of ACT over the last fifteen years, ACT is much more. It encompasses a philosophy of science that raises key questions about what we can and cannot know about the nature of truth and reality. It is grounded in a behavioral theory of language that challenges us to think differently about how we make mental connections among our experiences. Importantly, ACT also is a community, on an international level, with common purposes. The continuous cultural discussion that thrives in ACT training workshops, international conferences, supervision groups, and e-mail lists is a central and dynamic aspect of the ACT community. In recent years, intense interest has been percolating in all of these settings, including interest in the nature of human compassion and how ACT practitioners can engage compassion to help alleviate the suffering they encounter in their clients and in themselves. Metaphorically, the global ACT community is a family, and this family has begun to talk about how it can act more compassionately and, in that way, contribute to a more compassionate world.

In a recent e-mail discussion, the common topic of how ACT relates to Buddhism was raised, and many people responded, ACT cofounder Steven C. Hayes among them. For all of the common ground between Buddhist practices and ACT, such as mindfulness and an emphasis on the observing self, Hayes raised an important point of distinction. To paraphrase his response, he noted how application of the scientific method and ongoing research into fundamental psychological processes allows the ACT community, and Western scientists more generally, to engage in a focused and pragmatic strategy for developing empirical knowledge—a strategy that leads to a more rapid refinement of methods. The evolution of the ACT community's approach to human suffering can, in essence, progress and change as we gain a better understanding of our theory and technique. As we approach compassion from an ACT perspective, this empirical lens, grounded in functional contextualism, will open up new ways of seeing and knowing, along with new techniques and new possibilities for our clients.

Methods from CFT, FAP, and other compassion-informed disciplines serve as key elements in the work of bringing a focus on compassion to ACT. This provides both opportunities and challenges, as is so often true in our work at the frontier of applied psychological science. For example, when ACT practitioners encounter CFT, they find much that is familiar and encouraging, as well as clear distinctions between these approaches. CFT, originally developed by Paul Gilbert (2010) to better address shame-based difficulties across a range of diagnoses, is a form of evidence-based therapy that specifically targets the cultivation of compassion. Key processes, such as mindfulness, willingness, disidentification with mental events, and committed action in the service of valued aims, are present in both ACT and CFT. This allows ACT practitioners to deploy their clinical wisdom in bringing a focus on compassion to their work.

CFT strongly emphasizes a particular valued direction and motivation, for both therapist and client: developing the capacity for awareness of suffering and the motivation and ability to alleviate or prevent the suffering we encounter. ACT, on the other hand, has an implicit emphasis on compassion that is emergent in its model; however, compassion has not historically been the central feature of the therapy or prescribed as a necessary valued aim. In a sense, the emphasis on mindfulness processes rather than compassion in the ACT literature to date, relative to the CFT literature, mirrors the contrast of emphasis between the Theravada and Mahayana schools of Buddhism. Historically, the Theravada approach, which is older, suggests that compassion arises out of mindfulness itself, with an emphasis on vipassana meditation and ethical action in the world, whereas the Mahayana and Tibetan Vajrayana traditions have a much greater focus on the deliberate cultivation of compassion, putting this motivation in the center of their practices. In the Mahayana tradition, the ideal and experience of bodhicitta (the altruistic aspiration toward enlightenment of all beings) is prescribed as a key self-state to be induced and cultivated through imagery, meditation, and action. Similarly, CFT also places a great deal of emphasis on constructing a sense of a compassionate self in a way that may be new to many ACT practitioners.

FAP, which is closely related to ACT in the functional contextual family, engages the psychotherapeutic relationship to directly shape new, more adaptive behaviors for clients in real time, during emotionally courageous and compassionate exchanges. It requires therapists' honest engagement with their own emotional responses to others, and to their own suffering and personal history. In seeking to establish a sacred space of awareness where both client and therapist have an opportunity for personal transformation, FAP creates fertile ground and a wholesome context for the cultivation of compassion within an intimate and healing relationship. In bringing a focus on compassion to ACT, this context is key.

As you proceed through this book, we invite you to consider how each concept and technique might be relevant to your own clinical practice. ACT, FAP, and CFT share common values of openness and adaptability. Each of these modalities is both a process model and a freestanding therapy. As such, this work is meant to be an entrée to compassion-focused work for the ACT practitioner. Rather than suggesting a radical reinvention of ACT methods, casting off its previous developments, or welding together techniques in the name of psychotherapy integration, we suggest gently exploring how we can bring a compassionate focus into our ACT work, along with an understanding of the basic scientific rationale for this move, an appreciation of the workability of engaging compassion in psychotherapy, and an attitude of engaged and active curiosity. For all of the talk of suffering and all of the difficult spaces we can walk through on a compassionate journey as therapists, there is room for joy and flourishing in compassion-focused work. May we all allow ourselves to be open to some of that joy.

When concepts seem unconventional to a scientific tradition, the challenge is often one of appreciation and understanding, of cultivating a more expansive and elaborative engagement, rather than one of reductionism or dismissal. Importantly, one of the foundational papers in ACT was Steven Hayes's 1984 article "Making Sense of Spirituality," which brought the lens of functional contextual assumptions to dimensions of experience that were thought to be off-limits to "serious science." Interestingly, this paper was the seed for decades of growth in knowledge and research into flexible perspective taking and the self. Clearly, the strength and workability of the ACT rubric stands on its ability to approach the range of human phenomena, including compassion and the role of affiliative emotions in adaptive flexibility. We are committed to the ongoing evolution of compassion-focused ACT practice, and we offer this book in the service of that aim.

1

Compassion: Definitions and Evolutionary Roots

In these first decades of the twenty-first century, compassion and self-compassion are increasingly being researched and applied as an active, empirically supported process variable in psychotherapy. This might not seem surprising, given that compassion has been at the center of contemplative practices for emotional healing for at least 2,600 years. Shakyamuni, or Gautama Buddha, taught that cultivating compassion could transform the mind, and his philosophical descendants have built upon his observations and insights ever since. Furthermore, most of the world's major religions have specific prayers and imagery practices that involve the experience of compassion as a source of emotional comfort or redemption. In terms of psychotherapy, for some sixty years, starting with the work of Carl Rogers (1965), it has been proposed that empathy is central to psychotherapy. Since Rogers's work, different therapies have explored the value of warmth and empathy in the psychotherapeutic relationship (Gilbert & Leahy, 2007; Greenberg & Paivio, 1997). However, compassion, as a process in itself, has only recently come to be seen as a core focus of psychotherapeutic work.

As cognitive behavioral therapy (CBT) has increased its emphasis on applied mindfulness and acceptance-based approaches, it makes sense that mental training designed to intentionally foster a compassionate mind would become a growing trend in contextual behavior therapies like ACT and FAP. Contextual behavior therapies inherently address the interconnectedness between an organism and its context in a way that resonates with Buddhist psychology and the science of compassion. Additionally, this emphasis on compassion within behavioral therapies is a part of a trend toward greater integration of compassion-focused methods and Buddhist influences within psychotherapy across many theoretical approaches (Germer, Seigel, & Fulton, 2005). An effective approach to therapy that is grounded in compassion would target cultivation of compassion as a key process for enhancing emotion regulation, increasing psychological flexibility, and furthering well-being. Compassion-focused therapy provides us with a rapidly growing, evidence-based mode of psychotherapy that pursues these aims and is highly compatible with contextual behavioral approaches.

Definitions of Compassion

The word "compassion" is derived from Middle English via Anglo-French from the Late Latin com-pati, which means "to suffer with or sympathize." In current conceptualizations, compassion is rarely presented as a single emotion or cognitive process. Definitions of compassion usually suggest that compassion is made up of several processes that involve the following characteristics:

- Mindful attention to and awareness of suffering

- An understanding and felt sense of suffering and its causes

- Motivation to remain open to suffering with the intention or wish to alleviate it

In addition, conceptualizations of compassion often address the interconnectedness of human beings. While clinical psychology has yet to embrace a single definition of compassion, many writers, clinicians, and researchers have contributed to an ongoing scientific discussion regarding what is meant by "compassion."

Indeed, several specific definitions of compassion are commonly used in psychotherapy and research and are worth consideration in establishing a model that ACT practitioners can deploy in their clinical work. McKay and Fanning (2000) define compassion as a multicomponent process that includes acceptance, understanding, and forgiveness—a definition that emerges from their work on self-esteem and self-criticism. They propose that compassion can be an essential component of an integrative cognitive behavioral treatment for self-criticism. Notably, each of the current applied psychological definitions of compassion either includes a component addressing self-criticism or has emerged from working with clients who struggle with high levels of self-criticism and shame-based difficulties (Neff, 2003b; Gilbert & Irons, 2005).

Definitions Within Self-Compassion Approaches

Kristin Neff's definition of self-compassion (2003a, 2003b) is derived from social psychology and Buddhist traditions and has likely become the most prevalent model of self-compassion in clinical psychology at present. This is largely due to the widespread use of Neff's Self-Compassion Scale (2003a) as the instrument of choice in the psychological study of compassion. Derived from Buddhist psychology, Neff's model involves three essential experiential constructs: mindfulness, self-kindness, and a sense of common humanity. Mindfulness involves focused and flexible awareness, acceptance, and a clear view of the nature of suffering (Nhat Hanh, 1998; K. G. Wilson & DuFrene, 2009). Self-kindness involves regarding oneself with warmth and care, rather than criticism and harsh judgments. Finally, common humanity involves recognition that all human beings face suffering and pain as they move through life. Furthermore, a sense of common humanity also allows for insight into the connection between one's own experience and the experience of the whole of humanity. Higher levels of reported self-compassion have been found to be correlated with lower levels of depression and anxiety (Neff, 2003a; Neff, Hsieh, & Dejitterat, 2005; Neff, Rude, & Kirkpatrick, 2007), and these relationships persist even after controlling for the effects of self-criticism. The research of Neff and her colleagues has also demonstrated positive correlations among self-compassion and a range of positive psychological dimensions (Neff, Rude, et al., 2007), including life satisfaction, feelings of social connectedness (Neff, Kirkpatrick, & Rude, 2007), and personal initiative and positive affect (Neff, Rude, et al., 2007).

Definitions Within ACT

In ACT-consistent terms, Dahl, Plumb, Stewart, and Lundgren (2009) have outlined how compassion relates to psychological flexibility—the unified model of adaptive human functioning underlying ACT. Psychological flexibility has been defined as "contacting the present moment as a conscious human being, fully and without needless defense—as it is and not as what it says it is—and persisting with or changing a behavior in the service of chosen values" (Hayes, Strosahl, & Wilson, 2012, pp. 96–97).

According to the model of Dahl and her colleagues, compassion involves the ability to willingly experience difficult emotions; to mindfully observe our self-evaluative, distressing, and shaming thoughts without allowing them to dominate our actions or states of mind; to engage more fully in life pursuits with self-kindness and self-validation; and to flexibly shift our perspective toward a broader, transcendent sense of self (Hayes, 2008b). Hayes and colleagues (2012) specifically link compassion and self-acceptance to perspective-taking processes. According to the ACT model, the human ability to be conscious of our own pain involves awareness of the pain of others. Similarly, when we develop the ability to be less dominated by categorical, judgmental self-evaluations, we may more readily let go of condemnations and judgments of others. From this perspective, as we cultivate compassion, we are developing core elements of psychological flexibility, and as we become more flexible, we have the opportunity to grow in compassion.

Definitions Within Compassion-Focused Therapy

Paul Gilbert (2005) has drawn upon developmental psychology, affective neuroscience, Buddhist practical philosophy, and evolutionary theory to develop a comprehensive form of experiential behavior therapy known as compassion-focused therapy, or CFT. Gilbert (2007) describes compassion as a multifaceted process that has evolved from the caregiver mentality found in human parental care and child rearing. As such, compassion includes a number of emotional, cognitive, and motivational elements involved in the ability to create opportunities for growth and change with warmth and care (Gilbert, 2007).

Gilbert (2009a) defines the essence of compassion as "a basic kindness, with deep awareness of the suffering of oneself and of other living things, coupled with the wish and effort to relieve it" (p. 13). This definition involves two central dimensions of compassion. The first is known as the *psychology of engagement* and involves sensitivity to and awareness of the presence of suffering and its causes. The second dimension is known as the *psychology of alleviation* and constitutes both the motivation and the commitment to take actual steps to alleviate the suffering we encounter (Gilbert & Choden, 2013).

When we view these two dimensions of compassion in terms of our work as clinicians, we can connect with a felt sense of compassion in action. Imagine you have your first session or two with a young man who suffers from severe social anxiety. He is a bright and caring student and spends some of his free time volunteering as a tutor for students at the state university. His descriptions of his experience suggest that years of bullying by schoolmates and being emotionally abused by his father have fueled a hostile inner voice that savagely shames and criticizes him. When he thinks about meeting with friends at a party or concert, he expects that they will reject and judge him. Even just speaking about social meetups fills him with dread and despair. As you spend time with this client, listening with an open heart, looking into his eyes, and seeing the pain and shame he has experienced, you might be increasingly sensitive to his suffering. You may feel emotionally moved upon hearing about the abuse he suffered, experiencing a resonant sadness or anger when in his presence.

And as you come into contact with the client and understand more of his story, you might feel motivated to help him deal with his anxiety and distress. You might feel a sense of professional and personal commitment to help him feel grounded in the moment and step forward into a life that has greater meaning and opportunity for joy. Although taking those steps might mean the client comes into contact with great anxiety, your compassionate motivation wouldn't be soft or weak. You probably wouldn't feel compelled to help him to avoid social situations or curl up and hide.

Both of the psychologies of compassion would be awakened within you. You would feel an awareness of and engagement with the suffering you encountered in this therapeutic relationship, and you would feel a commitment and motivation to do something to help alleviate that suffering. Your compassionate mind would be active, and it might serve you well as an ally in the work of helping the client make important changes in his life. In time, the client may also learn to activate his own capacity for self-compassion, intentionally directing warmth and support toward himself and creating a range of new possibilities for meaningful action in the process.

While the clinical utility of Gilbert's CFT definition and theoretical model of compassion is readily apparent, it is important to recognize that CFT has developed its conceptualization of compassion from a foundation in basic science rather than clinical observation. The CFT model of the two psychologies of compassion—engagement and alleviation—links the processes that contribute to experiences of compassion and emotion with highly evolved neurophysiological systems, especially those associated with social behavior (Gilbert, 2007).

The Two Psychologies of Compassion and ACT

The emerging common ground across psychological science is that compassion is a complex and multimodal organization of human behaviors with clear antecedents in human evolution and emotional processes rooted in inheritable response patterns that develop even prior to birth. However, compassion also involves verbal learning and specific developmental experiences that occur in a social context. Understandably, the emphasis within ACT and contextual CBT upon the prediction and influence of human behavior with precision, depth, and scope is highly relevant to broadening our understanding of compassion. The contextual behavioral science (CBS) approach that underpins ACT invites us to examine the precise dynamics of both the verbal learning involved in human compassion and the emotional, biological, and inherited response patterns that contribute to our awareness of suffering and our efforts to address the pain we encounter in the world. In some instances, compassion can be viewed as involving a skill set that can be cultivated through mental training and serve as a significant part of the emotional healing process (Davidson, 2003; Gilbert, 2009b; Lutz, Brefczynski-Lewis, Johnstone, & Davidson, 2008). Importantly, compassion involves the activation of the emotions that arise in connected, intimate, and close relationships. We refer to these emotions, which involve empathy, warmth, and care, as *affiliative emotions*. Activation of networks of affiliative emotions can promote focused, flexible attention and a broadening of the range of possible actions in the presence of stimuli that typically narrow behavioral repertoires. Indeed, research has increasingly established that compassion can facilitate lasting change in the way we experience and respond to suffering (Gumley, Braehler, Laithwaite, MacBeth, & Gilbert, 2010; Hofmann, Grossman, & Hinton, 2011).

In accord with Gilbert's model of compassion described above (2010), here we will briefly conceptualize compassion and its two dimensions in terms of acceptance and commitment processes, and in accord with functional contextual assumptions.

The psychology of engagement: This dimension involves the ability to notice, turn toward, pay attention to, and engage with suffering. Engagement with compassion involves several aspects, all of which facilitate awareness of and sensitivity to suffering. These processes relate to experiential acceptance rather than experiential avoidance: turning toward the things that are difficult to bear with a motivation to engage with the suffering we encounter. In terms of the ACT model of psychological flexibility, processes that emphasize acceptance, willingness, and awareness are clearly related to the CFT psychology of engagement.

The psychology of alleviation: This dimension involves developing and maintaining the wisdom, skill, and behavioral capacity to take effective and personally meaningful action in the presence of suffering. Such action may involve direct steps to alleviate suffering and its causes, yet it may also involve developing the commitment to remain in the presence of difficult emotions with compassionate acceptance. The ACT processes of owning one's values and making a commitment to embodying those values are related to the psychology of alleviation.

Speaking to the healing quality of the experience of compassion, Christopher Germer states that "compassion is a quality of mind that can transform the experience of pain, even making it worthwhile. When we open to pain in a compassionate way, there is a feeling of freedom—of nonresistance, noncontraction—and a deep sense of connection to others—of expanding beyond ourselves" (Germer, 2012, p. 93). When flexible perspective taking affords us an opportunity to turn compassion inward, phenomenological qualities of mindful awareness, loving-kindness, and a broader sense of an interconnected self may become more apparent (Neff, 2011). This is territory that will likely be quite familiar to the experienced ACT practitioner, and that merits further expansion and exploration within the CBS rubric.

As we approach a functional understanding of compassion, there is a striking continuity between compassion and other concepts derived from contemplative practice that can contribute to well-being. Mindfulness, acceptance, and compassion are often described as interrelated processes. For example, several writers have established that training in mindfulness involves a willingness to contact the present moment just as it is and effects an emergent form of self-kindness and self-validation (Kabat-Zinn, 2009). Other writers have highlighted the ways in which mindfulness and compassion are complementary core processes in psychological health that remain distinct, describing mindfulness and compassion as two wings of a bird—a classic Buddhist metaphor (Germer, 2012). While these processes can be construed as interconnected or discrete to varying degrees, mindfulness training has been used as a preparatory practice for the cultivation of compassion and a healthy psychological perspective throughout thousands of years of contemplative practice (Tirch, 2010; Wallace, 2009). And although mindfulness and other healthy qualities of mind may be involved in the experience of compassion, we suggest that compassion is a distinct process, with a distinct evolutionary trajectory, quality, and functional application.

Clinical Example: Using Compassion in Working with a Client with a History of Trauma

The following is the first in a series of clinical vignettes that will illustrate how compassion can be used as an active process in psychotherapy. As we proceed, we will clarify and explain the details of how to work with these processes through specific techniques and exercises. While all identifying information has been changed, these vignettes are all drawn from actual sessions. When a therapist's emotional response is indicated, this is meant to describe the therapist's genuine, experiential connection with the affect experienced in the room. Importantly, bringing a compassionate focus to psychotherapy extends beyond mere validation of emotions to empathic bridging and affective connection and expression. Compassion in psychotherapy may often first be evident in the emotional tone and intention present in the relationship between client and therapist.

This first example illustrates the activation of compassion in the therapeutic alliance during an ACT session. Ella is a thirty-five-year-old woman meeting criteria for borderline personality disorder who is back in therapy specifically to deal with her history of sexual trauma. She and her brother were sexually abused by an uncle when they were between the ages of six and ten. She feels so much shame around what happened then that she never disclosed it in her previous therapeutic work. After six months of intense relationship-centered ACT work, she asked her therapist to address it, and they have spent the past three sessions doing trauma work.

Therapist: You're just so brave to have finally chosen to open up about this.

Client: (*Looks down.*) I don't think I'm brave. I've hidden it all these years and I feel so ashamed.

Therapist: In my eyes, you are even braver to share it when you feel so much shame. You know, I don't see what happened to you as anything to be ashamed of. I see it as something horrible. The thought of this little girl that you were being abused makes me so sad and angry. (*The therapist is visibly emotionally engaged with the client.*)

Client: (*Looks down and stays silent.*)

Therapist: What's going on right now?

Client: If you only knew how worthless I am, you'd hate me too.

Therapist: I understand how a part of you might feel that here and now. You've been carrying this for a long time. Can you see how sad I feel for that little girl and how sad I am that you had to go through that?

Client: I know you mean well and it's your job not to judge, but I am so ashamed of what I did.

Therapist: Ella, you did nothing. It was done to you.

Client: (*Starts weeping.*) It's worse than you think.

> *Whenever she approaches talking about the trauma, Ella is overcome by overwhelming feelings of shame. She liked her uncle and can even remember having felt pleasure during some of the abuse. Worse still, she recalls an instance of bringing her brother to her uncle, whereupon he was abused, and then telling her brother not to tell anyone. To this day she has never spoken to her brother about the abuse, and her sense of shame and self-hatred has only grown over the years. In a case such as Ella's, we believe that actively fostering a compassionate perspective on herself and the past actions of that abused, lost, and confused child is a key to recovery.*

Therapist: When you're ready to share more, I'll be here. What I do know now is that being sexually abused as a child is one of the most confusing and shaming experiences possible. And being abused by someone we trust or love can make it so much worse. How can we ever know who to trust? We can even come to believe we were somehow responsible for or complicit in the abuse.

Client: (Weeps softly.) I feel ashamed that I sometimes liked it—some of it. (Weeps more strongly.) Oh my god, I'm never going to dare to look at you again.

Therapist: I'm here for you. It's so incredibly painful and so incredibly courageous for you to share this. I don't know if you can believe this, but it makes me respect you more that you at last have the courage to break out of the isolation the abuse forced you into and are sharing this with me. I want to honor your courage as much as I want to respect your boundaries. (Becomes teary.)

Client: (Weeps softly.) Thank you.

Therapist: If you feel up to it, would you be prepared to look into my eyes and tell me what you see?

Client: I don't know if I can.

Therapist: It's okay if you don't. Take your time.

Client: (Raises her head and looks into the therapist's teary eyes.)

Therapist: What do you see?

Client: I see sadness.

Therapist: Do you see judgment?

Client: (Pauses.) No. I see that you are there for me.

Therapist: I am. My mind also goes back to that little girl. Is it okay if I speak to her?

Client: (Hesitates.) Yes.

Therapist: I'm so sad that you are going through this. It must be so frightening and confusing. You must feel so alone. I want you to know that you didn't choose what you have been put through, and that this is so very much not your fault.

Client: (*Weeps.*) I am so ashamed. I've been bad.

Therapist: You're in an impossible situation and you need someone to protect you.

Client: (*Cries softly.*) Yes. Thank you.

Therapist: I'm here for you. (*Pauses.*) And if you could go speak to that little girl, what would you tell her?

Client: I've hated you so much all these years. (*Weeps.*) But I know it wasn't your fault. You just needed someone to protect you, and no one was there.

Therapist: I want you to know that I can see your incredible pain and shame, and that I hope you and that little girl will, together, find your way through it. I think that what you both need is not more judgment or being shamed, but some kindness and compassion.

Evolution, Cognition, and Behavior: What Is Characteristically Human?

To place the experience of compassion in the context of human evolution, an individual's learning history, and the context of the present moment, we begin with an exploration of how compassion has evolved and how it relates to what is fundamentally human in us all. If we observe the simplest of living organisms, perhaps a single-celled life-form like an amoeba, we can notice it move away from a potentially harmful stimulus, like cold, heat, or touch. And we can also notice it move toward a source of food. Of course, an amoeba isn't thinking or making decisions in the way we might, but it still inherently responds to potential threats and potential life-sustaining conditions by either moving toward or away from them, discriminating between aversive and appetitive stimuli.

As life-forms evolve and become more complex, they are able to respond to what they encounter in their environment in increasingly sophisticated ways, yet that basic discrimination between moving toward life-sustaining (appetitive) stimuli and away from potential danger (aversive stimuli) remains present as the root variable controlling all behaviors. For example, consider a pet dog. We know that this dog can learn to respond to changes in its environment by increasing certain behaviors or decreasing other behaviors. The dog can learn to run toward the kitchen when it hears the sound of its food bowl being filled, a type of behavior that is under appetitive control. And the dog can learn to run away from the living room when it hears the angry voice of its owner, a type of behavior that is under aversive control. We humans also behave under either aversive or appetitive control, but since we have uniquely human capacities for symbolic thinking and complex emotional responding, discriminating between what is harmful or helpful to us can become infinitely complicated.

From a CBS perspective, the term "behavior" is used to represent anything and everything that a human being may do (Kohlenberg & Tsai, 1991; Törneke, 2010). From daydreaming to running, from digesting to feeling sad, from seeing to loving, from thinking to perceiving, the entire range of human actions and experience is seen as constituting behavior. This is in accord with B. F. Skinner's perspective (1974) and is particularly germane to a scientific approach because it helps us consider the whole of our experience, whether public (through our five senses) or private (through the mind's eye or inner sensations), as not being different in essence. In terms of psychological science, this is useful because the basic rules of how to predict and influence behaviors have been well studied in experimental psychology, and many of these rules apply to both mental and physical behaviors (Hayes, Barnes-Holmes, & Roche, 2001). It also helps with overcoming the philosophical conundrums inherent in dualistic positions regarding how one type of thing (mental stuff) could exert a controlling influence over something different in essence (physical matter).

Evolved Fusion

Research has repeatedly demonstrated that humans have a tendency to respond to symbolic, mental events as though they were literal events in the external world (Dymond, Schlund, Roche, & Whelan, 2013; Ruiz, 2010), a phenomenon referred to as *fusion* in ACT (Hayes et al., 1999). When called to mind, unpleasant things can put us under aversive control, whereas pleasant things can result in appetitive control. For example, consider a man who has lived with generalized anxiety disorder for decades and persistently worries about his finances. He's likely to often worry about how he might become destitute, lose whatever savings he may have, and perhaps even become homeless.

When his mind generates a range of worries and imaginary scenarios, these mental events are likely to influence his actions. He might be very averse to risk when making financial decisions and therefore miss important opportunities. Furthermore, he might be reluctant to assert himself in the workplace and live in fear of upsetting his supervisor or coworkers. Day after day, he is responding to his worries as if they were real, and his life becomes smaller and smaller as his range of activities becomes increasingly constricted. So, with the evolutionary emergence of complex human cognition some two million years ago, human behavior began to come under the influence of our thoughts and emotions, as well as our outer environment, which can be both useful and problematic. It can be useful in that it allows us to conjure up models of the world in our mind's eye and then test them out in the real world, leading to a technological explosion that's radically improved our survival prospects. But it can also have some problematic side effects.

Through fusion, our behavior can become so dominated by the influence of mental events that we are sometimes more controlled by inner representations than actual factors in the outside world (Strosahl, Hayes, Wilson, & Gifford, 2004). For example, if a woman's mental representation of a party involves a group of judgmental guests who are going to mock her under their breath and shun her, she may experience anxiety. Furthermore, she may attempt to avoid the party and experience physical symptoms of anxious arousal through the sympathetic nervous system, and her mind may generate debilitating thoughts such as *You can't handle parties* and *You're such a social reject*. These may come to such prominence that, if she takes them literally, even if she attends the party and all of the guests are friendly, she still may experience fear, self-criticism, and an attentional bias toward the negative due to the influence of mental events on her biology and behavior (Barlow, 2002; Greene et al., 2008).

When we are under the aversive control of mental events, we tend to try to mentally suppress or avoid such events. It makes sense that we may naturally want to run away from feelings, images, and ideas that are unpleasant because in the outside world, running away from dangerous things is usually a good strategy. The problem here is that the more we try to push away an unwanted thought or feeling, the more it tends to show up, and the more it may come to dominate our experience and control our behavior. How many of us have lain awake at night trying to avoid thinking about a problem at work or school the next day? Experimental and clinical research has repeatedly verified that suppressing thoughts or emotions has the paradoxical result that they show up with greater frequency, and that attempts at experiential avoidance are what drive a lot of psychological suffering (Ruiz, 2010; Wenzlaff & Wegner, 2000). Under the dominance of distressing mental events and subsequent embodied emotional responses, we become hooked into aversively controlled attempts at avoidance and control, which can keep us trapped in an endless cycle of suffering and a sense of being profoundly stuck.

Fusion involves mental events exerting an influence over our behavior—not just verbal behaviors, but also physiological responses, including emotional responses at a level that is not expressed or experienced in recognizably verbal terms. As mentioned, much of what we experience as humans, including many of our behaviors, is shared with other animals. In evolutionary terms, these response patterns are older than humanity. For example, territorial behaviors, sexual behaviors, affiliative responses, and emotions such as fear or disgust all have evolutionary precursors in prehuman animals. Similarly, elements of emotional experiencing are situated in bodily responses that are not dependent upon cognition.

While a single definition of emotion is elusive, emotions can be conceived of as evolutionary emergent psychophysiological phenomena that guide an organism in adaptation to environmental demands (Levenson, 1994); provide ingrained ways of preserving an organism's welfare (Panksepp, 1994); and have a heritable, universal nature that allows our present responses to be guided by our ancestral past (Ekman, 1992, 1994; Tooby & Cosmides, 1990). Considerable evidence from a wide range of animals, especially primates, supports the view that rudimentary forms of caring behavior, altruism, and other types of kindness are widespread (de Waal, 2009). And, undoubtedly, ancestral humans who practiced compassion, group protectiveness, sharing of food, and care for the young or sick were more likely to survive than those who were more indifferent to one another's welfare (D. S. Wilson, 2007).

Evolution, Cooperation, and Compassion

Contextual science theorists, notably Steven C. Hayes, are currently exploring an evolutionary context for understanding human verbal behavior and are situating their understanding of language and cognition in evolutionary terms (Hayes & Long, 2013; D. S. Wilson, Hayes, Biglan, & Embry, 2012). Hayes and

Long (2013) recently recalled B. F. Skinner's proposition that "all behavior is due to genes, some more or less directly, the rest through the role of genes in producing structures which are modified during the lifetime of the individual" (Skinner, 1974, p. 704). Hayes's integration of CBS and evolutionary science stresses cooperation as our chief evolutionary advantage, and the evolutionary antecedent of both human cognition and compassion (Hayes & Long, 2013).

While some of our behaviors are shared with our evolutionary ancestors, at least three domains—cognition, culture, and cooperation—are particularly important in understanding human behavior (Hayes & Long, 2013; D. S. Wilson et al., 2012). As discussed, in basic terms cognition involves symbolic thought—a representation of the world around us that can guide our actions (Hayes & Long, 2013; Von Eckardt, 1995). In evolutionary terms, culture stands for our capacity to communicate and transfer a body of learning across generations and among people. In this way, the acquired cognitions and response patterns that have been hard earned through our evolutionary history are not dependent upon the survival of a single generation of the species or a single group. Our collective learning can be transmitted into the future of our species—a transmission that has a huge impact on social contexts and on how genotypic potentials are phylogenetically and individually expressed (Hayes & Long, 2013).

Regarding the third element of human behavior that is characteristic of our species, cooperation, this represents our ability to work with one another to achieve specific aims. Humans cooperate at a level of complexity and consistency unknown in other animals, and as such we possess an evolutionary advantage through our ability to communicate and work with one another. Evolutionary theorists are beginning to hypothesize that cooperative behavior may have led to the differentiation of our species from other primates through the efficiency of between-group selection (Hayes & Long, 2013; Nowak & Highfield, 2011). More effective groups of early humans, working together and communicating in eusocial ways, were perhaps more likely to thrive than groups of other primates, where individual selection may have led to less efficient collective adaptation. In order to understand this better, imagine a group of early nonhuman primates competing for resources with the earliest humans. Our ancient ancestors would have had the advantage of being able to cooperate and communicate with one another in more precise and subtle ways than other primates, allowing them to use and share knowledge of tools, work together to accomplish aims, point out potential sources of danger, and look after one another when an individual was wounded or healing. Under the influence of the principles of adaptation, variation, and selection between groups, such a group might develop superior ways of flexibly interacting with the environment, promoting the survival and flourishing of the collective. The significant benefits of cooperation would logically contribute to the selection and elaboration of the human capacity for verbal communication and emergent symbolic or representational thinking.

Some animals do exhibit a capacity to respond to the perceived intentions of others, including apes and even crows (Call & Tomasello, 1999; Clayton et al., 2007), and these species may pool their behavioral resources for survival to some extent. However, it appears that humans alone respond to and use nonverbal gestures, facial expressions, and utterances in sophisticated cooperative ways that facilitate the transmission of emotional information (Call & Tomasello, 1999; Tomasello, Call, & Gluckman, 1997). In fact, human beings may be the only truly eusocial and cooperative vertebrates on our planet (Foster & Ratnieks, 2005; Hayes & Long, 2013).

The advantage of cooperation has probably played a role in the selection for and evolutionary emergence of human language. In turn, the development of human language likely contributed to the development of a verbal community that could selectively reinforce the development of human cognition (Hayes & Long, 2013; Hayes et al., 2012). As far as we know, humans alone can express themselves as speakers and listeners and experience themselves in a specific point in space and time, with a particular identity. In this way, the embodied evolutionary intelligence of genetically inherent motivations and emotions has interacted with the human capacity for symbolic representation to create the range of human behaviors, which are highly dependent upon social contexts, verbal learning, and the elaboration of internal networks of cognition. From this basis, humans experience themselves *as selves* and the human behavior of construing a separate self-identity emerges.

As we will explore throughout in this book, the human ability to construe a self in relation to another, capacity for perspective taking, and evolved tendency to experience soothing and stillness in the presence of affiliative emotional experiences are some of the seeds of our compassionate mind. And all of these qualities flow from our unique human experience of being within the cooperative, social context—the sense of "I-you," and the more important sense of "we." Interestingly, verbal processes also depend on a stable social context. That context, a function of cooperation in the verbal community, provides the basis from which a perspective of self, of the "I-here-now-ness" of being, gradually emerges as children learn to frame and relate their experience in relation and in contrast to "you-there-then" (Hayes, 1984). In this way, our deepest sense of self and emerging spiritual experiences arise as a function of verbal behavior and are mediated by a verbal community (Hayes, 1984). Thus, our sense of our own individual perspective involves the ability to imagine viewing the world through another's perspective, which further strengthens compassionate behavior, this time mediated verbally.

We believe this evolutionary contextual understanding of compassion can help make a great deal of sense of the connections between well-being, compassion, and psychological flexibility. As noted, Gilbert (2009a) emphasizes that compassion is an evolved human capacity that emerges from human behavioral systems involving attachment and affiliation, an argument supported by empirical research. Seeking proximity and soothing from caregivers in order to obtain a secure base for operation in the world is a mammalian behavior that predates human abilities for verbal responding and deriving a sense of self in relation to another, and predates the meta-awareness and observational capacity that arises in mindfulness training. The evolutionary advantage that we have in our capacity for cognition and verbal behavior is what has resulted in our particularly human quality of self-awareness, our ability to be aware of our awareness (i.e., mindfulness), and our ability to base our behavior on abstract thought and imagination, including our capacity to be sensitive to and moved by the suffering we witness. According to D. S. Wilson and colleagues (2012), this human capacity for symbolic thought affords us with an "inheritance system" that potentially has a combinatorial diversity similar to that of recombinant DNA. In this way, both our genetic and psycholinguistic evolution have led us to be soothed by the experience of self-compassion, and have allowed that experience of soothing and the ensuing courage to afford us with greater psychological flexibility and a secure base for functioning in the world.

Wang (2005) hypothesizes that human compassion emerges from an evolutionarily determined "species-preservative" neurophysiological system. This system is hypothesized as evolving in a relatively recent evolutionary time frame compared to the older "self-preservative" system. This "species-preservative" system is "based on an inclusive sense of self and promotes awareness of our interconnectedness to others" (Wang, 2005, p. 75). Relative to some other animals, human infants and children may seem defenseless, as they require a great deal of care and protection early in life. As a result, particular brain structures and other elements of the nervous and endocrine systems have evolved to promote nurturing behaviors of protecting and caring for others. Basic examples of this evolutionary progression can be observed by contrasting the parenting behaviors of reptiles and amphibians, for example, to those of mammalian species. The former lack even the most basic nurturing behaviors toward their young, while mammalian species observably display a wide range of caretaking behaviors.

Moving higher on the evolutionary ladder, Wang's review of the relevant literature suggests that the human prefrontal cortex, cingulate cortex, and ventral vagal complex are involved in the activation of this "species-preservative" system (Wang, 2005). These structures all play a role in the development of healthy attachment bonds and self-compassion. The development of both individually adaptive and group adaptive behavioral systems for dealing with threats can be viewed as an example of multilevel selection theory (D. S. Wilson, 2008); it reflects how our evolutionary history informs our verbal relational network in ways that connect us to one another, and also informs our place as an emergent species in the flow of life. Such an evolutionary perspective is intrinsically contextual in nature and reflects a potential area for multidisciplinary theoretical integration in the developing science of self-compassion.

2

Compassion and Psychological Flexibility

Although compassion in itself has yet to be integrated as a formal component of the ACT process model, ACT practitioners and researchers have been exploring the role of compassion and self-compassion in psychotherapy for some time now (Forsyth & Eifert, 2007; Hayes, 2008c; Luoma, Drake, Kohlenberg, & Hayes, 2011; Schoendorff, Grand, & Bolduc, 2011; Tirch, 2010; Van Dam, Earleywine, & Borders, 2010). In order to approach an understanding of compassion from an ACT perspective, we need to spend some time examining relational frame theory (RFT; Hayes et al., 2001), the underlying theory of cognition within CBS and the foundation for ACT. RFT provides us with an approach to understanding how human beings think and feel, based in the most basic behavioral principles. One advantage it offers is that, by building our knowledge about the basic units of mental functioning, we can develop and scientifically test new ways of addressing the complex problem of human psychological suffering. RFT describes the processes of mindfulness, self-development, and perspective taking, among many other mental phenomena. RFT also provides a useful way of considering how humans may develop a sense of self and a sense of others and how we frame our experience of time and space (Barnes-Holmes, Hayes, & Dymond, 2001; Törneke, 2010).

After just over a decade of widespread dissemination, RFT has become the foundation for a worldwide research initiative. This exploration of the fundamentals of cognition and language from the ground up is one of the most active research programs in behavioral psychology today. One of the central concepts involved in this field of study is a process called *relational framing*, or *derived relational responding*, which aims to provide a thorough account of exactly what takes place in human symbolic thinking. As we will discuss, all of this has particular relevance for understanding the emergent, applied science of compassion.

When training therapists in these theories that ground our work in a contextual understanding of language, we often invite our colleagues to look at the theory as something more than an academic exercise and see these concepts as essential and dynamic pieces of a vital psychotherapeutic process. Our assumptions inform how we view our clients and ourselves, and having a clearer understanding of the foundations of thoughts, feelings, and action will help us develop case conceptualizations, provide clear targets for interventions, and influence the style and flow of our conversations. Say that you are a more traditional psychoanalyst and your assumptions about how the therapy will work involve the resolution of a transference neurosis; everything from your facial expression to the degree of self-disclosure in the room will be influenced by those assumptions. Your aims will influence the directions that you suggest in the flow of the therapeutic discussion. Alternatively, if you are a Beckian cognitive therapist, interested in helping clients identify and directly change dysfunctional cognitions, you will have a different set of assumptions, and they will create quite different directions in relating to clients.

By taking the time to explore the evolutionary roots of our affiliative emotions and increase our understanding of the behavioral principles involved in cognition and language, we are opening ourselves to new assumptions and new possibilities for assessment, case conceptualization, and treatment planning. We are also bringing new dimensions of ourselves to the therapeutic relationship in the process.

Derived Relational Responding and Perspective Taking

As many ACT practitioners know, "derived relational responding" is a term used in RFT to describe verbal learning. Simply put, derived relational responding involves a person's ability to derive relations among stimuli, and as these relations are derived, the functions of the related stimuli can be transferred and transformed. For our purposes, when we say the "function of a stimulus," we mean the way that an experienced change in an environment (stimulus) can predict and influence the behavior of a person. For example, deriving a relation of equivalence between the word "dog" and the word "txakur" ("dog" in the Basque language) may transfer the functions of the word "dog" (appetitive or aversive, depending on one's experience with dogs) to the word "txakur." If someone were then to tell you to take care of your txakur because it was pacing by the back door and walking in circles furtively, you would know what to do. This form of learned relational responding depends upon contextual cues and derived relationships among stimuli that are not dependent upon formal properties of the stimuli (such as the sensory appearance qualities) or direct experience of them. For example, neither the word "dog" nor the word "txakur" is in any way similar to the direct experience of the animal, but both of these words, when serving as a stimulus, can have the effect of bringing to mind for the listener a host of associations and inner experiences related to dogs.

At this point, hundreds of studies have demonstrated derived relational responding's role in verbal learning and cognition (Dymond, May, Munnelly, & Hoon, 2010). Essentially, RFT suggests that derived relational responding is the fundamental building block of thinking, knowing, and speaking. As we explore the science of compassion for ACT practitioners, it is clear that an RFT account of compassion could help us better understand how compassion may function, how we may be able to develop methods to predict and influence compassionate behaviors, and how we can come to understand compassion with increasing precision, depth, and scope.

Relational Frames

Derived responding can involve different kinds of relations, which are sometimes referred to as *relational frames*, giving us the name for RFT. Here are a few examples of different kinds of relational frames:

- Comparative relations: for example, bigger/smaller and faster/slower

- Spatial relations: for example, above/below and behind/in front

- Hierarchical relations: for example, this is a part of that

- Perspective relations: for example, here/there, now/then, and I/you

In RFT, and therefore in ACT, the abilities to experience empathy, compassion, a sense of common humanity, and even a sense of self all are viewed as involving our learned capacity for creating perspective relations, a process known as flexible perspective taking (Hayes et al., 2012; Vilardaga, 2009). This is to say that, in RFT terms, the experience of self emerges from a particular form of learned derived relational responding that establishes a perspective—a point of view that is situated in time and space relative to other points of view. This form of verbal behavior is described as framing *deictic* relations, with the term "deictic" simply meaning "by demonstration."

When we use the language of behavior analysis, we can say that these deictic relations are trained relational operant behaviors shaped by ongoing social interactions (Barnes-Holmes et al., 2001). But because not everyone has a comfortable background in that kind of language based on behavior analysis, we will also simply say that deictic relations are the fundamental elements of how we mentally represent and experience the world, ourselves, and the flow of time.

RFT posits that the language training humans undergo in childhood results in our experience of having a self, which gradually develops through our interactions with others in our verbal community: our family and society in general. For example, a parent might ask a young child what she just did, or even who she is or what she will be doing tomorrow. Children might also be invited to contrast themselves with others. For example, a parent might say, "You were a very good girl today! Thanks for cleaning up your toys right away. Some girls at the party didn't even listen to their parents. Good job." RFT asserts that in order to establish consistency in our verbal communication, it's absolutely necessary for children to create a frame of reference and point of view, and hence a perspective. Over time, this perspective is experienced as a sense of self (Hayes et al., 1999; Törneke, 2010).

In RFT and ACT, deictic relations that involve I/you, here/there, and then/now all are viewed as involving perspective taking and represent the elemental processes that bring our experience of self into being. Furthermore, in order for the concept "I" to have any meaning, there must be a "you" involved. Similarly, in order for "here" to have meaning as a point of view, there must be a "there." Our sense of a self arises from this perspective taking, an experience of "I-here-now-ness" that emerges in the context of "you-there-then-ness." We can represent these perspectives symbolically in a number of ways. For example, we can imagine our perspective relative to another perspective: *How would I feel if I found myself having to raise that child on my own like she did?* or *What would it be like to be a soldier at war?* We can also imagine our perspective relative to all other perspectives: *I feel like I'm the only person in the world who feels this way!* Thinking from within the ACT model, the self is less a thing in itself and more a flow of experience. It might even be more accurate to say that we "engage in selfing" than that we "have a self."

Self-as-Context

When people are asked who they are, they often respond by telling some form of life story, or self-narrative. And these kinds of responses, such as "My name is Fred, I'm from Texas, and I'm an attorney," make perfect sense. From an ACT perspective, this sense of self is known as *self-as-content*. However, mindfulness and compassion allow for experiencing a different kind of self. This self exists as a sort of observer, a silent "you" who has been watching your experience, moment by moment, for a very long time and is always doing so "now."

Throughout history, many of the wisdom traditions that prescribe the cultivation of compassion as a method for alleviating human suffering also outline ways that meditators and other practitioners might access a transcendent sense of self. This sense of self has been referred to many ways, including "the observing self," "the clear light," "the ground of being," and "big mind." It is an experience that has been difficult to express in conventional language, let alone technical, scientific concepts. In ACT, this sense of self is seen as emerging from an experience known as *self-as-context* (Hayes et al., 1999). Self-as-context has been described as a convergence of major classes of deictic framing that results in an experience of the "I-here-now-ness" of being alive and an observing self.

How is it that this observing self, distinct from a narrative self, arises? In order to understand this, let's return to ACT's roots in research on human language and cognition—RFT. As discussed, part of human relational responding involves trained capacities for perspective taking. Through these processes, our experience of being includes a sense of ourselves as a point of perspective before which the entirety of our experience unfolds throughout life. In ACT, this sense of oneself as an observer is referred to as self-as-context because it is an experiential sense of self that does indeed serve as the context within which our experiences are contained (Hayes et al., 1999). As we respond to our own responding, this sense of an observing self is important because, while this observer can notice the contents of consciousness, it is not the same as those contents. Just as we have arms but are more than our arms, we have thoughts, but we are more than that experience. Emotions don't feel themselves, thoughts don't observe themselves, and physical pain doesn't experience itself. Throughout our lives, we can notice the presence of an observing self—which may be awareness itself—before which all of our experiences arise, exist, and, in time, disappear.

This sense of self-as-context is particularly important with regard to compassion. For example, it clearly links with the components of self-compassion as defined by Neff (2003b): mindfulness, self-kindness, and common humanity. Looking at the relationship between self-as-context and self-compassion in detail, we can see that returning to an awareness of self-as-context offers a non-attached and disidentified relationship to our experiences. In this way, Neff's self-compassion components of mindfulness and a sense of common humanity appear to represent the activation of the ACT process of flexible perspective taking that underlies the self-as-context mode of experiencing, as well as defusion (or disidentification) from our ongoing self-narrative, or self-as-content. The activation of these processes and the accompanying experience of self-compassion can help loosen the habitual influence that painful private events and stories hold over us. Furthermore, from the perspective of the "I-here-now-ness" of being, we can view our own suffering as we might view the suffering of others and be touched by the pain in that experience without the dominant interference of our verbal learning history, with its potential for shaming self-evaluations (Hayes, 2008a; Vilardaga, 2009).

When you remember clients who described being really stuck in their psychological problems—perhaps those who were mired in rumination and worry and waiting for their lives to start—what stands out about their experience? Do you recall how isolated they felt and how identified they were with their stories? In a recent session, one of our clients said, "I've been like this all my life. I just can't stop worrying about my health. I know I'm some kind of crazy person, and I wish I could be like the other people in my office, who have their stuff together. On top of that, it really, *really* feels like I'm going to get a brain tumor—that it's only a matter of time. This is too much for me." Under conditions of intense anxiety, people often have difficulty adopting a flexible perspective and stepping out of identification with their stories. For this client, obsessive worries related to contamination, radiation, and brain tumors didn't affect him as thoughts in his mind, but as genuine, looming threats in the world. He felt he was alone, bizarre, mentally and physically ill, and stuck in a place of perpetual anguish. He *was* his self-story and identified with it deeply.

When working with such clients, an ACT therapist, who is trained to notice obstacles to psychological flexibility and compassion, might make the following types of observations:

- The difficulty the client is having with flexible perspective taking

- How identified and fused with his self-narrative the client appears to be

- How persistent self-comparisons and lack of a sense of common humanity contribute to feelings of shame, dread, and difficulty in engaging with life

- How emotionally moving it can be to deliberately witness the pain of the client as he experiences a physically healthy phase of life as if it were a time of catastrophic illness

All of these processes are highly relevant to the cultivation of self-compassion, and all of them can be viewed through an ACT-consistent lens and approached through ACT-consistent therapeutic moves.

Compassion and Psychological Flexibility

Emerging from the CBS and ACT literature as a set of evidence-based psychotherapy processes, psychological flexibility involves the development of expanding and adaptive behavioral repertoires that can be maintained in the presence of distressing events that typically narrow behavioral repertoires. Psychological flexibility has a strong negative correlation with depression, anxiety, and psychopathology and a high positive correlation with quality of life (Kashdan & Rottenberg, 2010). Furthermore, psychological flexibility has been demonstrated to serve as a psychotherapy mediator in a large number of randomized controlled trials, and its component processes have been identified and supported by behavioral research, as well as neurophysiological research exploring the neural correlates of those components (Ruiz, 2010; Whelan & Schlund, 2013).

While psychological flexibility is a model of six elements (values authorship, commitment, self-as-context, defusion, willingness, and contact with the present moment), the model can be divided into two major areas of emphasis. The first area involves mindfulness and acceptance processes (self-as-context, defusion, willingness, and contact with the present moment). The second area involves the authorship of and engagement in valued patterns of action that contribute to living a life of meaning, purpose, and vitality (which inherently entails the processes of self-as-context and contact with the present moment). Although in ACT values are freely chosen and not prescribed, ACT cofounder Steven Hayes (2008c) has suggested that compassion may, in fact, be a value that emerges inherently from the psychological flexibility model—and the only value that does so. According to Hayes, the roots of both self-compassion and compassion may emerge from the six core processes that comprise psychological flexibility, sometimes known as hexaflex processes (Hayes, Luoma, Bond, Masuda, & Lillis, 2006), as illustrated in figure 1.

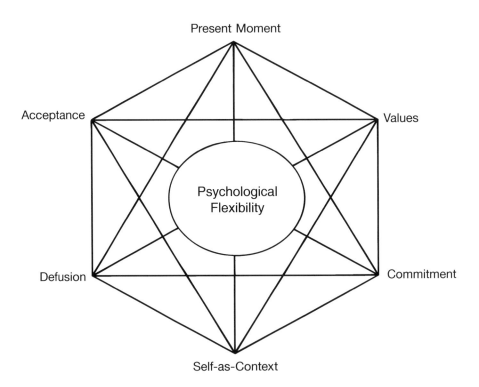

Figure 1. The hexaflex: Interacting processes in psychological flexibility.

Given your interest in this book, you may well be familiar with these processes and the growing body of interventions and techniques they inform. However, each component has a particular relationship to aspects of compassion and self-compassion, with implications for assessment, intervention, and treatment. And as we begin to explore these relationships, it is worth noting that these six processes work together interactively to several ends:

- Bringing people into direct experiential contact with their present-moment experiences

- Disrupting a literalized experience of mental events that may narrow the range of available behaviors

- Promoting experiential acceptance

- Helping people let go of overidentification with a narrative sense of self, or self-as-content

- Assisting in the process of values authorship

- Facilitating commitment to valued actions and directions

If we allow ourselves to mindfully reflect on what these processes represent and realize what it would mean to actualize them, we can approach a felt sense of how the ACT model encompasses and complements sensitivity to the suffering we encounter in the world and the motivation to alleviate that suffering. By examining how current conceptualizations of compassion relate to psychological flexibility, we can discover the foundation for the development and integration of a contextual and compassion-focused behavior therapy.

Self-Compassion, Mindfulness, and Psychological Flexibility

Both psychological flexibility and Kristin Neff's (2003a) conceptualization of self-compassion are multidimensional constructs that involve mindfulness, the experience of an expansive sense of self, and a commitment to serve specific valued aims. In the case of self-compassion, the alleviation of one's own suffering is an explicit aim, and in the case of psychological flexibility, a broader value of alleviating suffering and promoting life-affirming action is inherent.

As we consider the role of self-compassion in ACT, there is a temptation to find a way to fit self-compassion into the hexaflex model. Both psychological flexibility and self-compassion are constructs that have demonstrated clinical utility across a wide range of outcome and process studies (Neff, 2011; Ruiz, 2010). For example, controlled outcome research on mindfulness-based cognitive therapy has suggested that self-compassion may account for more variance in psychopathology than mindfulness alone (Kuyken et al., 2010). Similarly, Van Dam and colleagues (2010) found that self-compassion accounted for as much as ten times more unique variance in psychological health than a measure of mindfulness did in a large community sample.

Despite the natural pull to reduce or integrate self-compassion and the hexaflex in a seamless way, it is important to remember that neither self-compassion nor psychological flexibility is a technical term in the strictest sense of behavioral science. Neff's definition of self-compassion is an operationalization based on a reading of Buddhist concepts of compassion (Neff, 2003a), and the construct of psychological flexibility is based upon processes derived from basic RFT research on language, cognition, and rule-governed behavior. However, the hexaflex concepts are meant to be clinically applicable, middle-level terms for describing the underlying principles of RFT in somewhat everyday language. The hexaflex components are useful descriptors, but they need not represent everything that is involved in human well-being and psychological flexibility. What distinguishes CBS is the application of fundamental behavioral principles in accounting for the prediction and influence of human behavior. As we will describe, further CBS research may help identify more effective ways of working with the powerful psychotherapy process variable present in compassion for self or others. Similarly, compassion-focused techniques may expand the technical base of ACT in ways consistent with its theoretical underpinnings.

Relating self-compassion to psychological flexibility reveals both explicit and implicit levels of interacting processes. In terms of overt relationships between the models, we can see that the first component of self-compassion, mindfulness, is represented in the hexaflex as a form of flexible and focused attention that encompasses contact with the present moment, acceptance, defusion, and self-as-context (K. G. Wilson & DuFrene, 2009). The second component of self-compassion, common humanity, clearly relates to the experience of self-as-context, emerging as a function of flexible perspective taking. In terms of psychological flexibility, we can imagine a sense of common humanity arising with a shift from a narrow focus on the individual, narrative self to the sense of "we-ness" involved with being a part of the interconnected web of human experience (Gilbert, 1989; Hayes & Long, 2013). The third and final component of self-compassion, self-kindness, relates to treating oneself support-ively and with sympathy and includes "internal dialogues that are benevolent and encouraging rather than cruel or disparaging" (Neff & Tirch, 2013, p. 79). In the hexaflex, this type of deliberate engagement of warm regard and kind behavior toward the self is represented in the processes of authorship of freely chosen values and patterns of committed action to serve valued aims. This model of the relationship between self-compassion and psychological flexibility is illustrated in figure 2.

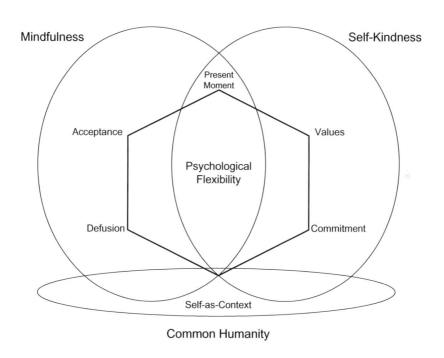

Figure 2. Self-compassion and psychological flexibility.

Beyond these obvious functional similarities between given processes, both models stress relatedness among their individual components. Accordingly, the relationships between self-compassion and psychological flexibility also contain subtleties and inherent relationships across processes. For example, while self-kindness appears to be more clearly related to values authorship and committed action, the very act of construing a self and regarding that self with the kindness we might extend to another is an act of flexible perspective taking and therefore related to the process of self-as-context. Similarly, for a person to consciously bring self-kindness to her flow of experience, she must be sufficiently in contact with the present moment to have the opportunity to facilitate such a shift. As a result, when working with self-compassion-based interventions, ACT practitioners can use their own clinical wisdom and insight to note the correspondences and relationships they discern in the lives of their clients.

The CFT Model and Psychological Flexibility

The model of compassion presented in CFT derives many of its constructs from research on developmental psychology, empathy, and affective neuroscience. Nevertheless, in CFT the core of the definition of compassion has its roots in ancient wisdom traditions. About 2,600 years ago, during the time of the historical Buddha, Siddhartha Gautama, there was a proliferation of contemplative traditions throughout the region along the Silk Road. These schools of thought emphasized the alleviation of suffering through meditative practices with a focus on the importance of cultivating compassion. Synthesizing these methods and innovating new perspectives and techniques, the Buddha developed a program for personal liberation from suffering that involved specific training in compassion. Since then, there have been many discussions of what compassion actually is and what it means, but a fairly standard definition has emerged, and it is used in CFT: sensitivity to the presence of suffering in oneself and others, with a commitment to try to alleviate and prevent such suffering. The definition points to the two basic psychologies of compassion discussed earlier:

- The psychology of engagement, which involves opening up to and working with suffering

- The psychology of alleviation, which involves working to develop the wisdom and skill necessary to alleviate or prevent suffering and its causes

Within the CFT model, these two central aspects of compassion each include several subcomponents, as shown in figure 3, where "Attributes" corresponds to the psychology of engagement, and "Skills Training" corresponds to the psychology of alleviation.

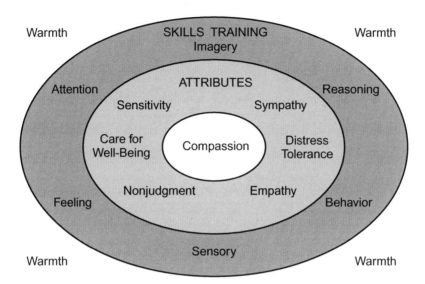

Figure 3. The compassion circle. (Reprinted from Gilbert, 2009a, with permission from Constable and Robinson.)

The psychology of engagement involves identifying and cultivating specific competencies, labeled as Attributes in figure 3: accessing the motivation to be caring, sensitivity to distress, sympathy, distress tolerance, empathy, and nonjudgment. These attributes are drawn from research on caregiving and altruistic behaviors, and they appear to be the foundational elements of a compassionate orientation (Gilbert, 2010). The psychology of alleviation (or prevention) involves further competencies for appropriate reflection and action, labeled as Skills Training in figure 3: attention, imagery, reasoning, behavior, sensory, and feeling. CFT uses a systematic approach to train and cultivate these capacities and skills and thereby develop compassion. The subcomponents of the two psychologies—of engagement and alleviation—are outlined below.

Components of the Psychology of Engagement

Importantly, the components of the psychology of compassionate engagement are interdependent. For example, the more we develop distress tolerance, the more willing and motivated we might be to develop compassion. Likewise, the more empathy we have, along with an ability to understand our own minds without judgment, the more we may be able to tolerate distress, increasing motivation. On the other hand, if any of these attributes falter, compassion itself may also falter. For example, it will probably be difficult to summon compassion if emotional engagement (sympathy) is low or distress tolerance or empathy are lacking.

Motivation to care for well-being. Although all of the components of the psychology of engagement are interrelated, in CFT we start by recognizing that motivation to be caring and try to alleviate or prevent suffering in oneself and others is central to the compassion journey. There are many reasons why clients may not be motivated to engage with suffering or interested in cultivating compassion. They may think that it will not help them, that it is weak, that it is undeserved, or that when they engage in compassion they will have overwhelming feelings of sadness and fear (Gilbert et al., 2012). Also, certain clients may have obstacles to motivation that are artifacts of their learning history and thus outside of their conscious awareness. Nevertheless, in CFT the experience of the compassionate mind begins with motivation to alleviate suffering as it is encountered and contribute to the welfare of living things.

Sensitivity. In CFT, sensitivity refers to how we pay attention to suffering, both our own and that of other people: how we come to notice it and hold it in our attention without turning away or trying to avoid it. This sensitivity involves present-moment awareness that is intentionally focused upon the presence of suffering as we encounter it in the world or in ourselves.

Sympathy. In CFT, sympathy refers to a reflexive and responsive emotional connectedness with suffering derived from the automatically engaged capacity to be emotionally attuned. For example, if you see a child stumble and hurt himself, this could trigger immediate unpleasant feelings within you. You might wince or feel compelled to act. This sympathy can also be directed within. When we pay attention to our own suffering, it is not an emotionally neutral experience; it comes with a feeling component, and the compassionate mind is capable of feeling into the pain.

Distress tolerance. Being motivated to engage with suffering, sensitive to the presence of suffering, and attuned to suffering with sympathy requires the ability to tolerate the difficult emotions, thoughts, and bodily sensations that arise. As described by Gilbert (2009a), this capacity for distress tolerance is closely related to acceptance: "Linked with but not identical to acceptance, tolerance is the ability to stay with emotions as they happen... Acceptance can involve tolerance, but it is also a deep philosophical orientation to one's difficulties. It's a coming to terms, 'letting it be,' not fighting or struggling any longer" (pp. 200–201). Neither acceptance nor distress tolerance is submissive resignation; rather, both speak to an intentional willingness to remain in the presence of challenging experiences in the service of compassionate aims.

Empathy. One of the more complex elements of the psychology of engagement is empathy, as it is both an intuitive process and a more deliberate approach (Decety & Ickes, 2011). For example, you might deliberately imagine what it would be like to find yourself in another person's shoes, as when viewing a client's sadness from an empathic perspective. However, empathy might also be implicit, such as having a discussion with a friend, simply noticing that he seems anxious, and having a hypothesis about his concern pop into your mind. Empathic responding has been described many ways, including theory of mind (Premack & Woodruff, 1978), mentalization (Fonagy, Target, Cottrell, Phillips, & Kurtz, 2002), and, as discussed, perspective taking (McHugh & Stewart, 2012), a central contextual behavioral concept. We may be better able to empathize with others when we are open to and aware of our own processes. For example, individuals who are frightened or avoidant of their own feelings (e.g., intense rage) or fantasies may struggle to understand or empathize with others in those states.

Nonjudgment. The final component of compassion is the ability to allow oneself to experience certain emotions and mental events without falling under the control of condemnation, judgment, or shaming. Nonjudgment doesn't mean indifference or apathy; rather, it represents a recognition that harsh evaluations, shame, and self-criticism can drive avoidance, contribute to emotional pain, and exacerbate suffering. So in CFT, we aim to "engage with the complexities of other people's and our own emotions and lives without condemning them" (Gilbert, 2009a, p. 205).

Components of the Psychology of Alleviation

The psychology of alleviation (which includes prevention) involves a set of skills that can create the potential to alleviate suffering in the context of psychotherapy and in daily life. A number of CFT interventions involve specifically training these skills to develop compassionate mind. These interventions include chair work, guided imagery, mindfulness training, compassion-focused exposure and response prevention, and working with compassion within the therapeutic relationship (Gilbert, 2009a; Tirch, 2012). Importantly, just as the attributes of compassionate engagement are interdependent, the skills of compassionate alleviation build upon one another. For example, compassionate behavior involves the wisdom of compassionate reasoning and can be guided by mindful, compassionate attention.

Attention. Training in focusing, guiding, and modulating attention is a significant element of CFT (Gilbert & Choden, 2013). Much of the preliminary attention training in CFT involves mindfulness, as this focused, flexible attention allows for disidentification and the ability to guide and move awareness. Indeed, mindfulness has served as a context for compassion training for millennia (Tirch, 2010). Additionally, CFT provides instruction in how to direct attention to the experience of compassion. For example, an exercise might be to devote mindful attention to people who are experienced as helpful throughout one day. Another form of such training might be a meditation practice of mindfulness of gratitude. Building on a foundation of mindfulness, focused attention training, and training in coherent breathing (Brown & Gerbarg, 2012), CFT extends to include guidance in directing attention to psychological, physical, and emotional domains.

Imagery. Imagery has increasingly been acknowledged as a powerful therapeutic tool in cognitive and behavioral therapies (Hackmann, Bennett-Levy, & Holmes, 2011). Imagery itself can stimulate a range of physiological systems and emotional experiences. In CFT, we share this insight with clients and point out that compassion imagery practices are designed to build the capacity for compassion, in part by stimulating related physiological systems. CFT makes use of a number of imagery exercises, including construction of a compassionate version of the self, imagining a compassionate and safe place, and creating the image of an ideal compassionate companion (Gilbert & Choden, 2013).

Reasoning. True compassion obviously isn't an unintelligent option; therefore, being able to stand back and take a wise, balanced perspective on situations is an important skill in the psychology of alleviation. It is important to think as freely and clearly as possible when engaging with compassion, because thinking through difficult questions and applying adaptive reasoning is often what helps us choose to develop compassion for things we don't like in others or ourselves (Loewenstein & Small, 2007). We may also take a compassionate perspective on our thinking itself and realize the ways in which thoughts can ensnare us in old, unhelpful patterns of action.

Behavior. Within the CFT model, compassionate behavior is basically any behavior that intentionally addresses people's suffering and tries to alleviate and prevent it. Behavior, in this sense, refers to overt behaviors rather than private behaviors in the mind; it refers to what we can do with our hands and feet to act upon and realize our motivation and intentions for compassion. Of course, such behavior would be wise and skillful, not simply reflexive rescuing, which may not actually help the target of compassion. Commonly, the cultivation of compassionate behavior involves courage as we come into contact with our awareness of suffering. For example, for a person who is agoraphobic, self-compassion does not mean sitting at home and avoiding difficult feelings; it requires practice in going out and facing the anxiety (Tirch, 2012). In essence, compassionate behavior means engaging with that which is causing suffering, and it is, of course, linked to commitment and willingness to engage.

Sensory experiencing. To some extent, the capacity for soothing through compassion, as an affiliative process, operates through the parasympathetic nervous system (Porges, 2007). It is therefore useful to help clients engage in more development of the parasympathetic nervous system. To do this, we use exercises that involve various breathing techniques and body postures. We also teach clients how to use facial expressions and voice to stimulate feelings of compassion within the body, and we use method acting techniques to help people experience engagement with the process of compassion. For example, when clients and therapists alike are first learning to build an inner voice and image of a compassionate self, CFT trainers invite them to bring mindful attention to the physical experience of smiling as opposed to having a neutral expression. Similarly, they are instructed to bring attention to the experience of listening to a warm voice greeting them, as opposed to what happens when a neutral voice greets them. Sensory sensitivity can guide our moment-by-moment experience of compassion and can stimulate the emotional systems involved in the compassionate mind.

Feeling. For the most part, compassionate affective experiences are associated with emotions involving connection, warmth, and kindness, partly because these are affiliative and soothing emotions that activate an experience of safeness and contentment, which can create a secure base for action. Compassionate emotions can also involve a sense of courage and willingness to face difficult things. Furthermore, there are times when feeling anger or panic might trigger compassion. An example would be anger at seeing indifference to starvation, as happened in the 1980s when Bob Geldof and Midge Ure created the charity supergroup Band Aid to raise money for alleviating famine in Ethiopia. Likewise, panic can activate compassionate feelings and action, as when someone realizes a child is trapped in a burning house and rushes in to rescue her. Clearly, it's not so much the quality of an emotion but its function and its link to the motivation to alleviate or prevent suffering that distinguishes the cultivation of compassionate emotions.

ACT Processes, the CFT Model, and Compassionate Flexibility

Each of the processes involved in the CFT model of compassion can be related to the ACT hexaflex processes that together effect psychological flexibility. Just as with Neff's model of self-compassion (2003a), these processes are all middle-level terms and do not precisely map onto one another. However, conceptually and technically integrating compassion and psychological flexibility in this way provides opportunities for clinicians to create focused interventions designed to help clients live adaptive and compassionate lives. In this way, examining a model of compassionate flexibility orients us toward adaptive, evidence-based processes and principles so that we can bring our clinical wisdom, creativity, and compassion to the human exchange we have with our clients.

Compassionate flexibility reflects a particular quality of engaged psychological flexibility. Drawing from previous definitions of relevant concepts (Dahl et al., 2009; Gilbert, 2010; Hayes et al., 2012; Kashdan & Rottenberg, 2010), we define compassionate flexibility as the ability to contact the present moment fully, as a conscious and emotionally responsive human being with the following qualities:

- Sensitivity to the presence of suffering in oneself and others

- Motivation to alleviate and prevent human suffering in oneself and others

- Persistent adaptation to competing and changing environmental, emotional, and motivational demands and commitment to returning attention and resources to the alleviation and prevention of suffering in oneself and others

- The ability to flexibly shift perspective and access a broader sense of oneself and others, involving the experiences of empathy and sympathy

- The ability to disentangle oneself from the excessive influence of evaluative, judgmental thoughts

- Maintaining an open and noncondemning perspective on human experience itself, thereby cultivating necessary and sufficient willingness to tolerate the distress encountered in oneself and others

The following elaboration of compassionate flexibility (illustrated in figure 4) provides a conceptual walk through the key elements of compassion as formulated within CFT theory, illuminating the hexaflex processes they relate to most significantly and how such processes might be targeted in the consultation room.

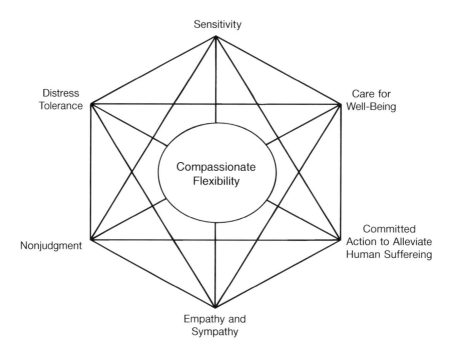

Figure 4. A model of compassionate flexibility illustrating some of the relationships between CFT processes and ACT's hexaflex model of psychological flexibility.

Care for Well-Being and Values

In ACT, living a life of meaning, purpose, and vitality in the service of freely chosen values is the core driving principle within the model of psychological flexibility. In a sense, all of the other processes come together to further increase engagement in personally meaningful actions. As discussed in ACT, values are neither goals to be attained nor rules to live by; they are inherently rewarding behaviors. A large part of values work involves clarification and authorship of behaviors that can be described as embodied intentions for how we wish to act in the world. Of course, some of the degree to which a behavior is intrinsically reinforcing may be related to our species's genetic history. Behaviors that have adaptive evolutionary functions, such as eating or having sex, are more likely to be reinforcing for most people than, say, vacuuming or watching paint dry. Similarly, the inherent adaptive, evolutionary nature of the caregiver instinct and cooperation has made motivation to care for well-being an inherently reinforcing and very strongly held value for most people throughout life.

The ACT literature stresses that values are freely chosen; however, as noted previously, compassion may be the one value that is inherent in the psychological flexibility model (Hayes, 2008c). In CFT, compassion begins with an emergent motivation to care for well-being, both our own and that of others. This speaks to the importance of human caregiving in our species's survival. CFT stresses the importance of evolved motives: values that issue from and are embedded in our deep evolutionary imperatives and embodied in evolutionarily ancient brain structures and functions. Motivation to care for well-being is clearly a value in the hexaflex usage of the term, yet it is also clearly related to some of the oldest behaviors exhibited by complex organisms on this planet. Nevertheless, individual learning history can interfere with how we contact and act upon this motivation. When people have encountered trauma in association with their experiences of support and warmth, they may have obstacles to their compassionate motivation.

Several techniques for values authorship derived from ACT and its psychological model are effective for enhancing awareness of and building compassionate motivation. These techniques include experiential imagery exercises in which the client envisions a day in the life of a future self who is living his values more fully. In another popular technique, the client imagines that she has died after living a full, rich life and is hearing what people offer as a eulogy for her, describing how she had realized a life of great personal meaning. These and other, similar techniques can bring clients into emotional contact with how they most wish to live their lives. When such work includes a compassionate focus, these practices can build the motivation to care for well-being and perhaps to be loving and open to love. Furthermore, even when these techniques are used without explicitly emphasizing compassion, many people are likely to contact how important loving relationships are for them.

The Psychology of Alleviation and Committed Action

Committed action represents an individual's ability to consistently engage in behaviors that support valued patterns of meaningful life activity and promote the realization of valued aims that create an experience of meaning, purpose, and vitality (Dahl et al., 2009). Because behavioral change rarely proceeds perfectly in an unwavering direction, committed action also involves returning to valued patterns after lapses in traveling the path we have set for ourselves (K. G. Wilson & DuFrene, 2009). For example, if a person who has been in recovery from alcohol dependence for thirteen months has a glass of champagne at a wedding, committed action may include halting the lapse and returning to 12-step meetings.

Many evidence-based therapy techniques, from exposure and response prevention to imaginal reliving, and from behavioral activation to practicing assertiveness, can be viewed as committed action steps in which people face difficult experiences in the service of their valued aims. In CFT, the range of techniques drawn from the psychology of alleviation are all committed behaviors that serve the value of cultivating compassion. Examples include compassionate imagery practice, engagement in refraining from addictive behaviors, compassion-focused exposure to fears, and developing authoritative, nonviolent assertiveness skills, all of which are forms of committed action. These techniques may serve various values, such as being a kind parent or living a more healthful lifestyle—values that in turn may serve the superordinate value of alleviating suffering where it is found, both in ourselves and in others.

Sensitivity and Contact with the Present Moment

In CFT, sensitivity means present-moment awareness that is directed toward engagement with the suffering we encounter in the world, which has an obvious relationship to mindfulness. As we cultivate greater present-moment sensitivity, we may be better able to simply notice the presence of suffering as it arises, holding it within an accepting awareness that does not turn away out of anxiety or aversion. Such sensitivity can also help us increase our awareness of the subtle dimensions of emotions and emotional memories. In this way, we may become better able, and better prepared, to encounter suffering and challenging emotions, with an increased sense that we have time to respond.

In the psychology of alleviation, this concept of sensitivity is used in a way that is similar to the psychological flexibility process known as present-moment awareness (Hayes et al., 2012). In fact, present-moment awareness, which is sometimes referred to as *self-as-process* (Blackledge & Drake, 2013), can be defined as purposeful, direct attention to the contents of the present moment as they unfold. In the hexaflex, present-moment attention also involves flexible awareness. Contacting the present moment means turning toward our experience, whatever it may be, in the moment, rather than turning away from the moment in pain or shame or getting lost in narrative content.

As the literature on mindfulness and attentional training has demonstrated, it is possible to cultivate and enhance an individual's capacity for flexible, focused attention to the present moment (Baer, 2003; Garland et al., 2010). Such attention can be trained using a number of present-moment awareness exercises during psychotherapy sessions and as homework. These practices may begin with simple movement of attention to different focal points in the body, or even in the environment. In time, these attentional practices may extend to deliberately bringing receptive awareness to one's experience during long periods of mindfulness meditation.

In classical mindfulness training, present-moment awareness served the aim of cultivating wholesome mental states, including compassion (Rapgay, 2010; Tirch, 2010; Wallace, 2009). When we bring a focus on compassion to such training, the present-moment awareness that is foundational to mindfulness serves as a context for cultivating states of mind conducive to compassion and well-being through a deliberate compassionate intention that also includes compassionate motivation and additional hexaflex processes involving the self and perspective taking.

Sympathy, Empathy, and Self-as-Context

ACT's psychological flexibility model holds that well-being and adaptive responding to the challenges of life are served by developing an ability to connect with and inhabit an experiential sense of the self as an awareness of our own awareness (Hayes et al., 2012). Throughout the many changes that occur in our lives and the myriad of contexts that will unfold for us, we humans maintain a sense of the "I-here-now-ness" of our experience. As mentioned, this sense of oneself as an observer of one's experience, separate from the content of consciousness yet observing the flow of experience, is referred to as self-as-context in the hexaflex model of psychological flexibility. Cultivating self-as-context allows for an experiential mode of self-reference that can serve as a foundation for the cultivation of compassion. In fact, this mode of self-reference has a discrete neuronal signature and involves distinct processes that can be trained (Barnes-Holmes, Foody, & Barnes-Holmes, 2013; Farb et al., 2007).

Flexible perspective taking can also involve an individual's ability to take the perspective of another and infer that person's intentions and feelings, as is the case with theory of mind tasks and mentalization. This ability allows us to step outside of ourselves and psychologically view the world from the perspective of another being, which may allow our painful mental events and emotional memories to hold less influence over us. Interestingly, at a preverbal level, tasks involved in flexible perspective taking are facilitated by efficient deployment of the parasympathetic nervous system, which is involved in relaxation and soothing (Porges, 2007). So from the perspective of the "I-here-now-ness" of being, you can view your own suffering as you might view the suffering of another and be touched by the pain in that experience, without being dominated by interference from your learning history, with its potential for shaming self-evaluations (Hayes, 2008a; Vilardaga, 2009). The biological context that can best contain this experience involves the activation of affiliative emotional response systems, along with an implicit or explicit experience that can be described as safeness or stillness. Accordingly, when you stand as witness to your own suffering or even suffering in others, you may be moved to take action to alleviate that suffering. In this way, stillness begins the movement toward action.

In contextual behavioral terms, CFT clients learn how to observe their experience from the vantage point of self-as-context and how to gradually disidentify from their self-stories and narrative, or self-as-content (Hayes et al., 2012). This process of disidentification, which is sometimes even referred to as "depersonalizing," has been a central psychotherapeutic move in CFT for some time; but only now is it beginning to be conceptualized in contextual terms.

Importantly, two of the central attributes of the psychology of engagement—which is to say two of the primary components of our evolved capacity for compassion—involve flexible perspective taking. These attributes are sympathy and empathy. These terms are used very differently from one another in CFT, though both involve dimensions of flexible perspective taking.

In CFT, sympathy is defined as a reflexive, emotional response to our awareness of the distress we witness in others or even in ourselves. When we are moved by the presence of suffering on a resonant emotional level, sympathetic responses occur, without elaborate cognitive analysis. This sort of emotional resonance is captured by eighteenth-century philosopher David Hume, who compared the transmission of emotional responses between humans to the harmonic vibration of violin strings (2000). In sympathetic responding, we automatically and effortlessly adopt the emotional perspective of another, are moved by the suffering we experience, and are compelled to do something to respond.

In contrast, within CFT empathy is defined as a heightened, focused awareness of the experiences of another person that includes understanding, perspective, and an ability to derive and construe what that person's experience would be like.

CFT offers a range of imagery and contemplative practices, as well as in-session interpersonal exercises, that provides training in flexible perspective taking, sympathy, and empathy. The following clinical example illustrates a few of these approaches.

Clinical Example: Cultivating the Observing Self and Compassionate Intention

Gene is a twenty-five-year-old client who presents with depression and social anxiety. He hates himself for his shyness and displays high degrees of fusion with a conceptualized self. To create the conditions for Gene to experience compassion in the presence of his shame and self-hostility, the therapist works within the relationship to facilitate flexible perspective taking and the emergence of some self-compassionate intention.

Client: I'm shy. I've always been shy. In my family I'm known as the shy one—the weakling, if you will. Basically, I'm just a depressed loser who will never dare to do anything worthwhile. I can't even get a girlfriend!

Therapist: I'm sad to hear that you've been walking around with this notion of yourself as shy and weak. How long has it been like this?

Client: For as long as I can remember. It's not a notion; it's who I am.

Therapist: So for all this time, the thought of being weak and shy has pretty much summed up your sense of who you are.

Client: It is who I am. They used to make jokes about this in my family. Now they don't dare joke anymore, but I know they still think it. In a way, that makes it even worse.

Therapist: Ouch! That must hurt.

Client: Yes. But they're right. I am weak and shy.

Therapist: So "weak" and "shy" are the two words that stand for who you are?

Client: Yeah. Pretty much. (*Looks down.*)

Therapist: That sounds so painful. (*Pauses.*) But can we look at these two words for a minute?

Client: What do you mean?

Therapist: (*Writes the words on a piece of paper and holds it a few feet from the client's face.*) Can you notice them standing there, as it were?

Client: Yes.

Therapist: Can you notice them telling you that's who you are?

Client: Yes.

Therapist: Can you notice how it feels to have your sense of self reduced to these two words?

Client: Yes, it's painful…and depressing.

Therapist: I'll bet. I can hear how much you identify with these words. When I see how much this causes you pain, I really wish for this suffering to cease. How about you?

Client: Me too.

Therapist: So you can notice that too. And can you also notice that there is a part of you noticing these words and how they make you feel?

Client: Errr….Yes, I think so…

Therapist: Can you notice that you are here, and that these words and how they make you feel are, so to speak, there? (*Holds the piece of paper a few feet from the client's face again.*) They are present, and they are painful, and you can also notice them being present and notice the pain that comes with them.

Client: Yes?

Therapist: So, there's a part of you that notices and hears these words, an "observer" part of you. This "observer you," the part of you that can notice both the words and the feelings the words evoke—would you describe this observer you as weak and shy? *(Pauses.)* Would you describe this observer you by the feelings that arise when it's criticized by these words, such as anger or anxiety? Or would you describe this observer you in a different way?

Client: Hmm....That's a weird question....I guess I would say it's different. It's somehow more distanced. Maybe it hurts less?

Therapist: Uh-huh. So you can notice the pain, notice your wish to make it go away, and also notice that you're noticing it. There sure is a lot going on in our tricky brains. Could it be that at every moment, there's a part of you that's there and can notice whatever shows up, painful though it may be? Isn't it the case that this observer you is just there, along for the ride, noticing and experiencing each moment, moment by moment?

Client: Yeah. It's just that I hate it.

Therapist: As I look at you, I'm starting to realize how long you've carried this sense of yourself as weak, carried this pain around the word "weak." *(Exhales.)* I'm wondering, when is it easier for you to bear this pain? Is it easier when you're judging your suffering and fighting with it? Or is it easier when you're simply noticing this emotional suffering and allowing some caring intention to be here now, allowing yourself this...wish that the pain might somehow relent?

Client: I guess it's when I stop the judging and just allow myself that wish.... Then the pain might fade.

Therapist: That feels like warmth in your voice now...not forcing the pain away, but standing back and looking upon yourself with a kind intention.

Client: Well....I guess it does feel somehow warmer or softer.

Nonjudgment and Acceptance

In the hexaflex model of psychological flexibility, the concept of acceptance is different from a conventional notion of acceptance as resignation, giving in, or giving up. Crucially, in ACT acceptance includes an element of willingness, defined as a voluntary choice to be in contact with difficult mental events and emotional experiences. This form of psychological acceptance is defined as "the adoption of an intentionally open, receptive, flexible, and nonjudgmental posture with respect to moment-to-moment experience" (Hayes et al., 2012, p. 77). In terms of compassion, this process of acceptance means choosing to remain open to our awareness of suffering as we encounter it in the world and in ourselves, even when it is difficult to bear. Of course, it is all too easy to engage in avoidance and control strategies when we encounter experiences that we don't wish to face, yet experiential avoidance also drives much of our suffering (Ruiz, 2010).

In order to help clients face their fears, their shame, and even their self-criticism, CFT aims to help them adopt a sensitive, nonjudgmental, and accepting awareness of the pain inherent in being human. This is not a white-knuckle or masochistic striving to remain in the presence of suffering for the sake of suffering. Compassion is not about just sitting in the cold, dirty bathwater of life so you can "feel your feelings" or "be accepting." As the psychological flexibility model suggests, acceptance in the service of compassionate motivation involves a willingness to be in contact with suffering as we encounter it (through the psychology of engagement), and a willingness to feel the pain involved as we begin to take action to do something about the suffering we encounter and move toward greater well-being (through the psychology of alleviation).

Clinical Example: Cultivating Acceptance, Nonjudgment, and Compassion

We return to the example of Gene for an illustration of how we can use a compassionate therapeutic relationship to help train clients to disidentify from their thoughts and emotions, access their inner wisdom through a functional analysis of their inner critic, and move toward willingness from a place of self-kindness and courage. Gene has been offered a gallery show for his paintings, but rather than work on this, he has been staying in bed, smoking marijuana, and binge-watching TV programs, bringing on a barrage of self-criticism. He has been responding through profound experiential avoidance that has been keeping him from engaging in activities that give him a sense of meaning, purpose, and vitality. This session takes place a few weeks prior to Gene's gallery opening, and Gene has been completely avoidant in the week preceding the session.

Client: So, I've been beating myself up all week again. I've hardly gotten out of bed. I just smoke weed and play video games most days. I'm disgusting.

Therapist: Well, this week has been very much like the rest of the month. You've been curling up and hiding. That's very sad, really.

Client: Yeah, I wish I were getting out to see my friends or to the studio, but I just feel like I can't face it anymore. I can't even think about painting.

Therapist: What is your anxiety?

Client: My anxiety? Hmm. I guess that I'm afraid that if I bump into anyone, I'm going to remember that I suck, that everybody dumps me, and that I am not working hard enough. I need to get more done and get my work in for the gallery show, and I'm screwing up.

Therapist: That part of you that tells you "you suck" and "you're not enough"—what emotions show up when that part drags in that old story?

Client: Ugh. You know how it is, Doc. Despair, misery, and total dread.

Therapist: "Despair, misery, and total dread." This is a pretty heavy trio you've got showing up. It's tragic, really. *(The therapist is clearly moved by this sadness but is half smiling in the presence of these emotions.)* Sometimes this life just feels like shit, doesn't it?

Client: *(Laughs and allows a few tears.)* Yes, indeed, it does. That's why we're talking.

Therapist: Exactly. That *is* why we are talking....Let's dig into this experience a bit, shall we? *(The client nods.)* So let's imagine that we had a magic pill like in the movie *The Matrix*—you know, the movie where everything that was going on was like an illusion in a computer? Let's say we have this magic pill, and if you took it, the part of you that tells you that you suck would go away forever. You could walk right out that door and never have the ability to tell yourself "you suck" or "you're not enough" again. What would you be most afraid would happen if you took it?

Client: That would be great. Nothing bad would happen.

Therapist: Well, okay, maybe that's the case. But what would your anxious self be afraid of if you took this pill and left my office without that harsh inner critic telling you your flaws?

Client: I see what you're doing here. Okay, my anxious self would be most afraid that I would be lazy—that I wouldn't get out of bed or live up to my potential.

Therapist: Okay, so that anxious self believes that the criticism is needed to keep you living your life effectively? Right?

Client: Yes.

Therapist: So, the critic is trying to help you to live up to your potential?

Client: Uh-huh. That critic is trying to protect me from failing.

Therapist: I see. So we can imagine that this critic has an intention to help you. But, is it really helping you?

Client: No effing way! This voice shows up telling me that I'm a piece of garbage, and I feel so exhausted by it that I just want to check out and cry. That's the irony. I'm afraid that if the criticism would stop, I'd be lazy, but all it does is make me shut down and hide, which is basically the same thing. I feel so trapped in all of this.

Therapist: "Trapped." Your mind tells you that you're trapped, that you can't get out of bed. That is just so sad and so heavy. What part of that experience of being criticized and trapped are you least willing to feel?

Client: Least willing to feel? Hmm. Well, I think it would be feeling ashamed that I'm not working hard enough. That's very tough.

Therapist: It sounds like it is. It's a feeling that's led you to stay in bed and be very stoned, checked out, and all alone. That is tough. I hear you telling me that the part of this that you really don't want to feel is this sense of shame for not doing enough. Please tell me, what would you have to stop caring about to not feel bad about ignoring your work?

Client: What would I have to stop caring about? Okay. Well, if I were going to totally stop feeling ashamed of blowing off my art and my work, I would have to basically not care about being an artist.

Therapist: Are you willing to do that today? Are you willing to leave this office and not care if you're working on your art and your craft?

Client: No. My art means everything to me. It really does.

Therapist: Yes! It does. That's a beautiful thing. So, if feeling sad and ashamed was a necessary part of carrying your life forward and being the version of yourself you wish to be—being the artist you wish to be— would you be willing to feel sad and ashamed?

Client: I'm feeling sad and ashamed anyway! But, yes, if facing those feelings was a part of living my life and being the artist I can be, I guess I can feel them.

Therapist: That, Gene, is compassionate courage. That's acceptance and willingness. Can you feel what it's like to touch that accepting part of you?

Client: Yes. I don't like to feel the dread and anxiety that show up with this criticism, though. It sucks.

Therapist: What a leap you've made there, Gene. You've moved from "I suck" to "It sucks to feel so criticized"! You can *feel* bad without buying into the idea that you *are* bad. That's a huge step. We've seen how much you care about being an artist and how you've learned to have an inner critic who keeps telling you that you suck and that you're awful. And when we looked at that critic's intention, we could sort of see how he was aiming to protect you from failure…

Client: *(Speaks with animation, eager to join in.)* And we also saw how all he's doing is making me feel worse by telling me "you're awful." It's funny how that part of me tries to get me moving and succeeding by telling me the same sort of critical crap that my stepmother told me for years. I don't respond to that kind of abuse. It makes me just shut down.

Therapist: That's a remarkable connection. So the part of you that hears this criticism is like you were when you were a boy. That part tries its best to do what makes the critic happy while listening to relentless criticism. When we think of that boy, with all of his hopes and fears, what might we want to say to him from a place of compassion and strength?

Client: I would want to tell him to just keep on going. I want him to get up and go to the studio, even when those voices are saying he's shit. He doesn't have to give in, and he doesn't have to give up. Even if the critic keeps going on and on, he can do it.

Therapist: That's very moving. You're finding a kind of bravery in your acceptance and compassion. So, it seems you're willing to carry this and live your life deeply.

Client: Hey man, it's easier said than done, right? But, yes, I definitely want to do that.

Therapist: One last thing on this. That critical part of you that thinks it's helping by badgering you and calling you names—the part that's really bringing you down? What would you want to say to that part from a place of wisdom, compassion, and strength? If you could, imagine what it would be like to speak from that compassionate courage and tell the critic what you want to say.

Client: *(Sits up straight.)* I would say this: "Listen, buddy, you're going about this all wrong. I don't respond to abuse, so if you want to help me get moving, you've got to speak to me like a human being. I know you're trying to help, but could you just lighten up a little?"

Therapist: That's wonderful, really. How did it feel to say that?

Client: I think I get it, Doc. I can get moving this week, even if the critic keeps it up. Phew! This is exhausting work today.

Therapist: Yes, it is. But you're doing it. You're looking out for yourself. I'm glad you're facing these things here.

Client: I need to face them somehow.

Distress Tolerance and Defusion

The evolved nature of human cognition, symbolic representation, and derived relational responding has resulted in a tendency to respond to the literal meanings and stimulus functions of our thinking in ways that strongly influence our subsequent behavior (Blackledge & Drake, 2013). We will be getting into quite a bit of detail about this process as we continue. For now, we can note that imaginal events can exert control over everything from our biological systems to our overt behaviors. In order to tolerate distress, we must have sufficient freedom from the influence of mental events to be able to remain in the presence of painful experiences while engaging in freely chosen actions. In ACT's model of psychological flexibility, defusion represents a trainable ability to disrupt or transform the effects of mental events, providing some liberation from being dominated and controlled by events arising in our evolved minds (Hayes et al., 1999). ACT offers many empirically supported techniques for facilitating defusion, which are present throughout the CBS literature. More recently, these methods have begun to be adapted into compassion-focused therapies for anxiety (Tirch, 2012).

The CFT concept of distress tolerance differs from defusion in many ways. In fact, distress tolerance is highly involved with acceptance and willingness (Gilbert, 2010). However, the capacity to stand back from the historically determined influences that mental events may have upon us and act differently than we have habitually involves defusion from the functions of these events. For example, consider a client who experiences chronic shame and self-criticism and needs to give a presentation at work. If his mind is telling him that he needs to stay home to avoid the anxiety he will face in public speaking, his ability to tolerate the distress he will feel when standing before his colleagues will call upon his capacity to defuse from the dominance of past events.

The relationship between defusion and acceptance is very close and interdependent, with the two processes combining to form what, in ACT parlance, is referred to as an *open response style*. In CFT, distress tolerance and nonjudgment interact in a similar way. As we are able to defuse from our habitual responses, ease the grip of self-condemnation and judgmental thinking, accept the difficult experiences that face us, and tolerate distress, we are better able to face suffering and take steps to alleviate it. Furthermore, activating our evolved capacity for affiliative emotions, centeredness, and compassionate motivation can enhance our ability to be accepting and open. In this way, these somewhat parallel processes in the psychological flexibility model and the psychology of compassion interact, in each case affording both new perspectives on how to relate to our experience and a range of methods for moving toward greater compassion, flexibility, and well-being.

Clinical Example: Training Acceptance and Defusion with a Compassionate Focus

John is a sixty-five-year-old man who complains of incapacitating attentional difficulties, though doctors haven't found any evidence of cognitive impairment or attention deficits. He manages a well-liked natural food store that hosts a number of community activities. He's been involved in community projects all his life and genuinely loves being of service to others. Yet he often feels like a fraud and experiences significant social anxiety and fears of public speaking. Lately he has become acutely preoccupied with his "memory issues." He feels so guilty about them that he finds it hard to pay attention to what others are saying and has become deeply depressed.

Therapist: How's it going?

Client: Bad. On my way here, I crossed to the other side of the street so I wouldn't have to meet this lady I know from the shop. I couldn't remember her name or what she talked to me about just yesterday! It was some upsetting family matter, but I can't remember what. My damned memory! So I crossed the street to avoid her. I'm not sure if she saw me. I hope not! I feel like such a coward, and like such a fraud for the "emotional support" I gave her yesterday. If I can't remember it now, it must not have been worth much. *(Sighs heavily.)*

Therapist: It's really tough to feel so bad and so preoccupied with the thought that you can't remember what people tell you.

Client: Yes, it's hard.

Therapist: I hope you can find relief from the weight of that.

Client: Can I?

Therapist: I hope you can. It would be a relief because it's so hard for you to be going through that.

Client: Yes, and I feel it's only getting worse.

Therapist: I'm having an image of this painful thought, about not being able to remember, standing between you and the people you're talking to. Where does it stand? *(Raises his hand and holds it several inches from the side of his own head.)* There? *(Brings his hand closer to the side of his head.)* There? *(Brings his hand in front of his eyes so his line of sight to the client is blocked.)* Here?

Client: *(Raises his hand in turn and brings it in front of his eyes.)* More like here.

Therapist: Wow. I want to stop for a moment to acknowledge how painful it is for you to have this thought effectively blocking you from being fully present with other people. I know how important others are to you.

Client: Yes, it's really hard.

Therapist: And you must feel so alone. It's as if it's cutting you off from others.

Client: Yes. Even my wife can't fully understand how I feel.

Therapist: Maybe we can make some room for how terribly painful it is for you to have this thought stand in your way and isolate you so much.

Client: How do I do that?

Therapist: Well, John, I don't think it makes you a fraud to have it there. I just think it makes life very hard for you.

Client: It sure does.

Therapist: So when life is so hard, what could help you most—bringing more harshness and judgment into the equation? Or do you need more kindness?

Client: I guess kindness. But I'm not very good at being kind to myself.

Therapist: Perhaps we can also make room for that as you learn how to be kinder to yourself and the difficulties you're going through.

Client: (*Smiles.*) I'd like that.

CBS, Compassion, and Buddhist Psychology

Western science continues to advance our understanding of compassion and the central role it can play in human psychological growth, adaptive behavioral functioning, psychological flexibility, and wellness. The scientific method allows us to expand our understanding and test its applications. However, we can continue to find wisdom in the thousands of years of prescientific phenomenological research conducted by contemplative traditions. In Buddhist psychology, several different aspects of compassion are discussed, and each reflects a nuance of the experience of compassion. For example, the concept of *metta* represents loving-kindness and a desire for all beings to be happy and at peace. Another Buddhist aspect of compassion, bodhicitta, is very significant to an ACT formulation of compassion, as it provides an illustration of how an individual's sense of self might be intimately involved in the experience of compassion.

Bodhicitta represents an altruistic aspiration for the end of suffering for all beings. It is said to arise among advanced meditators after they have recognized and encountered a sense of self that acknowledges and experiences the interconnectedness of all things. If we were to view the prescientific concept of bodhicitta in the way we would view a scientific hypothesis, we might posit that ongoing mindfulness practice leads to a shift in the sense of self such that all mental phenomena become insubstantial. In addition, this shift in sense of self allows for recognition of the interconnectedness of all things and all beings, with all conceptual divisions and separations being merely verbal constructions and acts of relating symbolic events in the mind. In this way, the arising of bodhicitta may involve letting go of evaluative self-concepts, which, by definition, place us in a position of opposition to others. Indeed, even the concept of a self may be viewed as an ongoing process of relating moment-to-moment experiences to one another, creating a conceptual process of experiencing reality that is actually based upon formlessness and *sunyata*, or emptiness. This shift of perspective is hypothesized to evoke a desire to alleviate all suffering in all beings. Therefore, in Buddhist psychology, compassion arises from a fundamental shift in perspective away from a content-based sense of self and toward an experience of self as a stream of bare attention. Clearly, there is a high degree of conceptual continuity between such a formulation and CBS concepts of flexible perspective taking, with the experience of self-as-context being crucial to liberation from suffering.

By shifting the focus away from a content-based self and adopting a psychologically flexible perspective, the ongoing pursuit of high self-esteem (and its attendant downsides in terms of narcissism and damaging social comparisons) can be avoided. This may help explain why the practice of self-compassion leads to more beneficial outcomes than the cultivation of self-esteem (Neff, 2009). Psychological flexibility obviates the need to judge or evaluate a content-based self as good or bad, given that the self is seen as an experiential process rather than a reified entity. This may facilitate a reduction in shaming and blaming self-talk and an increase in the ability to be kind to oneself in contexts of suffering. Psychological flexibility also allows individuals to commit to courses of action that align with their core values, perhaps helping to explain why self-compassion is linked to greater motivation. As was the case with exploring contemporary theories of compassion in applied psychology, exploring the relationship between psychological flexibility and Buddhist psychology's conceptualization of compassion also reveals a window of opportunity to further a science well-suited to addressing the problem of human suffering.

3

CFT: Origins, Evolutionary Context, and Opening Practices

While CFT is often practiced as a freestanding therapeutic modality in its own right, its methods have been designed in such a way that they can be used by practitioners who operate primarily in other therapy models. As Paul Gilbert has often stated in trainings, "We call this compassion-focused therapy, and not compassion therapy, because it is a way of bringing a compassion focus to the therapy that you have learned to practice." As a result, many practitioners of CBT, ACT, and other forms of psychotherapy have integrated elements of CFT and compassionate mind training into their practice without divesting themselves of their prior learning and becoming "CFT therapists" in every sense. There is clear value in exploring training in CFT, in its own right and in an undiluted form—indeed, two of the authors of this book have made the theory, research, and practice of CFT central to their professional missions. However, just some exposure to the literature on the science of compassion and the methods of CFT can provide ACT therapists with an evidence-based entrée into integrating this approach into their practice, and alert them to theoretical and practical possibilities for bringing processes and procedures from CFT into an ACT-consistent intervention, creating a compassion-focused ACT.

The Parallel Paths of ACT and CFT

ACT and CFT began to develop in quite distinct scientific communities, under different cultural circumstances and working with differing sets of assumptions. For many years these approaches developed in isolation from one another. For example, whereas ACT has emerged from the behavior analytic tradition, CBS, and the philosophy of functional contextualism, CFT has arisen more from affective neuroscience and developmental psychology research (Gilbert, 2009a). Nevertheless, both ACT and CFT have shared some assumptions in their orientations. For example, both have followed a bottom-up approach to developing treatment, have emphasized the importance of evidence-based processes and principles over treatment packages, and have rooted their clinical assumptions in basic science. Furthermore, both CFT and ACT have drawn upon elements of contemplative traditions, humanistic therapies, and the use of imagery and metaphor to generate integrative, experiential approaches to behavior therapy (Gilbert, 2010; Hayes et al., 1999). After years of growth along parallel paths, a number of factors have come together in recent years to bring the sciences of compassion and psychological flexibility together and engage them in a growing discussion that is facilitating new perspectives and clinical techniques. Many of the antecedents of the integration of CFT and CBS involve research, applications, and theory, and this chapter will discuss all of these factors.

Compassion-Focused Research

Over the last few years, the research base for compassion psychology generally and CFT specifically has been growing at a remarkable rate, with a rapid increase in the number of research and clinical publications addressing compassion. For example, the last ten years have seen a major upsurge in exploration into the benefits of cultivating compassion, especially through imagery practice (Fehr, Sprecher, & Underwood, 2008). One early study (Rein, Atkinson, & McCraty, 1995) found that people who were guided in compassion imagery experienced positive effects on an indicator of immune functioning (S-IgA), whereas being guided in anger imagery had negative effects. Furthermore, neuroscience and imaging research has demonstrated that practices of imagining compassion for others produce changes in the frontal cortex, the immune system, and overall well-being (Lutz et al., 2008). Notably, one study (Hutcherson, Seppala, & Gross, 2008) found that even just a brief loving-kindness meditation increased feelings of social connectedness and affiliation toward strangers. Another study of the benefits of compassion meditation (Fredrickson, Cohn, Coffey, Pek, & Finkel, 2008) allocated sixty-seven participants to a loving-kindness meditation group and seventy-two to a waiting list control. It found that engaging in six one-hour weekly group sessions with home practice based on a CD of loving-kindness meditation decreased illness symptoms and increased positive emotions, mindfulness, and feelings of purpose in life and social support. Yet another study (Pace et al., 2009) found that compassion meditation over the course of six weeks improved immune function and both neuroendocrine and behavioral responses to stress. Finally, an exercise as simple as writing a compassionate letter to oneself has been found to improve coping with difficult life events and reduce depression (Leary, Tate, Adams, Allen, & Hancock, 2007).

All of this research is of potential value for ACT practitioners, as most of these studies have proceeded without the burden of a particular set of mechanistic assumptions and often aren't based in a particular theoretical orientation. And as demonstrated in chapter 2, the underlying processes and potential procedures involved in applied compassion psychology are largely ACT consistent, leading to new avenues for the CBS community to explore.

In further relevant research, several compassion-focused intervention components that are entirely ACT consistent have been found to enhance psychotherapy outcomes, and to serve as mediator variables in outcomes. For example, one study (Schanche, Stiles, McCullough, Svartberg, & Nielsen, 2011) found that self-compassion was an important mediator of reduction in negative emotions associated with personality disorders that chiefly involve anxiety, fear, and avoidance (Cluster C disorders), and recommended self-compassion as a target for therapeutic intervention. Another study (Beaumont, Galpin, & Jenkins, 2012) compared CBT to CBT plus CFT in clients with a history of trauma and found a nonsignificant trend for greater improvement in the CBT plus CFT condition. In this study, CFT was associated with significantly greater improvement in self-compassion, a finding that led the authors to suggest that developing compassion could be an important adjunct to therapy. In a study of the effectiveness of mindfulness-based cognitive therapy for depression (Kuyken et al., 2010), researchers found that self-compassion was a significant mediator between mindfulness and recovery. In fact, in a meta-analysis of research concerning both clinical and nonclinical settings, compassion-focused interventions were found to be significantly effective (Hofmann et al., 2011). Research has shown that self-compassion can be distinguished from self-esteem and predicts some aspects of well-being better than self-esteem (Neff & Vonk, 2009). And in correlational research using the Self-Compassion Scale (Neff, 2003a), self-compassion has been found to offer protection against anxiety and depression, even when controlling for self-criticism. People who report high levels of self-compassion on the Self-Compassion Scale also report high levels of many positive psychological traits, including autonomy, competence, and emotional intelligence (Neff, 2003a; Neff, Rude, et al., 2007).

In addition to the growing body of research supporting compassion as a beneficial process in psychotherapy and in everyday life, CFT itself is seeing increasing empirical support through outcome research. An early clinical trial involving a group of people with chronic mental health problems who were attending a day hospital (Gilbert & Procter, 2006) found that CFT significantly reduced self-criticism, shame, sense of inferiority, depression, and anxiety. Another study (Ashworth, Gracey, & Gilbert, 2011), which was an uncontrolled trial, found CFT to be a helpful addition and focus for people with acquired brain injury. Additionally, an important randomized controlled trial using CFT for people with psychotic disorders (Braehler, Harper, & Gilbert, 2012) found significant clinical improvement and increases in compassion, as well as high levels of tolerability and low attrition, as compared to a treatment-as-usual condition. Similarly, a clinical trial (Laithwaite et al., 2009) found significant improvements in depression, self-esteem, and sense of self, as compared to others, in a sample of patients in recovery from psychosis in a forensic mental health setting. In other outcome research, CFT has been found to be significantly effective for the treatment of personality disorders (Lucre & Corten, 2012), eating disorders (Gale, Gilbert, Read, & Goss, 2012), and heterogeneous mental health problems in people presenting to community mental health teams (Judge, Cleghorn, McEwan, & Gilbert, 2012). As CFT continues to become more widely disseminated and growing numbers of clinicians and researchers acquire understanding and skill in its methods and philosophy, increasing outcome research will further test the model, leading to innovation and improvement.

And even as CFT and compassion psychology have been experiencing a rapid expansion of process and outcome research, ACT and its model of psychological flexibility has continued to generate an exponentially growing body of research, applications, and therapeutic innovations. Clearly, contextual approaches to behavior therapy have assumed a central role in the cultural discussion regarding evidence-based therapies. Additionally, contextual behavioral science has increasingly situated its model of language and cognition within evolutionary theory (D. S. Wilson et al., 2012). Because evolutionary theory was the conceptual birthplace of CFT, starting with the earliest intimations of CFT concepts in *Human Nature and Suffering* (Gilbert, 1989), this has drawn ACT and CFT further onto common ground. Thus, in CFT and ACT we see two approaches that have a great deal of commonality, even as they look at the question of human suffering through somewhat different lenses. It appears that a common focus is possible, and that the dialogue and diversity provided by any friction between these complementary perspectives can generate as much light as heat.

Contextual Compassion-Focused Applications and the CBS Community

As evidenced by the existence of this book, the integration of compassion psychology and contextual psychology is proceeding, in terms of both applications of CFT and developments in the CBS community. Over the last few years, a number of ACT psychologists have integrated compassion-focused techniques into their work, from adding elements of compassion psychology into interventions and training (Forsyth & Eifert, 2007; Wright & Westrup, in press; Yadavaia, 2013) to researching self-compassion as a process variable in ACT self-help books (Van Dam, Sheppard, Forsyth, & Earleywine, 2011) to examining how compassion may relate to the process of values authorship (Dahl et al., 2009). Much of the early compassion-related work within ACT, in both research and practice, involved the concept of self-compassion as delineated by Kristin Neff (2003a). In response to this trend, Neff's model of self-compassion has been translated into psychological flexibility processes (Neff & Tirch, 2013). As noted, there is a good amount of conceptual continuity between the two models, particularly concerning how both emphasize the importance of mindfulness, disidentification, and an experience of common humanity as being central to well-being.

Over the past several years, CFT has increasingly been involved in building bridges with the contextual behavioral science movement, which forms the scientific foundation for ACT treatment development. This has occurred through training initiatives, theoretical discussion panels, and research collaborations involving CFT founder Paul Gilbert and many members of the Association for Contextual Behavioral Science (ACBS), including the organization of the Compassion-Focused Special Interest Group within ACBS. In terms of treatment development, a recent CFT self-help–based intervention for anxiety has integrated elements of the psychological flexibility model (Tirch, 2012). Furthermore, members of the research team involved in the first randomized controlled trial demonstrating the effectiveness of CFT in the treatment of psychosis (Braehler et al., 2012) are now studying how ACT processes may be useful for the treatment of depression after psychosis (White et al., 2011). Clearly, the core of this conversation has evolved from the relationship between CFT's two psychologies of compassion and ACT's model of psychological flexibility.

The Roots of CFT in the Treatment of Shame-Based Difficulties

Compassion-focused therapy was developed with and for people who have high levels of shame and self-criticism, elements that are transdiagnostic for vulnerability to psychopathology (Gilbert & Irons, 2005; Zuroff, Santor, & Mongrain, 2005), and that can seriously interfere with therapeutic progress (Bulmash, Harkness, Stewart, & Bagby, 2009; Rector, Bagby, Segal, Joffe, & Levitt, 2000). Cultivating compassion and affiliative emotions is a core process for addressing shame and self-criticism (Gilbert & Irons, 2005), which often involve preoccupation or fusion with thoughts of self-condemnation and emotions of anger (Kolts, 2012), anxiety, or disgust (Gilbert & Irons, 2005; Whelton & Greenberg, 2005). Furthermore, anxiety and depressive symptoms across several diagnoses are correlated with higher levels of shame and self-criticism (Kannan & Levitt, 2013; Zuroff et al., 2005) and lower levels of self-compassion (Neff, 2009).

Moreover, when people's experience is dominated by such threat-focused thoughts and threat-based emotions, they often have narrowed attention and behavioral repertoires, as well as a reduced capacity for empathy (Fredrickson, 2001; Hayes & Shenk, 2004; Negd, Mallan, & Lipp, 2011; Wachtel, 1967). These effects may lead to fewer sources of reward and less access to a meaningful, purposeful life (Eifert & Forsyth, 2005). Research (Whelton & Greenberg, 2005) has shown that the negative effects of self-criticism are brought about in part by emotions of disappointment, anger, and contempt that accompany self-criticism, and not solely the form and content of thoughts.

Paul Gilbert has described how he initially began developing a compassion-focused approach twenty years ago when using cognitive behavioral therapy to help people reevaluate and reframe their depressed or anxious thinking (Tirch & Gilbert, in press). Gilbert found that when people were trying to generate evidence-based thoughts, the inner tone of these alternative thoughts was often still hostile or frightened (Gilbert et al., 2012). Inner dialogues characterized by self-hostility and shaming did not seem to respond as well to cognitive disputation as they did to a shift in tone toward a warm, kind, and compassionate emotional experience. This set in motion an exploration of the basic psychological science of affiliation, attachment, and emotion regulation by Gilbert and his colleagues in the UK and internationally—an exploration that has continued to this day. Interestingly, the period of this initial development is roughly synchronous with the earliest innovations of CBS and ACT in the United States.

CFT and Evolutionary Theory

A key focus of CFT is using evolutionary insights as a basis for psychoeducation and helping people address shame and self-criticism by depersonalizing the contents and processes of the mind. As noted, this is resonant with the ACT process of defusion. Contextual behavioral science, as its name implies, is highly focused on the contexts that give rise to mental events. In a related way, CFT contextualizes mental events and human suffering in three primary domains:

- Suffering arises because we are evolved beings with biological bodies that are easy to injure and that deteriorate, become diseased, and die. Moreover, our brains are evolved to enact species-appropriate (archetypal) motives and behaviors, such as forming attachments to parents, joining groups, seeking status, being selected as a sexual partner, or acting as a parent. This places mental suffering in an evolutionary context that has given rise to a brain full of conflicting motives, emotions, and ways of thinking and therefore is rich in its potential for suffering. Thus, much of what goes on in the mind is not our "fault"; however, we can learn to cultivate skills and approaches that are helpful.

- Suffering arises within the context of the individual's learning history, including the ways in which life experiences have influenced phenotypic development not only at the physiological level, but also at the level of safety strategies, goals, values, and self-identities.

- Suffering arises within the present-moment context of the individual: the multitude of factors that may be giving rise to moment-by-moment experience.

The Evolutionary Context

Using an evolutionary approach to the issues of mental health (Gilbert, 1989, 1998; Nesse, 1998) makes it easy to recognize that our minds are set up in such a way that they are full of compromises and trade-offs (Brune et al., 2012; Gilbert, 2001). So CFT generally begins with introducing a psychoeducational model based upon current evolutionary understanding. Over time, this model has become more sophisticated and central to the process of de-shaming and depersonalizing the contents of the mind.

The Reality Check

There are various CFT methods for helping clients situate their experience in an evolutionary context, including stories, psychoeducation, metaphors, and the development of a collaborative case conceptualization that takes the evolutionary functions of human emotions into account. Early in therapy, most CFT therapists use a semistructured discussion known as the Reality Check to introduce clients to the context of evolution, and help them see that much of their life experience has been beyond their choosing and that suffering is a natural part of human life.

Within CFT, a lot of what appears to be psychoeducation is actually a way of engendering a fundamental and philosophical shift of perspective, through a process of guided discovery facilitated via discussions between the therapist and client. While the theory and practice of many forms of therapy appear to be separate aspects of the work, engaging with the evolutionary model in CFT is an essential part of cultivating mindful insight into the nature of being human, an approach that can evoke compassion. Adopting an engaged, open, and deliberately emotionally evocative demeanor, CFT practitioners often begin their work in this way to help clients experientially apply insights from evolutionary psychology regarding the nature of the mind.

Intervention: The Reality Check

The Reality Check is a collaborative discussion that involves stories, metaphors, and guided discovery. Together, client and therapist explore the evolutionary context of human suffering by reflecting on the fact that we all are of the same species and share our common humanity. The therapist may begin by explaining, "We are all built by genes in more or less the same way, and this has given rise to our very tricky brain. Everyone's brain has common emotions, motives, and ways of thinking. Some of these mental experiences are very helpful, such as problem solving in the face of environmental challenges. Other mental events can be quite painful, such as worrying about events far in the future that we can't have any control over." The client and therapist may then engage in further guided discovery in which the therapist uses Socratic questioning to explore the client's reaction to her role as an emergent being in the flow of life.

As the CFT therapist hears the client's reactions and questions, he engages in *affect matching*, validating the client's emotional response through nonverbal communication, affective expressiveness, and de-pathologizing language. Even at this early stage in therapy, the therapist may also use *empathic bridging*, slowing down the dialogue and deliberately using mindfulness of the therapist's own emotional processes to evoke flexible perspective taking on the part of the client. From the outset, CFT therapists are aiming to understand the world through their clients' eyes, while thinking *with* clients and not for them.

Following the introduction of the evolutionary model, the CFT therapist reflects on the fact that because we are biological beings, life is full of suffering.

The therapist provides a range of examples of this, such as, "There are millions of potential viruses and diseases that can afflict the human condition, and we are quite easy to injure, sometimes with long-term consequences. Our lives are relatively short, about twenty-five thousand to thirty thousand days on average, and during this time we may flourish for a while, but we will gradually deteriorate and lose functions."

Following this, the therapist makes the social contextual point that anyone is "only one particular version of himself or herself, shaped by his or her social learning history." CFT therapists often use the following example to illustrate the point: "If I had been kidnapped as a three-day-old baby and raised by a violent drug gang, what kind of person would I be today? When they grow up, the sons of drug enforcers in cartels conduct violent crimes as part of the family business. As much as I don't want to think I could be that sort of person, it is possible that with such a learning history, I would be a very different version of myself." The therapist invites the client to reflect on this in some detail. As the client gains insight into the fact that the therapist himself might have become aggressive or even murderous, possibly incarcerated or already dead—in other words, a very different type of person—this can initiate a shift toward recognizing that we are all just versions of ourselves. Indeed, early experiences can even affect genetic expression and the maturation of different brain areas—that is how powerful social contexts are. Then, not surprisingly, the next question the therapist poses is: "Is it possible to start to train and choose versions of ourselves that will organize our minds and sense of self in a way that is more conducive to well-being?"

Far from being mere psychoeducation, the Reality Check is a first step on the way to helping clients practice acceptance and defusion. Furthermore, at the same time they are beginning to take responsibility for engaging in change processes and for cultivating mental states conducive to their well-being.

The Interaction of the Old Brain and New Brain

To show clients how potentially destructive the human mind can be—as well as highly caring and compassionate—CFT therapists typically draw an outline of the brain and begin to label it as shown in figure 5.

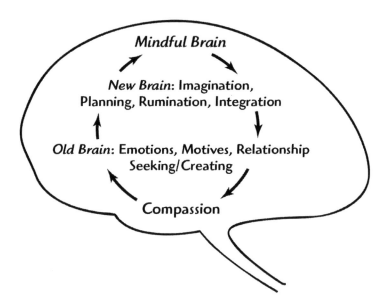

Figure 5. Interactions between mindfulness, compassion, and older and newer brain functions. (Reprinted from Gilbert & Choden, 2013, with permission from Constable and Robinson.)

In discussing brain functions that evolved earlier, for the sake of simplicity the therapist refers to them as *old-brain* psychology. This includes many behaviors, social motivations, and emotions we share with other animals, such as being territorial, having conflicts and aggressive interactions, belonging to groups, forming alliances, having sexual desires, looking after offspring, and, crucially, responding to affection and affiliation by becoming more calm.

This is a point of distinction between CFT and ACT. Whereas CBS proceeds from a set of assumptions wherein the act of an entire organism in context is the agreed upon unit of analysis for the prediction and influence of behavior, CFT explores the brain as an emergent, collective set of evolved capacities in the context of the flow of life on earth. While this is a contextualism of a certain stripe, CFT looks within the organism for an evolutionary functional analysis of emotion, rather than viewing mental events explicitly as dependent variables. Both conditioning principles and embodied affective processes are essential in CFT. This is a part of the centrality of emotional responding within CFT theory, leading to a strong emphasis on processes of emotion regulation, attachment, and affiliation throughout the model. So, the idea is to help people gain clear insight into the fact that these motivational and emotional systems have been built into us, not by us. As a species, we simply find ourselves here, with a mind that has many old-brain functions and intense, compelling, and emotionally driven patterns of action (Gilbert, 2009a).

Next, CFT therapists explore human problems related to the evolved *new brain*, or thinking brain. Indeed, humans have been referred to as the thinking ape (Byrne, 1995). Unfortunately, our evolved capacity for thinking creates both problems and benefits. As mentioned in chapter 1, around two million years ago humans began to develop a whole range of new cognitive abilities: imagination, reasoning, reflecting, anticipating, and generating a sense of self. And as discussed, contextual behavioral theory and research suggest that these mental abilities are based upon the way humans began to derive relations among stimuli in our environment (Roche, Cassidy, & Stewart, 2013). For humans, a "combination of our genetically evolved capacity and a history of reinforcement by a social community" (Hayes et al., 2012, p. 360) has resulted in the range of capacities that CFT refers to as *new-brain psychology*: language use, symbolic understanding, problem solving, and elaboration of learning through cognition.

One of the core principles in CFT is understanding the way these new-brain competencies link into, stimulate, and are stimulated by old-brain systems of motivation and emotion. While emotions may emerge from preverbal, old-brain evolutionary response patterns, the human experience of emotion is expressed and derived from our cognitive and verbal behaviors, which are shaped by social contexts and involve our new-brain capacities. CFT posits that the interaction of hardwired emotional and motivational responding, determined prior to birth with new-brain cognitive abilities, is part of the source of much human suffering. Take an intelligent mind and fuel it with tribal vengeance, and you can end up with horrendous atrocities and nuclear weapons. Equally, take a mind with new-brain competencies and link these into motivational systems that are concerned with caring and helping others, and you find the sources of compassion (Gilbert, 2009b).

CFT therapists help clients experience and understand the interaction of old-brain and new-brain abilities using metaphors and examples, such as imagining a zebra running away from a lion. Once the zebra gets away, it will quickly calm down and go back to eating or other zebra activities. Whereas the zebra's threat-based emotions may return to baseline calm within minutes, this is unlikely for humans because of our capacity for cognition, with which we predict events and create internal representations of possibilities. If a zebra thought as humans do, it might start to ruminate, imagining what might have happened if the lion had caught it and what it might encounter tomorrow. This zebra would then experience intrusive simulations, images, and fantasies related to being eaten alive, or what might happen if it doesn't spot the lion tomorrow, or even the disaster of two lions turning up! While the human brain can solve problems and give rise to science and culture, it can also trap us in terrible internal loops because our thoughts and imaginations allow us to run simulations of numerous possibilities in our mind, stimulating physiological systems involving evolved motives and emotions. This is the essence of Robert Sapolsky's famous book *Why Zebras Don't Get Ulcers* (2004).

Emotion Regulation Processes in CFT

CFT is focused on deep, evolved emotion and motivational systems and the stimulation and cultivation of specific affect regulating systems. It follows the psychological scientific view that emotions serve evolved and emergent motives, and that emotions also build and strengthen motives. As Silvan Tompkins (1963) said many years ago, while one can be motivated for anything, with emotions it matters, and without emotions it doesn't. However, motives and emotions follow important evolutionary trajectories, such as being part of a group, gaining status, developing friendships, finding sexual partners, creating attachment, and caring for offspring (Gilbert, 1989, 2009a), and also signal how well or poorly we are doing. These evolutionary trajectories relate to social and other behaviors that are inherently reinforcing.

So emotions are evolved to orient our actions in real time, and the anticipation of emotions is what often guides motives and behaviors. Evolutionary analysis and affective neuroscience research (Depue & Morrone-Strupinsky, 2005) suggest that there are at least three types of emotional systems (figure 6). Sometimes referred to as the three-circle model, this CFT model of human emotions is a description of the complex interacting processes involved in human emotion regulation, and it aims to make sense, in a clinically applicable way, of some complicated science. As such, the model might run the risk of oversimplifying things. Nevertheless, it forms a bridge that allows us to bring an understanding of the evolution of human emotion into the consultation room as we work directly with clients and their own compassionate wisdom.

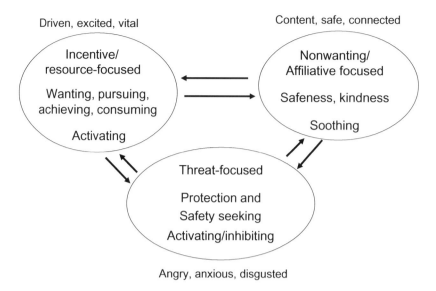

Figure 6. The three major emotion regulation systems. (Reprinted from Gilbert, 2009a, with permission from Constable and Robinson.)

The Incentive/Resource-Focused System

The first of the three emotion regulation systems in the model is the *incentive/resource-focused system*, which involves the range of human behaviors that contribute to pursuing aims, consuming, and achieving (Gilbert, 2007, 2009a). These are emotions of joy, pleasure, and excitement. They are associated with achieving, winning, and succeeding and serve the motive of acquiring resources that enhance survival and reproductive success. The incentive/resource-focused system likely activates dopaminergic (reward) systems to a greater degree than do other emotion regulation systems. When we are engaged in pursuing aims and seeking excitement and feel a drive toward acquisition and accomplishment, this emotional system is activated and plays a key role in how we act and respond to the world around us.

Importantly, CFT recognizes that many dimensions of our experience are affected when a particular emotion system is activated. For example, imagine that you discover you won a huge, multistate lottery and would soon have hundreds of millions of dollars wired into your bank account. What might you feel in your body? What thoughts would likely be triggered in your mind? What emotions might move through you? Would your attention be focused and tight, or broad and wandering? What urges would arise? Might you find yourself up all night, wondering what to do with all of this new money and new possibility? Clearly, as an environmental event—or even just the thought of such an event— activates the incentive/resource-focused system, many dimensions of our being are affected and influenced.

The Threat-Focused System

The second emotion regulation system in the three-circle model is the highly sensitive *threat-focused system*. Our genetic ancestors, who faced the persistent presence of threats such as predators, disease, and natural disasters, evolved to possess a "better safe than sorry" process for quickly detecting threats in the environment and responding rapidly. The threat-focused system involves some of the older evolutionary structures in the brain, including the amygdala and the limbic system, and the serotonergic system (Gilbert, 2010), which activates defensive behaviors, such as the classic fight, flight, or freeze response. The emotions involved are along the lines of anger, anxiety, and disgust (LeDoux, 1998). We often describe this system to our clients as the "always-on, 24/7, better-safe-than-sorry, threat-detection mind." Whether because of or in spite of that excessive verbiage, clients immediately know what type of emotional state we are referring to.

The Nonwanting/Affiliative-Focused System

In contrast, the third emotion regulation system in the three-circle model, the *nonwanting/affiliative-focused system*, is based on the experience of contentment and connection. When animals are not under threat or seeking to fulfill survival and reproduction needs, they can be quiescent, hence the evolution of emotions and states that serve the functions of "rest and digest" and offer the experience of safeness and peacefulness. For many animals, calming can occur simply by removal of the threat. However, during the evolution of mammalian attachment, the rest and digest system underwent adaptations such that affiliative signals could also trigger a calming response and signal a state of safeness (Carter, 1998; Porges, 2007). Thus, when an infant is distressed, the presence of the parent and physical contact can downregulate threat processing and calm the infant. This is reflected in affiliative-oriented experiences and emotions, such as nurturance, validation, and empathy, which involve the oxytocin and opioid systems (Gilbert, 2007).

In this way, humans have evolved to naturally respond to kindness and warmth through a downregulation of the anxiety systems and a felt sense of soothing. This involves a genetically predisposed capacity to feel a sense of safeness and soothing in the presence of stable, warm, empathic interactions with others (Gilbert, 2010). This affiliative-focused safeness system is activated by experiences that evoke the stable, caring context that an engaged and effective parent establishes with her child (Bowlby, 1968; Fonagy & Target, 2007; Sloman, Gilbert, & Hasey, 2003). Accordingly, the evolution of caregiving and nurturing in humans has influenced the structure of the vagus nerve, the functions of the autonomic nervous system, affect regulation, and human social behaviors (Porges, 2003). In many ways, the affiliative-focused emotional system is central to the experience of compassion.

Context Matters

Each of these three emotional systems, when activated by events in the environment or even in the mind, serves to organize our actions and mental events. We may become prepared to fearfully run from physical danger or to joyously run downfield to win the big game, depending on what the environment triggers in our emotional world. Compassion involves our experience of safeness, contentment, and inner authority in ways that aren't always obvious, and such experiences can be empowering in a lasting manner. By deliberately deploying mindful awareness and activating our experience of compassion, we may be finding a place of stability and readiness from which to step forward into a meaningful life.

Attachment, Soothing, and Affiliative Emotions in CFT

There is now considerable evidence that as mammals evolved live birth for immature offspring, the attachment system became central to the organization of emotional regulation between infant and parent (Cozolino, 2010; Mikulincer & Shaver, 2007a; Siegel, 2012). With the evolution of the human capacity for language and cognition, the size of the human brain expanded, so that we have a brain that, at around 92 cubic inches (1,500 cc), is nearly three times the size of that of our nearest evolutionary relative, the chimpanzee. As such, the human brain would grow far too large for offspring to pass through the birth canal if humans were to develop more fully than they currently do in gestation. Therefore, we humans are born with our brain development "half-baked," so to speak. Human infants are very vulnerable and we have a low birth rate, factors that require behaviors of protection, support, and caring for our species to survive. As noted, this has resulted in significant evolutionary modifications to the parasympathetic and sympathetic nervous system to enable the parasympathetic nervous system to produce a calming response in the presence of others who are caring, safe, and affiliative (Porges, 2007).

In addition, a range of specialized brain systems for detecting and responding to affiliative signals evolved, including the oxytocin system (Carter, 1998). Oxytocin helps build trust and affiliative relationships and is stimulated in and by affiliative relationships (Uvnäs Moberg, 2013). Moreover, oxytocin exerts direct effects that calm threat processing in the amygdala (Kirsch et al., 2005). So there is now considerable evidence that the experience of affiliative behavior regulates emotion to a high degree, and particularly emotions related to threats (Uvnäs Moberg, 2013). Attachment theorists suggest that the affiliative emotional experiences involved in healthy attachment bonds serve as a secure base from which people can begin to explore their world and face challenges (Bowlby, 1969, 1973; Mikulincer & Shaver, 2007).

CFT builds on attachment theorists' approach while recognizing that internal working models of others may be problematic as sources for a secure base. Many people have experienced abuse, trauma, or neglect by caregivers or in the context of caregiving behaviors. This can cause activation of the soothing system to be associated with increased threat through classical conditioning principles, which can result in fear of compassion and difficulty with activation of soothing (Gilbert, 2010). Therefore, compassion-focused therapy seeks to stimulate the affiliative-focused emotional system as an internal point of reference and organizing process in a manner that is gradual and not overwhelming. In the chapters to come, we will describe a number of techniques, visualizations, and practices that can cultivate compassionate mind and generate compassionate flexibility. However, in CFT the cultivation of compassion begins with deployment of attention and the deliberate engagement of the soothing system through a blend of mindfulness and slow, rhythmically steady breathing (Gilbert, 2009a), via such exercises as Soothing Rhythm Breathing (Tirch, 2012).

Intervention: Soothing Rhythm Breathing

In CFT, clients are typically introduced to Soothing Rhythm Breathing, a compassion-focused variant on mindful breathing, early in the course of therapy. Thereafter, the technique becomes the foundation and first step in a succession of practices involved in compassionate mind training. In part, the practice is derived from elements of Buddhist concentration meditation and mindfulness meditation, with adaptations to create a brief and clearly understandable form that is useful in the context of psychotherapy. The meditation is an invitation to find a point of stillness in the experience of breathing from which it is possible to observe the comings and goings of the mind. This stillness involves activation of the parasympathetic nervous system and the attendant calming and relaxation, all resulting from coherent breathing (Brown & Gerbarg, 2012). Similar practices are a part of classical mindfulness (Rapgay & Bystrisky, 2009), Tibetan *samatha* meditation, and Zen meditation.

Below, we present instructions for Soothing Rhythm Breathing (adapted from Tirch, 2012) to assist you in guiding and structuring the practice, whether for yourself or for clients. (For a downloadable audio recording of this practice, please visit http://www.newharbinger.com/30550; see the back of this book for more information.) As is the case throughout this book, allow your experience to lead you, using your own words and pacing rather than adhering rigidly to the script. The key to it, as in much of compassionate mind training, is to direct attention and access a state of body and mind that is conducive to the experience of compassion. This exercise is usually conducted in a seated position with the back upright yet supple. The ideal setting is a comfortable place, free from distractions or interruptions.

As we will often begin our practices, please find a comfortable place to be, where you can place both of your feet on the floor and allow your back to adopt an upright yet supple posture. As much as you can, allow yourself to feel settled and grounded into the experience. When you feel willing, allow your eyes to close, perhaps adopting a friendly or relaxed facial expression, perhaps smiling slightly. Begin to draw your attention to the gentle flow of the breath in and out of the body. Feel your connection to the breath as you inhale and exhale. As best you can, hold your focus on the breath with a gentle and allowing spirit, not aiming to change or correct anything, but simply being with the act of breathing.

As you begin to deepen your awareness of the flow of the breath, feel your breath descend into your belly, noticing the rise and fall of your abdomen and chest. As best you can, allow the air to reach the bottom of your lungs. As you exhale, notice the falling or gentle shrinking of the abdomen. Feel the muscles under the rib cage moving with each inhalation. As you notice the rising and falling of the belly, allow your breath to find its own rhythm and pace, simply allowing the breath to breathe itself and giving way to your breath's own rhythm, moment by moment. With each in-breath, feel as if you are breathing attention into the body, and with each out-breath, feel your entire body letting go.

Now extend and lengthen the out-breath, and allow the breath to settle into a slow, soothing rhythm. Breathe in for a count of three seconds, pause for a moment, then breathe out for a count of three seconds, and briefly pause again. As you're able, extend this rhythm to a count of four seconds for each in-breath and out-breath, and then five seconds. Hold this timing lightly, using it as a guide and a pulse. Whenever your mind wanders away to thoughts, images, or distractions, gently remember that this is the nature of mind; upon the next in-breath, bring your attention back to this soothing rhythm of the breath.

Remain with this attention to the soothing rhythm of your breath as much as you can, feeling each inhalation descending through the lungs, noticing the rising and falling of the abdomen, and sensing the release of the exhalation.

After practicing breathing in this soothing rhythm for a few minutes, allow yourself to notice when you are ready to bring this practice to a close. Then exhale and let go of this exercise entirely. At your own pace, bring your awareness back to your surroundings, opening your eyes and returning to your experience right now.

The Soothing Rhythm Breathing practice aptly illustrates how CFT accesses particular bodily and mental states in preparation for engaging more deeply with life's challenges. In this context, the concept of soothing refers to the experience of centeredness, preparedness, and mindful awareness that develops from the activation of affiliative emotions and secure attachment experiences. For the ACT practitioner, this experience of stabilization in the present moment represents the foundation of psychological flexibility, linking the cultivation of compassion to the development of broader repertoires of adaptive responses to the difficulties that arise on the road to a life well lived.

4

Training Self-Compassion
in Clinical Practice

Regardless of their theoretical approach, clinicians often notice that successful therapy leads to a profound sense of self-reconciliation. We believe that compassion for oneself and one's inevitable failings, past, present, and future, is a key element in such self-reconciliation. Pierre Cousineau, a clinician friend of ours, likes to say that if he could give his clients only one skill, he would give them the skill to be self-compassionate. Unfortunately, our evaluative and comparing minds make it so easy to fear or hate our selves, histories, thought patterns, emotions, behaviors, and the self-concepts that inevitably come to filter our experience and seemingly limit our options.

Yet when we are at war with ourselves or some part of ourselves, what could a victory possibly look like? Who would win and who would lose? What would become of the loser, and what would be left of the winner?

From a compassionate perspective, nothing is to be gained by prosecuting a war against those parts of our experience or ourselves that evoke discomfort and stubbornly resist our attempts at change. It's only natural to dislike aversive experiences such as fear, sadness, or self-doubt. From there, it is only a very short distance to hating them and the vessel that contains them. Then comes hatred for the kind of person who feels or does such things; in other words, oneself.

Our culture disparages weakness and negative experience and makes this dislike abundantly clear in myriad ways—including, quite often, through our early caregivers. As we learn how to relate to our private world from our early caregivers, we may adopt a hostile, dismissive, avoidant, or invalidating attitude toward difficult inner experiences, perhaps based on the assumption that we are supposed to think rationally and feel good, supposed to be confident and optimistic. We may believe we are expected to "just do it" regardless of inner obstacles. These messages are pervasive to the point where it can feel unsafe to publicly show any sign of weakness.

When the evaluative mind enters the fray, these social processes become highly potentiated and the war against inner experience starts in earnest. If only we felt differently, if only we could see the good side of things, if only we'd had a different history; if only we had a less negative vision of ourselves, more self-esteem, less self-doubt, more of this, less of that…then we would finally be complete and whole. Verbal processes trap us in endless evaluative frames from which we nearly always emerge at fault.

In this context, training self-compassion can be seen as the overarching goal in therapy. If we all had the skill and courage to make space for our own suffering and be kind to that part of ourselves that stumbles and sometimes falls, change would become so much easier. Through self-compassion, mistakes cease to present us occasions to berate ourselves, shame dissipates, and we become our own best friend, coach, or ally, providing ourselves with whatever support we need to make it through and move toward what really matters to us.

This chapter explores the clinically relevant processes that make us hate ourselves, the forms they can take, and the functions they can serve. It then outlines a number of key skills that can assist clinicians in training self-compassion and briefly discusses psychological barriers to self-compassion from a learning theory perspective. Then, through the lens of our clinical practice, we'll explore the elements of the deep reconciliation that can arise from self-compassion and offer some clinical approaches that may be helpful in getting clients to engage in this process.

The Ultimate Frontier in Self-Reconciliation

When therapy works at a deep level, it brings clients to a place of profound reconciliation. In that place, the past has not been erased, nor has pain disappeared, yet clients' resonance and relationship with the self are transformed. Of course, personal flaws, pain from past history, judgments of the evaluative mind, and scary emotions do not disappear, though they often become less intense. They still play out on the stage of our private personal experience; however, instead of igniting an inner war, they can now lead to a kind inclination of the heart and a softness born of taking the full measure of the struggle and its costs. Clients develop a new sense that they are able to speak to themselves in the way they need to be spoken to in order to provide the support that will allow them to move toward what is important in this difficult and beautiful life.

In our clinical experience, one characteristic common to clients who have effected deep and lasting change in their behavior is a sense of having made peace with the parts of their experience and past that they had been warring against or fearful of. Their problems have in no way been magically solved, and they will assuredly know suffering again. Yet they seem to approach their entire selves with a new sense of kindness and reconciliation. At this point, names and tags fall away, and it is not uncommon for clients to even wonder about the diagnostic labels that have been applied to them, as they have come to see more broadly that suffering is an integral part of the human experience—one that informs what is centrally important to us and can be held with the same kindness and willingness as our deepest values. What, then, would be the sense in trying to not have suffering, to dismiss it, avoid it, or somehow invalidate it?

Clinical Example: Holding Yourself in Kindness

Below is a dialogue with Carl, who has come to the end of a twelve-session course of ACT. When Carl started ACT, he was forty-two and came with a twenty-year history of therapy, sometimes in inpatient facilities. He had at various times been diagnosed with depression, generalized anxiety disorder (GAD), and obsessive-compulsive disorder (OCD). From his point of view, his main difficulties were anxiety and a lack of self-esteem. After ten weekly sessions, he took a break from therapy and came back three months later, then once again three months after that. Below is an extract from that twelfth session. For the past six months, he's been gradually improving.

Therapist: So, how do you feel about our work? What has changed?

Client: Well, it's strange to say, but the main thing for me is how I've stopped being so hard on myself.

Therapist: How so?

Client: I used to constantly judge myself and feel ashamed because of my anxiety. Then I would judge myself for making lists, seeking reassurance, and doing my rituals. Of course, I would judge myself for having OCD, depression, and—what do they call it again? DAG, AGD, GAD? Who cares about these labels anyway? Then, after we started our work together, I would judge myself for judging myself! I basically used to hate the Carl that did all this.

Therapist: Ouch!

Client: Yeah. Well, I wanted to be someone else, someone better, someone without anxiety. Now I see that I was at war with a part of myself. How could I win against myself? Now what's important to me is to move in directions I care about. Of course I'll stumble and even fall. And that will be hard. But it's okay, because when I fall, I now know not to treat myself so harshly. Everybody stumbles sometimes, right? So yeah, I'd say the main change is I've made my peace with myself.

Three years later the therapist met with Carl again. He'd made the choice to end his relationship of ten years with his partner. Most importantly to him, he'd changed jobs, moving out of banking and into providing support to teenagers who were struggling in school. He'd also stopped smoking and started exercising. The job change was tough and money was tighter, but he loved his new job, working in a school and helping troubled kids, and he was good at it. The dialogue below is from that follow-up session.

Therapist: How did you manage to make these difficult changes?

Client: Becoming kinder to myself allowed me to follow my heart, even though I knew it would be difficult and scary at times.

Therapist: And was it?

Client: (*Laughs.*) Oh yes! But nowhere near as bad as the stories my mind used to sell me! What I do now is just proceed, knowing it may be hard. And when it is, I give myself gentle encouragement. I guess I speak to myself a bit like I wish I'd been spoken to as a kid—and, come to think of it, a bit like I speak to those kids I work with.

We contacted Carl again as we were writing this chapter. It has been six years since he was last in therapy. He has a new partner, and they're in the process of buying a house together. He still loves his job helping teenagers. On the occasions when he feels down, he goes back to the observer perspective and practices receiving his distress with kindness. There is no question that he is finally leading a rich and meaningful life.

Carl's story is evocative. It is particularly interesting to us in that, more than six years after a brief treatment that helped him get unstuck from over twenty years of struggling with obsessions, compulsions, worry, and poor self-esteem, he reports three skills as being central to maintaining the gains of treatment: an ability to take an observer perspective on his experience, choosing directions rather than rigid goals, and receiving with kindness the experiences he cannot change. In other words, though Carl does not specifically name compassion and his therapist did not engage in explicit compassion work, Carl has learned to be self-compassionate.

What Makes Us Hate Ourselves?

From an ACT perspective, fusion with self-as-content can be one of the most potentially damaging processes we face. Indeed, long histories of punishment for a wide array of behaviors, augmented by the attendant verbal punishment that minds deliver, can result in people becoming fused with self-critical or self-shaming constructions their minds insist are their true selves. Clients (and if we are honest, most of us) therefore walk around with fused notions of who or what they really are, and more often than not hate or shame themselves for it. Depressed, anxious, shy, ugly, socially inept, unlovable, complicit in abuse, ne'er-do-well, coward, idiot, misfit, defective, and so on—the list is endless. But whatever particular set of epithets the vagaries of our personal history have led us to fuse with, one thing most of us share is that we intensely dislike and often criticize ourselves for whatever self-concept we hold.

Derived relational responding is the driving force in this dynamic. Most of these labels arose from painful moments in our history. Through the transformation of stimulus functions that lies at the heart of relational framing—a largely involuntary process—the pain, and often shame, that these events elicited became attached to the memories of the events and the labels our behavior, experiences, or entire self received on those occasions. When that content is, in turn, put into a frame of equivalence with the self, then our very notion of self becomes aversive—something to move away from. This can lead to self-hatred and self-shame and take many forms, including suicidal ideation, self-harming behavior, self-chastising or self-aggrandizing talk, putting on a mask and pretending, ruminating, self-shaming, and dissociating.

Fusion of our sense of self with content or labels of experience is often prompted and reinforced by caregivers or peers, through statements like "Little Joe is such a shy boy," "You asked for it!" "You're such an idiot for not seeing this," "You'll never amount to anything," "Look at this big baby crying again," and so on. Soon enough, that other-initiated talk can turn inward and become self-sustained disparaging self-talk. Is it any wonder that deep-set self-hatred is so prevalent? Because of this dynamic, it is clinically crucial to promote a more flexible sense of self that can help clients disentangle themselves from rigid self-concepts and the limitations they impose on behavior.

Learning History and Emergence of Sense of Self

As mentioned, our self-concepts are largely the products of our learning histories, especially in relation to our caregivers and attachment figures. From a functional contextual point of view, the self is a function of verbal behavior and emerges as a product of becoming a verbally competent human (Hayes, 1984; Kohlenberg & Tsai, 1991). Developmentally, the acquisition of verbal behavior goes through a number of phases. At first children learn to name objects, then subjects and actions, often as whole functional units containing all three: "Baby eats apple." "Baby sees doggy." "Daddy reads book." As children grow more sophisticated in their use of language, the functional units become increasingly smaller, separating subjects from objects (baby from apple) and objects from actions (apple from eating). In normally developing children, this process is relatively straightforward as regards publicly observable objects and actions. Most children are presented with a great many opportunities to use and respond to functional verbal units and get fairly consistently reinforced for correct uses and responses. This is a form of multiple exemplar training that is ubiquitous, and a consistent history of reinforcement is a central condition for successful multiple exemplar training.

Early on, children have no more language for their inner experience than they do for the experience of their senses. And whereas learning to orient to sensory experience is necessary for physical survival, the world of inner experience, as Skinner (1974) noted, only acquires significance because it is important to other members of our verbal community. In this way and through social interaction, we learn modes of interacting with our inner experience. This is why it is so common for people to recognize their caregivers' voices in their self-talk.

How does the individual learn to recognize and name that part of the universe that only he can observe? How do we learn to name what we feel when no one can see it? Because our caregivers do not have direct access to the objects or actions involved (bodily states and sensations), a certain amount of guesswork is necessary, often based on what can be observed of the child's behavior. This means that, even at best, our descriptions of private events can never have the precision of our descriptions of publicly observable objects or events (Skinner, 1974).

A consistent learning environment requires that caregivers devote exquisite attention to subtle cues, and that they flexibly adapt to new information available from further observation. When caregivers are stressed, absent, overworked, avoidant of or overcome by emotion, or themselves the product of an inconsistent learning history, chances are they will not respond in ways most conducive to children learning how to recognize and name their inner experience and accept it as normal. Under these conditions, children might be told that they are angry when they are in fact hungry, that they are hungry as the clock strikes noon, that they are not (or should not) be sad when they are feeling sad, that they want ice cream when in fact their caregiver wants ice cream, and so on.

Repeated such experiences during early development may lead to children having difficulties in learning to name what they feel or want with any precision and under the control of internal stimuli (i.e., what they really feel, think, or want). Instead, they may have to take cues from others to know about their "own" thoughts and feelings. Their inner experience might have received so little attention that they have no words to describe it. In many cases, they will have learned to fear, deny, or judge their inner experience rather than notice and accept it as one may notice and accept the changing weather. In extreme cases, such as when early attempts to name feelings, thoughts, and desires have been consistently or unpredictably punished, they may present with a veritable phobia of experiencing or expressing their inner experience.

The world of inner experience can thus become an unfamiliar, unstable, treacherous territory, full of darkness, threats, and defects. And that, in turn, will further feed self-hatred, shame, fear, and a sense of unrelenting inner conflict. Clinically, clients may say that they do not know how they feel or think. They might be unable to describe inner sensations or name their emotions, perhaps only locating feelings in their heads; or they may react aversively to any attempts at helping them contact inner experience, such as through eyes-closed mindfulness exercises.

Attachment and Self-Compassion in Context

How caregivers respond to a child's instinctual bids for affiliation can also have a profound impact on affiliative behavior. Whether those bids have been consistently reinforced, ignored, punished, or responded to inconsistently (at times reinforced, at times punished or ignored) can contribute to the development of the child's attachment patterns (Mansfield & Cordova, 2007). A history of consistent reinforcement for affiliation bids could result in a secure attachment style. A history in which such bids were consistently ignored may lead to an avoidant attachment style. A history in which those bids were consistently punished could produce an attachment style that's fearful. And because few learning histories are perfectly consistent, different combinations of reinforcement, punishment, and ignoring could lead to a mixed attachment style with either a dominant style or, in cases where inconsistency is the norm, a disorganized attachment style. Because we learn our relationship with our inner experience and concepts of self largely from our attachment figures, these styles could in turn be reflected in individual styles of relating to inner experience: secure and accepting, avoidant and dismissive, fearful and critical, or disorganized and unaware. Of these, only the first style would naturally incline the individual toward self-compassion. The others would naturally fuel different forms of self-hatred, self-shame, and inner conflict.

It thus takes a specific learning history and a deliberate verbal context and community to build an accepting and kind relationship to one's own experience and self-concept—a relationship that consistently reinforces compassion for one's own aversive experiences and those of other people. It makes sense that when that history is missing, a healing relationship, such as the therapeutic relationship, might provide a privileged context for building a new learning history that fosters and reinforces affiliative responding and self-compassion skills, something we'll discuss in detail in chapter 6. In this way, the therapeutic relationship offers a setting in which a different approach to the self and one's own experience becomes possible. This can range from helping clients learn to receive their negative self-concepts with strength, wisdom, and kindness to helping them transform a sense of self that is unstable or disorganized. Within this context, clients can also adopt a more flexible sense of self.

Verbal Processes and Self-Compassion

We have discussed how the verbal community is central to learning one's relationship to one's own private experiences, thoughts, and emotions. Now we will briefly look at the influence of verbal processes on self-criticism and self-compassion. Understanding the verbal processes that lie at the root of self-hatred and reinforce it can help clinicians devise targeted interventions to gradually undermine self-critical behavior and foster a more compassionate approach to how hard it is to live in this world. This approach highlights the importance of being kind to oneself in order to have a chance to move toward what is important in life, even in the face of deep-seated and painful inner obstacles.

As previously noted, fusion with the content of one's experience and verbal constructions is the process that fuels self-criticism and self-hatred. The fruit of derived relational responding and the transformation of functions, cognitive fusion is ubiquitous and constitutes the normal mode of mind. Through derived relational responding, inner experience acquires the aversive or appetitive functions of sensory experience. Though it is useful and at the root of our ability to think abstractly, fusion makes it highly probable that individuals will define themselves by the content of their experience. From there it is natural to evaluate one's self-concept and classify it as aversive. Thus, clients will judge themselves as bad because of what they have experienced (for example, trauma) or still experience (anxiety, sadness, fear, doubts). They may condemn their present selves for past actions. They may feel ashamed of having intrusive ego-dystonic thoughts. They may fear their inner experience and equate their feelings of emptiness with proof that they are somehow less than others.

Self-Compassion Versus Self-Esteem

Whereas traditional cognitive approaches may recommend helping clients reevaluate their self-definitions more rationally, from an ACT perspective the problem with self-hatred does not arise from the content of one's self-concept, which would prescribe changing the problematic content, but from excessive fusion with one's self-concept, or self-as-content. If the problem is not primarily how one evaluates the content of one's self-definition, then trying to move evaluative constructs, such as self-esteem, might not prove most helpful.

From an ACT perspective, trying to directly modify one's self-evaluation (i.e., improving one's self-esteem) runs the risk of investing self-evaluations with excessive importance. Then, through derived relational responding, the risk of increasing or strengthening negative self-evaluations arises. A positive evaluation marshaled in the service of weakening a negative sense of self might serve to put both in a frame of coordination that can result in the aversive functions of the original evaluation being transferred to the proposed alternative evaluation. Thus, the intended positive self-evaluation becomes associated with the same experience of suffering as the original negative self-evaluation. Furthermore, high self-esteem in itself is not necessarily correlated to better social or general functioning. When insensitive to context and attached to one's self rather than one's actions, positive evaluations are liable to lead to higher degrees of narcissism and lower levels of prosocial behavior (Morf & Rhodewalt, 2001). In addition, such artificially inflated, conditional self-esteem is fragile.

A potentially more fruitful approach to dealing with negative self-evaluations, and one that carries fewer risks of unintended side effects, would be to cultivate compassion for aversive self-concepts. In this work, the key processes are defusion, acceptance, and fostering experiential contact with a sense of an observer self, or self-as-context. The central focus is on cultivating the ability to take perspective and receive one's suffering and negative evaluations as they arise.

Establishing an Effective Context for Training Self-Compassion

We believe that effectively training a more self-compassionate approach to one's suffering is greatly enhanced by various prerequisites and key skills. From a contextual point of view, it is crucial to establish a context that will prove most effective in fostering compassion. Foundational elements for establishing such a context include a deliberate focus on acceptance in the therapeutic relationship, the skill set of the therapist, presentation of a rationale for the work, establishing a functional contextual point of view, and orienting to function and workability rather than form.

Establishing an Accepting Relationship

In psychotherapy work, the therapeutic relationship is the primary context in which change takes place. We believe it is essential for the relationship to be based on acceptance, kindness, compassion, and reciprocity. As suggested by the promoters of functional analytic therapy, the therapeutic relationship can be established as a sacred space that can compassionately hold everything clients think and feel, along with all of their history and the whole of who they are (Tsai & Kohlenberg, 2012). It can also become a model of a truly intimate relationship, which, in the definition offered by Cordova and Scott (2001), is a relationship in which behaviors that are liable to be socially punished, such as sharing vulnerabilities, opening up to one's hopes and dreams, or showing one's soft side, are not only not punished but in fact reinforced. Such a relationship can offer a supportive environment for the cultivation of self-acceptance and self-compassion. In chapter 5, we will further detail how to use the behavioral tools of functional analytic therapy to promote such a relationship.

Cultivating the Therapist Skill Set

ACT has its roots in a model of normal functioning in which evaluative verbal processes inherently feed cognitive fusion and experiential avoidance and can lead to unclear values and lack of contact with the present moment. In turn, fusion with the self-judgments that the interactions of these processes can create is a universal human experience. And just as ACT clinicians are all the more effective when they embody compassionate flexibility around their own fusion and values, training self-compassion is best done by clinicians who practice self-compassion around their own struggles, self-judgments, and shame.

To effectively foster curative relationships, clinicians must themselves possess a flexible repertoire for intimate relating, including the skills or behaviors they seek to train in their clients. Direct experiential work is key. This can be accomplished by working through the clinician exercises proposed in this book, and by attending experiential training workshops in ACT, CFT, and FAP. Clinical supervision or participating in a peer consultation group with like-minded clinicians can also be helpful in developing these skills in both personal and professional life.

Beyond the clinic, practicing deliberate acts of kindness with loved ones and strangers, keeping a log of compassionate interpersonal risks and acts of self-care, cultivating mindfulness, and engaging in compassion-focused imagery practices can all contribute to learning to stay within a mindful, compassionate space. Mindful movement practices, such as yoga or tai chi, can also be helpful.

Presenting an Overall Rationale for the Work

A key aspect of creating a context for compassion-focused work and enhancing client motivation is presenting a rationale for the work. While there are a number of ways to do so, we believe that an effective rationale stems from the functional contextual point of view and includes several key elements. The first step is to establish mindfulness—a focus on what happens in the present moment—as the favored arena for training and learning new skills. Following from that, the therapeutic relationship can be presented as a context in which familiar difficulties can and will show up, providing precious opportunities for present-moment work. Drawing clients' attention to this dimension of the work can help normalize emotional and affective issues that will arise in or about the therapeutic relationship. It also provides the groundwork for the clinician to turn to clinically relevant behavior when it shows up in session. As defined by FAP, and as we will detail in chapter 5, clinically relevant behavior is problematic or improved behavior that occurs in session and in the therapeutic relationship and that is an instance of problematic or improved client behavior outside of session (Kohlenberg & Tsai, 1991).

Establishing a Functional Contextual Perspective on Compassion

The functional contextual viewpoint on compassion can be set forth by presenting psychological flexibility as becoming able to do what is important even in the presence of inner obstacles such as unpleasant or painful emotions, thoughts, or self-judgments. This can be presented in a number of ways, such as through a metaphor suggesting that we cannot control the waves of our emotions but can learn to surf them. Another effective way to present the functional contextual viewpoint on developing compassion is through the ACT matrix (Polk & Schoendorff, 2014).

Intervention: Presenting the ACT Matrix

The ACT matrix, shown in figure 7, is a diagram that helps orient client and therapist toward increased psychological flexibility and compassion. It can provide an effective way to establish a functional contextual point of view with clients in everyday language. The matrix can be introduced in a number of ways.

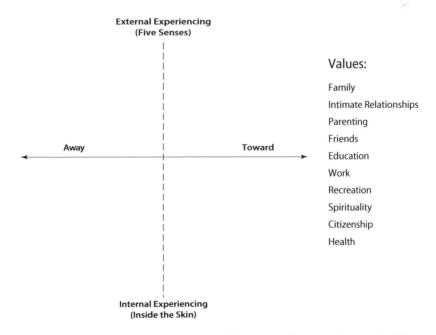

Figure 7. The ACT matrix. (Reprinted from Polk & Schoendorff, 2014, with permission from New Harbinger Publications.)

One effective way of presenting it is to invite clients to name who or what is important to them and ask them to note it in the lower right quadrant of the diagram. Common responses include family, children, spouse, work, or health. Whatever clients may name, it is written down. Next, ask if they always do what would move them toward who or what they identified as important. In other words, do they always embody their values? Of course, none of us do; there are always obstacles that stand in the way. Take a moment to differentiate between external obstacles (material circumstances, other people, or both) and internal obstacles (thoughts, emotions, bodily sensations, and memories, some of which may arise in the presence of external obstacles), then invite clients to list some of their inner obstacles to moving toward who or what is important and place them in the lower left quadrant of the matrix. Common obstacles include fear, anxiety, guilt, shame, pain, painful memories, and thoughts of being unworthy, stupid, not good enough, and so on.

Next, invite clients to list some of the things they can or could be seen doing (if, say, a video camera recorded their actions) to move away from these inner obstacles—behaviors that they usually engage in response to these obstacles or to cope with them—and place them in the upper left quadrant. These are often resistant or avoidant behaviors and commonly (but not always) stand in opposition to behaviors that would move them toward what really matters. Typical away moves include avoiding, drinking, taking drugs, distracting with television or video games, shopping, working, arguing, seeking to be right, blaming, compulsions, doing sports, cleaning, seeking reassurance, and so on.

Finally, ask clients what they can or could be seen doing (on the video camera) to move toward who or what is important to them and list these responses in the upper right quadrant. Common toward moves include spending time with loved ones, playing with one's children, going on date nights, planning a vacation, reconciling, exercising, and doing sports.

As the examples we listed illustrate, some behaviors can be considered either toward or away moves depending on whether they are under aversive control of unwanted inner experience or appetitive control of values. For example, you could go to the gym as a move away from anxiety, a move toward health, or a bit of both. And just as only clients themselves can notice who or what is important to them and what they don't want to think or feel, only they can tell if a particular behavior is more of a toward move or an away move. When clients are unsure, asking them to ascribe percentages to toward and away can be useful. Through skillful questioning, you can orient a client toward experiencing the perspective of an observing self that can notice inner experience and whether behavior is performed in the service of moving away from unwanted inner experiencing (or at times moving toward wanted feelings, such as when using substances) or toward values.

Once the matrix has been set up and clients are noticing that the self, or "I," lies at the center of the matrix—and the therapeutic process—you can ask which life clients would choose if presented with two options: doing more things to move away from what they don't want to feel or think, or doing more things to move toward who or what is important. Thus far, every single one of our clients has voted for the option of moving toward life and what is important. You can then wrap up the process by explaining that the work in therapy will be about becoming better able to choose moving toward who or what is important, even in the presence of inner obstacles—a definition of psychological flexibility that's accessible to the layperson.

Presenting the matrix sets up a context for therapy under clear appetitive control of values (i.e., moving toward). In this respect, the functional contextual approach differs radically from other approaches, which largely seek to help clients move away from aversives, either by reducing the occurrence or intensity of aversive thoughts and feelings, or by helping them change their behavior to escape aversive consequences (such as when promoting abstinence from alcohol and other drugs). We believe that setting up an appetitive context as explicitly as possible is crucial for establishing long-term motivation that can last beyond the removal of aversive consequences and reductions in distress. Furthermore, it provides an ideal basis for fostering more approach behavior toward aversive inner experience and self-concepts, which is a key element in training compassion clinically.

Orienting to Function and Workability

Behavior cannot be understood in isolation from its context. For example, looking at different options may be useful before engaging in a course of action but not so helpful once action has been taken and there is no possibility of changing course or outcomes. Whereas other cognitive and behavioral approaches tend to focus on the content of clients' thoughts, a functional contextual approach seeks to orient to the function of a particular thought or behavior in a given context.

Orienting to function involves looking at the effects of behavior, thoughts, emotions, and memories in a given context. Do thoughts of being hurt in the past that arise in the context of meeting a new potential partner serve as obstacles, or do they facilitate opening up? Does the behavioral response to these thoughts and feelings serve to move toward valued ends? These two questions— what behavior follows a particular inner experience (thought, emotion, memory, or image) and whether this behavior represents a move toward a valued direction—help orient to function. Orienting to function can prevent clinicians and clients from getting trapped in the content of inner experience and the often futile attempts to change that content.

From an ACT perspective, once the unworkable function of a particular inner experience has been identified, defusion and acceptance strategies, along with orienting toward values, are the preferred means of changing the verbal context and increasing the workability of behavior.

Validation of the Struggle

Self-compassion implies unconditional validation of one's own aversive experiences and feelings. It involves opening up to the entirety of one's experience and having the wisdom to know that one's emotions and thoughts are valid. Many clients struggle with self-validation. Deeply understanding and acknowledging inner experience, particularly emotional experiencing, is a singularly uncommon skill. Even clinicians, who are professionally trained in validating clients' experiences and emotions, may struggle with this process when turning it inward.

Analyzing the Workability of the Struggle

From an ACT perspective, an effective first step toward validation includes a functional analysis of clients' struggles to move away from unwanted inner experiences. In such an analysis, the clinician invites her client to consider how effective his away moves have been, in both the short and the long term, and whether they have served to help him move toward who or what is important.

Often clients report that away moves are effective in the short term. This provides an opportunity to validate the fact that the client engages in them. After all, they do work; they are valid, even if not the most effective approach in the long run. Indeed, most clients report that their away moves are ineffective in the long term, causing negative consequences or even making unwanted inner experiences more frequent, more intense, and generally more important in their lives. This provides a further opportunity for clinicians to validate clients' experiences of being stuck in away moves.

Finally, asking whether away moves have been effective in helping clients move toward who or what is important helps reorient the work toward their freely chosen values. As mentioned, some behaviors can be either away moves or toward moves, depending on the context. For example, clients can go out with friends or engage in physical activity as a move away from loneliness or anxiety. Yet if friendship and health are important to them, they could also do the same behaviors under appetitive control of their values. This insight can help clients appreciate the potential for increasing the appetitive control of many of their away moves. Here, the power of derived relational responding can come into play, gradually bringing a range of hitherto aversively controlled behaviors under appetitive control. For example, say the compulsive away moves of a client presenting with OCD are running, reading, calling family and friends, cooking, and doing crossword puzzles. As the client comes to see that these are all also moves toward values, he can gradually begin to engage them under the appetitive control of values, rather than the aversive control of anxiety and obsessions. Indeed, we had such a client once who, by the end of treatment, did not meet criteria for OCD anymore while still engaging in largely the same range of behaviors; the difference was that he did so now under the appetitive control of values (Schoendorff, Purcell-Lalonde, & O'Connor, 2014).

Through this kind of analysis of the way clients have struggled—often referred to as *creative hopelessness* in ACT texts—clients can learn how addictive and powerful away moves can be and how they result in people feeling stuck, unable to free themselves from entrapment. The first step toward freedom is to acknowledge this valid experience of being stuck. The next step is to stop struggling with the trap itself—in other words, defusing from rigid interaction with language.

Defusion from Self-as-Content

Fusion with negative self-concept is a major obstacle to fostering a more self-compassionate stance. If clients take the negative self-conceptions their minds produce literally—self-conceptions that often echo the words of developmentally influential figures—self-criticism and self-invalidation can become their default behavior. By presenting the mind as an evaluating organ, useful for judging whether things fit in the world of five-senses experiences but not so useful when it comes to controlling inner experiences, the clinician can create more space in which clients can start gaining some distance from what their minds tell them.

Clinical Example: Targeting Self-Judgments and Criticism

Given how common negative self-evaluation is, it may be possible fairly early in treatment to zero in on negative self-judgments and criticism as they appear in the moment. Asking clients how effective self-berating has been and how they would like to be able to behave toward themselves instead can help. The dialogue below, which occurred in the second session of therapy, illustrates such an intervention. Ted is a thirty-two-year-old man presenting with depression, professional difficulties, and a high level of marital conflict.

Therapist: So, Ted, what did you notice in your matrix over the past week?

Client: It looks like it's been mostly away moves. I am just such a loser. I don't know why you bother with me.

Therapist: Ouch! First let me congratulate you for noticing away moves. Minds generally don't like it when we start noticing this, and one thing they often do in reaction is beat us over the head with the fact that we've noticed away moves. Could this be what has happened?

Client: Yeah. *(Sighs.)*

Therapist: That must have been really painful. Is it something new, or is this something your mind usually does, judging you harshly and calling you names?

Client: Oh, I'm used to it. I'm just a loser anyhow.

Therapist: It sounds to me that it's almost as though "I'm a loser" stands guard to stop you from going anywhere beyond where it's kept you all these years.

Client: What do you mean?

Therapist: Well, here you are doing something new: noticing toward and away moves. Yet "I'm a loser" won't let you do it. It picks up the away moves you notice and tries to use them as sticks to beat you back into the "I'm a loser" corner.

Client: Yeah. That's exactly it.

Therapist: I wonder if that's what you need? Do you really need to be more beaten down?

Client: Well, no. But what else can I do?

Therapist: How would the person you want to be handle this? By calling you a loser? Or would some other words help?

Client: I guess I'd need more encouragement.

Therapist: Great! Let's start by encouraging you to notice when your mind wants to pick up the loser stick and beat you with it. That's kind of like level two of noticing.

The client is fused with the negative self-concept "I'm a loser," which functions to limit what he can do in a given context. The clinician works on making apparent to the client how fusion with this negative self-concept determines his behavior, picking up on the self-judgment and helping the client defuse from it by pointing to its function: beating the client into a corner. Making that function apparent provides the space in which the client can identify an alternative, more compassionate behavior: offering himself encouragement.

Intervention: The Mother Cat Exercise

Self-blaming and a harsh approach to our inner distress can become the default mode of interacting with the self-judgments and other parts of our inner experience that we dislike. Noticing how we receive our aversive inner experience can help lay the foundations of a more compassionate approach to our suffering. The following exercise in discrimination can be very useful in helping clients develop a more compassionate stance toward their experiences, behavior, or past. The exercise builds on a number of aspects of compassion-focused work and starts with a little story.

Imagine you're observing a mother cat tending her litter of six kittens in a box. Of the six, one is black and white, and from the moment it opened its little eyes, it has shown itself to be more adventurous than its siblings. One day, as the mother cat is nursing her kittens, the little black-and-white kitten, who has ventured away from her line of sight, suddenly emits shrieks of distress. The mother cat instantly makes a beeline to where the black-and-white kitten is, catches it by the scruff of the neck, and carries it back to the box, where she drops it and licks it until it's soothed. This mother's behavior is not peculiar to cats; it's present in some form in many species and nearly all species of mammals—well, perhaps not quite all species of mammals.

When it comes to humans, we may not always make a beeline for our little one in distress, perhaps saying, "I don't have time for this now!" or "Wait until your dad gets home." We may not immediately bring it back to a safe place, instead demanding explanations: "Why did you get into trouble again?" We may judge: "If you behaved there as you behave in the box, no wonder you came to grief!" We may invalidate: "You have no good reason to cry!" We may threaten: "Stop whining, or you'll be sorry!" We may mock: "Look at that big baby crying again—not such a brave adventurer now!" We may turn away: "Don't come near the box. I only want happy kittens here!" In short, unlike a mother cat, we humans may display a large palette of behaviors other than instinctively approaching a young one in distress, bringing it to a place of safety, and comforting it until it is soothed. What stops us from approaching distress and providing comfort? Getting hooked by the mind's judgments. We all learned how to receive and respond to our own distress by witnessing how distress, both our own and that of others, was received by those giants we grew up amongst.

How about you? When your own kittens of inner distress start shrieking in the distance or when your self-judgmental thoughts start rumbling from afar, when that long-ago child starts hurting again, what do you do? How do you receive that kitten or that child? Do you turn toward it with an open heart and an intention to soothe the pain, or do you turn away, push away, ignore, belittle, argue, demand explanations, invalidate, scrutinize, mock, or engage in any number of behaviors other than approaching and receiving your inner distress with compassion? Just notice. And then notice if you can find some space to give that hurt part of yourself, that painful self-judgment, doom-laden prediction, or panic-stricken feeling, some of the mother-cat care it needs.

This exercise can be helpful for both therapist and client. It promotes discrimination between two modes of relating to aversive inner experience, whether those experiences are thoughts, self-stories, judgments, memories, or emotions. Often, when clients simply notice how they receive their inner experience, it can allow them to gradually notice the unworkability of not comforting their suffering.

We like to invite clients to try to identify the attachment figures from whom they might have learned their nonsoothing behavior. To aid in this, we volunteer our own experience, such as hearing a parent's voice loudly disapproving of our behavior when we make even a minor mistake. We observe that sometimes the blaming words in this tone of voice come so fast that there is little to be done about them other than noticing them as a hook and validating how painful it is to have this experience.

Clinical Example: Using the Mother Cat Exercise with a Depressed Client

Below is a dialogue with Ted that illustrates use of the Mother Cat exercise.

Therapist: So, over the past week, were you able to notice how you received your inner distress when it showed up?

Client: It's strange, but I could really see it as the little Ted getting so angry and frustrated about not being listened to.

Therapist: And how did you meet him—like the mother cat, or in some other way?

Client: My first reaction was to try to push him away and…I guess shame him in some way. Like, *Look at you, little so-and-so, feeling pissed off again! Can't you just stop it?*

Therapist: Ouch! That feels harsh.

Client: It is. And I could almost hear my mother's voice talking to him.

Therapist: Wow! What did you do?

Client: It's strange, but when I noticed it, I thought of your mother cat image and was able to approach him with more kindness, to not meet anger with anger.

Therapist: I find this really touching.

Client: Yes. But you know, I didn't make those calls to potential employers we discussed last week, and I lashed out at my wife when she tried to remind me.

Therapist: What's showing up for you now?

Client: That I'm useless and not a good client. *(Pauses.)* I feel ashamed and angry.

Therapist: That must be hard, and it's hard for me to see you like this. I wonder how you're receiving what you're feeling and thinking right now. Is it more like a mother cat or in some other way?

Client: *(Laughs.)* I guess more the other way!

Therapist: And what would the Ted you want to be do with that little kid showing up in anger and shame?

Client: Be more like a mother cat.

Therapist: I wonder what your mother cat would do right now.

Client: I guess she would say that it's tough to feel this way and that she's going to just be there for me.

Therapist: Yes, and I will be there for you too.

In this dialogue, after the client reports having practiced the discrimination introduced the previous week, the therapist catches an in-session moment when the client veers back toward self-judgment and self-shame. In response, she invites him to practice the discrimination in real time. This exercise is an example of how offering clients a values-based discrimination, such as the one conveyed by the Mother Cat metaphor, can help them recognize and change unhelpful patterns of relating to their inner experience. In the course of therapy, it is not uncommon for clients' minds to turn the therapeutic tools or exercises they receive into a way to feed the self-judging machine, as Ted did. In our experience, guiding clients to notice when their minds turn on them and gently shaping a more compassionate approach to old wounds and judgments can greatly speed progress.

Training Self-Compassion More Directly

The war against ourselves that our minds convince us to prosecute cannot be won. Accepting what we dislike about ourselves is the only basis for deep self-reconciliation. Clinical experience suggests that making peace with oneself is a hallmark of deeply transformative therapies. Peace is not about the end of pain; it is about not going to war against pain and suffering and instead receiving these experiences as they are, with a kind inclination of the heart. By promoting defusion and acceptance and orienting clients toward their values, ACT can serve to promote this kind of compassionate peace effectively.

Cognitive fusion, which from an ACT perspective plays a central role in many pathological processes, also affects self-conceptions and can result in highly aversive self-constructions. The resulting behaviors of self-judgment and self-shaming are fundamental to the verbal entanglements that narrow people's life choices and unduly increase suffering.

The emergence of a sense of self is a verbal product of our early interactions with our caregivers. Central to this process is the ability to recognize and name inner experiences. This learning requires a caring, consistent, and accepting social environment, which is rarely the case due to the vagaries of both family and cultural environments. In addition to purely verbal processes, our history of reinforcement or punishment for affiliation bids can impact our relationship to our own experience and our capacity to provide ourselves with the comfort we need. Within this context of verbal and attachment history, people can become fused with particularly painful and rigid forms of self-evaluations and self-shame. Rather than trying to change the content of such evaluations and emotions, it may be more fruitful to foster a more compassionate relationship with them. Because the relationship we have with our inner experience was learned in the context of relationships with our closest caregivers, a close and intimate therapeutic relationship can provide a context ideally suited to helping clients foster a more accepting and compassionate relationship with their inner experience and self-evaluations.

Some key elements of working on compassion clinically include establishing a validating, accepting, and intimate therapeutic relationship; presenting a cogent therapeutic rationale; establishing a functional contextual point of view; and focusing on the function rather than the form of inner experience and behavior. The ACT matrix can be an effective tool in establishing a functional contextual point of view. An integral part of this work is validating clients' struggles against their own experience, helping them see that it is often effective in the short term, and also orienting them to its long-term unworkability, both in terms of reducing their suffering and, crucially, in terms of moving toward a valued life.

5

Using the Therapeutic Relationship to Train Compassion

Imagine that you wanted to learn to surf. Would you choose lessons in which all you did was talk about your surfing attempts over the past week and what you could try to do differently in your next week of surfing? Or would you rather take lessons in which you got a chance to practice surfing in front of your coach so she could guide you as you practice new moves? Furthermore, would you choose lessons in which the teacher mostly talked about the theory of surfing, or in which most time was devoted to practicing? Finally, would you pick a teacher who is a technically proficient surfer, or one who has read numerous surfing books, been a spectator at major competitions, and knows the lingo but could never stand up on a board?

In therapy, as with surfing, the best learning occurs through experience, and the most effective practice is that which can be observed and coached in the moment by a therapist who herself possesses the skills she is hired to impart. Thus, when it comes to training clients to become more compassionate and self-compassionate, in-session practice is key, and compassion and self-compassion on the part of the therapist are a must.

Self-criticism and self-shame are damaging forms of interacting with one's self and one's personal experience. From an ACT point of view, they are a function of various inflexibility processes. Fusion with self-judgmental thoughts and nonacceptance of aversive experiences feeds a sense of self that is limited to the aversive content of one's past and present experience. Difficulty in contacting values and engaging in valued actions also undermines self-worth, getting clients further into their heads and keeping them stuck in a painful cycle of ineffective action, self-depreciation, and shameful hatred of personal history. By increasing their flexibility, clients can come to learn how to surf the waves of negative thoughts, aversive experiences, and self-denigrating stories so they can move in valued life directions.

To a large extent, what happens in therapy happens in the context of the therapeutic relationship. And as is the case in the analogy of surfing above, ineffective behavior is best observed directly, rather than through the filter of clients' reconstructed verbal accounts. Likewise, the skills that will help clients progress are best practiced in session, allowing clinicians to coach clients toward a more compassionate and self-compassionate stance. This emphasis on the present (therapeutic) moment is ideally suited to using operant learning principles, which are focused on providing consequences in the moment. This chapter will describe how operant learning principles can be used in session to help clients become adept at surfing self-critical thoughts and shameful self-directed emotions as they navigate toward a valued life.

Self-Compassion as a Condition of Compassion

From an ACT perspective, compassion and self-compassion are highly related. Being truly compassionate implies being truly self-compassionate and vice versa (Hayes, 2008c). Both compassion for others and self-compassion imply embracing difficult feelings, noticing judgmental thoughts without becoming entangled in them, connecting with a flexible sense of an observing self, and gently carrying one's history forward into a life of engagement with deeply held values. Furthermore, practicing both compassion and self-compassion is a central part of a therapist's skill. And just as for clients, these qualities are best fostered by cultivating compassionate flexibility and extending kindness and self-validation to whatever difficult experiences and self-judgments may arise.

Using Positive Reinforcement to Train Compassion

The functional contextual approach has its roots in learning theory principles and, more particularly, in the principles of operant learning. Countless experiments have shown positive reinforcement to be the most effective tool of behavior modification.

Positive reinforcement denotes a relationship between two events in which the event that follows a behavior increases the future probability of the behavior. Animal models have shown that the effectiveness of the reinforcing event depends on its temporal proximity to the behavior. The closer the reinforcer is to the behavior, the more effective it is likely to be in making that behavior more probable in the future. It can be important to remember that positive and negative reinforcement denote an arithmetic operation in the sense that a consequence is added to or subtracted from the environment, rather than the reinforcer having a positive or negative valence or feeling. For example, sometimes parents will criticize a child's behavior at length only to find that the behavior criticized actually increases. In such cases, criticism serves as a positive reinforcer, even though it may feel negative to both child and parent.

Positive reinforcement is fairly straightforward when applied to nonverbal animals, and the marvelously elaborate behaviors that animals accomplish on film attest to its effectiveness (Pryor, 2009). In such contexts, reinforcers consist of physical or physiological events. However, when it comes to verbal humans, the effects of derived relational responding make reinforcement much more complex. Through derived relational responding, the functions of inner experiences (such as bodily sensations, emotions, or images) and symbolic stimuli (such as words or thoughts) are transformed in ways that are governed by complex relational networks, which themselves are the product of unique and complex individual histories.

Once derived relational responding comes into play, it becomes harder to identify the contexts in which a given event will be reinforcing. For example, with one client a compliment might serve to increase the behavior complimented, whereas for another client it will have the effect of punishing (i.e., decreasing) the behavior. In the latter case, it is probable that the client's verbal history has served to transform the functions of compliments into a punishing consequence. This does not negate the power or effectiveness of positive reinforcement, but it does make the clinician's task more complex. It is therefore particularly important for clinicians to pay close attention to the potential reinforcing or punishing functions their behavior may have on clients.

Functional Analytic Psychotherapy and Compassion

Functional analytic psychotherapy can be of particular interest to clinicians seeking to foster and train compassion and self-compassion in their clients. It can serve as both a model and a series of techniques that apply operant learning principles to therapy and, specifically, to the therapeutic relationship. FAP focuses attention on clinically relevant behavior (CRB), meaning in-session client behaviors that are functionally similar to their behaviors outside of session. There are two main classes of clinically relevant behavior:

- CRB1, denoting instances of client problematic behavior

- CRB2, denoting improved behavior as compared with CRB1

FAP invites both therapist and client to notice CRB1 and the client to practice CRB2 within a reinforcing environment: the therapeutic relationship.

Clinically relevant behaviors are defined idiographically. For example, expressing criticism might be a CRB2 for a client who has difficulty being assertive, but a CRB1 for a client whose relationships are negatively impacted by a high propensity to criticize others. In FAP, the therapist cultivates awareness of client behavior, has the courage to invite the client to notice when clinically relevant behavior might be present, and lovingly reinforces CRB2 while paying close attention to the reinforcing (or punishing) functions of therapist behavior. The therapist offers the therapeutic relationship as a sacred space (Tsai & Kohlenberg, 2012), a safe context in which clients can try out new behavior without fear of overly punishing consequences or a break in the relationship. Such a loving and reinforcing context is ideally suited to helping clients work through self-shame and self-hatred while exploring the practice of compassion and self-compassion.

FAP uses behavior modification tools to promote CRB2. One of the most important of these tools is shaping by successive approximations. In shaping, one first observes the behavioral repertoire such as it is and seeks to reinforce the slightest step in the direction of the desired behavior. When a further step is taken, that new step is reinforced in preference to the previous step, and so on, until the behavior is fully shaped. So in the example of expressing critical thoughts as CRB2, the therapist will initially reinforce any sign of a negative reaction to her behavior, then any form of critical speech, then only critical speech that is likely to be well received by others (for example, including empathic validation of the person criticized). Once the behavior is ready to be taken "on the road," the therapist encourages and promotes generalizing the improved behavior into the client's life beyond the therapeutic relationship.

The Five Rules of FAP

Kohlenberg and Tsai (1991) have proposed five clinical rules to guide the practice of FAP. More recently they have described FAP as being based on awareness, courage, and love (Tsai et al., 2008); and, as you will see, these qualities are highly relevant to the five rules of FAP.

Rule 1: Notice CRB. FAP invites both therapist and client to identify CRB. Noticing CRB implies *awareness* of client behavior. This awareness implies presence, mindfulness, and empathic connection.

Rule 2: Evoke CRB. FAP requires that CRB be present so that it can be worked on. Evoking CRB requires *courage* on the part of both therapist and client. Both are invited to be honest and authentic, take risks, show vulnerability, ask bold questions, and gently confront avoidance.

Rule 3: Respond contingently to CRB. The therapist seeks to reinforce CRB2 while responding appropriately to CRB1. This is inherently compassionate and a demonstration of *love*. By truly caring for and gently tending to clients, tirelessly supporting them, authentically acknowledging them, and deeply appreciating and respecting them in both their difficulties and progress, therapists can most effectively reinforce improved behavior and help clients modify problematic behavior.

Rule 4: Notice the reinforcing effects of your behavior. This invites more *awareness* as the therapist seeks to observe whether her interventions have been reinforcing or not. Here, a willingness to hold interpretations lightly and ask clients how her behavior has impacted them is helpful.

Rule 5: Promote generalization of improved behavior. This last rule implies *awareness*, *courage*, and *love* as the therapist helps clients recognize similarities in the functions of CRB and the functions of behavior in outside life and encourages appropriate risk taking in the presence of similar antecedents outside of session.

Applying these rules encourages clients to become more mindful of their behavior in the moment and can help them identify as CRB1 those clinically difficult moments when noticing their unworkable behavior leads to further self-criticism and shame. Promoting mindfulness of such behaviors and conceptualizing them as teachable moments can be a powerful way to promote compassion and self-compassion.

Finally, these rules are not meant as rigid prescriptions but more as gentle invitations to try new behavior. If by doing so you contact your own reinforcers in the shape of deeper and more effective therapeutic relationships, you may find yourself using them regularly.

Clinical Example: Noticing the Self-Critical Mind in Action and Defusing from It

The self-critical mind is often hyperactive and will use everything it can to fuel the fires of self-hatred. In the example below, Sam had been invited to notice, over the week between sessions, actions he took to move toward who and what is important to him and actions he took to move away from what he didn't want to think or feel.

Therapist: So, what did you notice?

Client: I had never realized how many away moves I engage in. It's pathetic. [CRB1]

Therapist: I notice you're putting yourself down. Do you also put yourself down when you're with other people? (*Applies FAP rule 1: noticing CRB and offering a parallel between client behavior in and out of session.*)

Client: Yes, I'm always putting myself down because of my lack of self-esteem. (*Confirms CRB1.*)

Therapist: And is being harsh on yourself a toward move or an away move? (*Applies FAP rule 1: noticing CRB.*)

Client: I guess an away move....See, I did it again! [CRB1]

Therapist: Ouch! That's harsh. How about noticing your toward and away moves—is that a toward move or an away move? (*Applies rules 2 and 3: evoking CRB and responding contingently to CRB.*)

Client: A toward? [CRB2]

Therapist: What's showing up for me is how easy it is for you to get hooked by your critical mind, and then it's as if you grabbed the bat yourself and started banging away on yourself. (*Applies rule 1, missing an opportunity to apply rule 3: reinforcing CRB2.*)

Client: Yes. You see? I told you. [CRB1]

Therapist: (*Makes a gesture to go grab an imaginary baseball bat behind her chair.*) Here it comes again! (*Applies rule 3: responding contingently to CRB.*)

Client: (*Laughs.*) Okay, I see it now. [CRB2]

Therapist: So how about noticing when your mind hands you the bat and just letting us know? (*Applies rule 2: evoking CRB.*)

Client: I think I can do that. [CRB2]

Therapist: So tell me about your toward moves over the week. (*Applies rules 2 and 3: evoking CRB and reinforcing CRB2.*)

Client: I called my parents, took my son for a walk, and talked to my wife about going out to dinner together. [CRB2] But really, it wasn't much… [CRB1] Oh, here comes the bat! [CRB2] (*Laughs.*)

Therapist: So if you didn't grab the bat, what would you say? (*Applies rules 2 and 3: evoking CRB and reinforcing CRB2.*)

Client: That I'm glad I did these things, and I feel proud. [CRB2]

Therapist: Great, Sam. How was this whole exchange for you? (*Applies rule 4: noticing the reinforcing effects of therapist behavior.*)

Client: At first it was hard, but I think I got the hang of it and could catch myself before going for the bat. And it's true that it makes a difference.

Therapist: I'm also happy you could notice your toward moves. (*Applies rule 3: reinforcing CRB2.*) Would you be willing to continue doing that over the week, even when your mind tries to gang up on you? (*Applies rule 5: promoting generalization of CRB2 to life outside of session.*)

In this exchange, the therapist is focusing on present-moment processes and inviting the client to do the same. The therapist offers a parallel between in-session behavior and potential problematic behavior outside of therapy. When the client offers an explanation (lack of self-esteem), the therapist does not get into the content and instead remains focused on CRB, gradually shaping a CRB2 of noticing the CRB1 of being harsh on oneself, and reinforcing the CRB2 of naming toward moves without depreciating them in the next breath.

Shaping Compassion in Session

The stance of the FAP therapist is one of deep compassion for her clients, their suffering, and their learning history. Seeing behavior as the result of a learning history, she does not hold her clients responsible for their suffering, their thoughts, or their emotions and stands ready to walk with them through their suffering and toward more workable behavior. Seeing behavior as the result of learning history, she appreciates that providing her clients with a safe learning environment (the therapeutic relationship) can help them choose more effective behavior outside of session, setting a new course for their relationships and their lives.

FAP invites the therapist to reinforce clients naturally, noticing how her heart responds to their improved behavior and letting them know how she genuinely feels. As in ACT, the FAP therapist also opens her heart to her clients' suffering with a deep wish to see that suffering diminish and a courageous willingness to stand by her clients and their suffering. The FAP therapist makes a commitment to responding with authenticity and kindness to her clients, including being willing to cry with them.

Clinical Example: Using FAP
Principles to Promote Compassion

Below, we illustrate how a therapist can use FAP principles to promote compassion in an example from a session with Joe, a teacher and community activist who is beset by deep self-shame. Although he obtained a PhD and is a well-respected member of his community, Joe has gone through life with an unshakable sense of being a fraud and undeserving of others' regard. His community involvement is a function of his values, but he has always felt inferior to his peers: less intelligent, less handsome, less well-read. To this day, he feels he received his PhD by some sort of fluke, being certain he was the dullard among his peers in graduate school. Now, at the age of sixty, he feels his cognitive abilities are declining and complains of attention deficit and an impaired memory.

Client: I think people should work harder. [CRB1]

Therapist: You sure have worked hard all your life, not just teaching, but also as a community activist. (*Applies rule 2: evoking CRB.*)

Client: (*Looks uncomfortable.*) I didn't work that hard, really, and I only got involved in my community because of my religious beliefs. [Probable CRB1, harshly judging himself and others]

Therapist: I'm noticing that your mind is being harsh on both you and other people. Does it happen just in here or does it show up elsewhere? (*Applies rule 1: noticing CRB and offering a parallel between in- and out-of-session behavior.*)

Client: Well, you know, that's the way I was educated. We had it hard. But even so, I managed to remain the laziest of the bunch. [CRB1] But yeah, my wife always tells me I'm too harsh on my daughters. Mind you, I try to be extra nice to my granddaughters. They're so sweet! [CRB2 to shape]

Therapist: It's lovely to hear that you're sweet with your granddaughters. And it makes me sad to think you have to live under the yoke of such a critical mind. I wonder if, deep down, the person you want to be gives voice to the most critical thoughts your mind comes up with. I mean, I know religion means a lot to you, and I wonder: If you could choose, would you choose to be known as harsh, or more as a compassionate person? *(Applies rule 3: reinforcing CRB2 and seeking to shape further CRB2.)*

Client: Compassionate, I guess. [CRB2 to shape]

Therapist: And if no one ever knew or if it wasn't a question of reputation but of the impact you really had on others, would you choose to align with your harsh mind or with a more compassionate stance? *(Applies rule 3: aiming to further shape CRB2.)*

Client: The same. I would be compassionate. [CRB2]

Therapist: That is so touching to hear you say this when I know your mind is waiting to ambush you at any second. *(Applies rule 3: naturally reinforcing CRB2.)* How about we use our time here to help you behave in this more compassionate way, as you'd like—could that make a difference? *(Applies rules 2 and 3: evoking and reinforcing CRB2.)*

Client: Do you think I can do it? [Probable CRB2]

Therapist: I'm sure you can, and I'm here to help. *(Applies rule 3: reinforcing CRB2.)*

In this dialogue, the therapist focuses on clinically relevant behavior as it shows up in the room rather than on what the client is saying about his life outside of therapy. By paying close attention to how the client progresses and by introducing values, the therapist is able to get him to move to a more compassionate stance and choose compassion as a valued direction.

Helping Clients Accept Compassion from Others

The therapeutic relationship is peculiar in many ways. In contrast to "normal" relationships, it does not exist for its own sake. It is a professional relationship. Yet unlike other professional relationships, and due to its nature—being a space into which clients bring their most difficult personal problems and vulnerabilities—it cannot be limited to a surface relationship in which the clinician as a person remains hidden behind a veneer of professional distance. FAP invites clinicians to open their hearts to their clients and foster relationships that are every bit as deep as relationships in outside life, and often deeper. Yet the therapeutic relationship remains significantly different from other relationships in that at all times it is in the service of the client's therapeutic goals and best interests. Within such a relationship, clinicians can use their own reactions to shape more compassionate behavior in clients.

Clients with deeply ingrained histories of self-criticism and shame, perhaps as a result of childhood trauma, are commonly fused with the most painful forms of self-hatred, shame, and guilt. Histories of physical or sexual abuse often lead to a sense of guilt on the part of the victim. In cases of physical or sexual abuse at the hands of a caregiver, it is not uncommon for victims to feel they deserved it and carry a crippling burden of guilt and shame. That shame and guilt can make it exceedingly difficult to truly accept genuine care and compassion from others. In such cases, establishing a profound therapeutic relationship can provide a context in which clients can gradually open up to compassion and care—first to receiving it from the therapist, and then to evoking that compassion from themselves, toward themselves.

Clinical Example: Using the Therapeutic Relationship to Shape Acceptance and Compassion

In the following extract the therapist invites his client to connect with a past situation in which shame arose. As a child, Clare was for years sexually and emotionally abused by her father. She has been carrying a crippling burden of guilt and shame related to the abuse. Although she has mentioned the abuse to others in her family and distanced herself from her parents long ago, it is still difficult for her to contact her tangled feelings around what she has been through. Clare and her therapist have been working on interpersonal issues for over six months, and she now feels ready to address the abuse.

Client: I feel so guilty because I feel like I used my body. I've hated it ever since.

Therapist: It makes me sad to hear this. Would you be willing to close your eyes and bring to mind one of the situations from your childhood that you feel ashamed of?

Client: I can try.

Therapist: Where are you, and how old are you?

Client: I'm twelve and in my parents' living room. My father is there.

Therapist: What can you see around you?

Client: I can see the sofa. I can see the pictures on the walls and the sunlight through the bay window. I see my father sitting in his recliner. He's reading a newspaper. He's not paying attention to me.

Therapist: Can you notice what you are feeling? *(Pauses.)* What you are thinking? *(Pauses.)* What do you do?

Client: I feel bored. I… *(Pauses.)* I am striking provocative poses. *(Starts sobbing softly.)* I feel so ashamed! This is really hard!

Therapist: Could we just pause here for a minute? I want you to stay with that twelve-year-old Clare. Would you be willing to stay with her and how she feels?

Client: *(Speaks softly.)* Okay…

Therapist: Imagine that we could both go together and meet her. You can see what she sees, hear what she hears, and feel what she feels. *(Pauses.)* Could we just ask her, "What do you need right now?"

Client: *(Speaks in a little-girl voice.)* I just want to play. I want to go outside and play. I want to see people and have fun! *(Sobs.)*

Therapist: Yes, you just want to go outside and play. You want to see people. Those are perfectly normal needs for a twelve-year-old girl. You need attention. And that's a perfectly normal need for a twelve-year-old girl. *(Pauses.)* And the only way you know how to get attention is by doing what you're doing.

Client: *(Sobs.)* Yes.

Therapist: Clare, do you think we should condemn that young girl for that?

Client: No, of course not.…She doesn't know any better.

Therapist: What could we do to help her?

Client: Could I just hug her and tell her I love her?

Therapist: Let's do that. Give her a hug and tell her that you love her. (*Has tears in his eyes, obviously moved by the client's pain.*) She just needs to be seen and loved, and to feel safe. Is there something more you can tell her?

Client: Just that I love her and that it's not her fault. (*Sobs.*)

Therapist: No, it's not her fault. It's all she knows how to do. (*Pauses.*) Clare, take your time, and when you feel ready, you can come back to this room with me and open your eyes.

Client: (*Opens her eyes.*)

Therapist: I feel so moved that you had the courage to go there with me. How are you feeling now?

Client: I trust you. I think you're a good person. It's the first time that I've realized I don't have to hate myself for what happened and what I did. I didn't know any better. I've known these things intellectually, but this was the first time I could actually feel it.

Therapist: How could you have known any better? How could anyone who'd been through what you went through know any better?

Client: Yes.

Therapist: Do you think that now, when guilt shows up, you can go back and give that little girl the support and love she needs?

Client: I can try. At least now I know I don't have to hate myself and my body.

In this exchange, the therapist invited Clare to go back not to a moment of abuse, but rather to an episode that evoked the most shame for her: her provocative bids for attention from her father and abuser, the only way she could get some of the attention she craved. In contact with that memory, the therapist invited Clare to take the little girl's perspective and notice that, at the time, she did not have other options. From that experiential realization, and with gentle coaching from her therapist, Clare got to *feel* that she was not to blame for what happened, nor for the behaviors that have brought her the most shame over the years and fed her deep hatred of her body and sexuality. Such a realization could not have arisen through intellectual discussion or argument. The experiential element was essential to the work, and the therapist used the strength and sacred space of the relationship and the sense of trust within it to ease Clare into this very difficult experience.

Using the Therapeutic Relationship to Train Compassionate Perspective Taking

Combining compassion-focused ACT and FAP can lead to very powerful interventions in which clients can directly experience, through perspective taking, compassion and ultimately self-compassion. As they become better aware of what they do when they become more compassionate and self-compassionate in session, they are more likely to do it outside of the therapeutic relationship. From an ACT position, perspective taking involves inviting clients to shift as fully as possible from the perspective of their here-now experience to a different spatial and temporal perspective, contacting as fully as possible their own experience there-then or someone else's experience. Taking someone else's perspective is part of the definition of empathy. Taking one's own perspective at a different time and place can thus help foster empathy and compassion for oneself in those other situations. Combining these different aspects of perspective taking can provide the clinician with a powerful means of training compassion and self-compassion.

Clinical Example: Using the Therapist's
Experience to Evoke Perspective Taking

In this example, we return to Joe, the teacher and community activist who is worried about cognitive decline and attention deficits. Leading up to this dialogue, it has been two weeks since Joe's previous session, and Joe's therapist was fifteen minutes late to this session. He'd made a mistake when writing down Joe's appointment time, a fairly common occurrence for him. In the dialogue that follows, they are discussing Joe's interpersonal risk log, a FAP-inspired exercise in which the client keeps a daily record of intentionally taking at least one interpersonal risk.

Therapist: How did it go with keeping an interpersonal risk log?

Client: It worked really well for about a week, and I did feel that I was able to connect with others. But then I realized that all of this was superficial because I called a lady I know by the wrong name. I keep on making the same mistakes, like forgetting people's names. In my position, that's unacceptable. I'll never be able to really connect with other people.

Therapist: Oh yeah, the mistakes we make....Five minutes ago I got here fifteen minutes late. That's exactly the type of situation in which I feel like a jerk and where I get really self-judgmental. But when I got here you were really nice about it and immediately made me feel at ease.

Client: (*Laughs.*) Actually, it did cross my mind that you'd done it on purpose just to show me that I don't judge you harshly because of a small mistake!

Therapist: No, it really was a mistake. I goofed up. It's the kind of mistake that's all too frequent for me, as you know. But it's true that I immediately felt accepted by you—so much so that my habit of coming down really hard on myself when that happens sort of dissolved.

Client: Well, everyone can make mistakes, and you have other qualities...

Therapist: Sure, but this is one mistake I make too often, so it's particularly meaningful to me that, having been on the receiving end of it a few times, you could still accept me with such kindness. (*Pauses.*) Joe, I'd like to ask you to imagine that you're looking through the eyes with which you looked at me when I goofed up. But now, I'd like you to imagine being beamed back to the situation in which you called that lady by the wrong name. As you do so, look at yourself as if you were witnessing the scene from a little distance. Take your time... (*Pauses.*) What do you see?

Client: (*Pauses.*) Well, I see a kind man. He wants to help and he gets the name wrong....A man with his weaknesses. I see a man I rather like, a man for whom it's not easy... (*Pauses. His face softens and looks sadder.*)

121

Therapist: Yes, Joe. This man is the Joe I know: a man who has his weaknesses, but also a warmhearted man who lives by his values. A man I feel touched by…

Client: Yes, it's true.

Therapist: I have to tell you that I'm getting teary right now. It's the first time since we've started working together that I've seen you give yourself the compassion that you have for others, and that made you choose your line of work. It's as if you finally allowed yourself to see yourself as a human being like any other…

Client: Yes, it's true. (*Pauses, then laughs.*) But you know my mind doesn't agree. It's still trying to say I don't deserve to be forgiven for my mistakes.

Therapist: Sure, that's what minds do. Could you describe what you did just now when you looked at yourself from that more compassionate perspective, and how it felt?

Client: Well, I relaxed my shoulders, I relaxed my chest, and I think I opened my heart a tiny bit… (*Pauses.*) It's not easy to say. I wonder if I'm not reconstructing it now…

Therapist: Not easy to say, and yet you knew how to do it. See if you can do it once again. So you're standing in front of that lady and you get her name wrong. Okay, relax your shoulders and chest…

Client: (*Pauses.*) Okay, I see. (*Pauses, then laughs.*)

Therapist: Thanks for trying this. I want to invite you to see if you can notice yourself doing some of that in the coming week and include it in your interpersonal risk log, only now as an interpersonal risk you are taking with yourself, so to speak.

Client: Okay, I'll do that, even if I'm not too sure how I'll do it.

This dialogue marked a turning point in Joe's therapy, being the first time that he behaved in a deeply compassionate way toward himself. He did not just say compassionate words about himself and his memory lapses; he did so from a place of feeling. When the therapist could see him visibly soften, he felt touched and expressed that.

In this exchange, the therapist invited Joe to shift perspective by looking at himself in the situation that generated shame and self-criticism from the perspective he took when looking at the therapist's mistake. Here again, the key to this intervention was inviting the shift in perspective from an experiential rather than intellectual place. The therapist then reinforced Joe's new behavior by openly sharing how Joe's self-compassionate behavior impacted him (CRB2) and by inviting Joe to notice what he had done to direct compassion toward himself, thereby promoting generalization to situations outside the therapeutic relationship (FAP rule 5).

As discussed, within the ACT model, flexible perspective taking is a key component of psychological flexibility. In our experience, perspective-taking exercises often elicit self-compassion in clients. For example, inviting a client to experientially return to particularly hurtful childhood events to meet the child she was then and give or say something to that hurt or frightened child typically evokes more compassionate behavior toward that child and her suffering, as illustrated in the dialogue with Clare.

Clinical Example: Using Self-as-Context to Train a More Self-Compassionate Stance

Other approaches to perspective taking can also be useful in training clients to approach their present life difficulties from a more empathic and self-compassionate stance, as illustrated in this dialogue with Mike, who is in therapy for severe OCD accompanied by intense shame and self-disparagement. Mike has made good progress with the ACT model and, in particular, has become quite adept at sorting his experience with the matrix. Because sorting into the different quadrants of the matrix implies being able to look at one's experience, rather than being fused with it, an ability to do this indicates a capacity to take the observer perspective.

Therapist: I'm quite impressed by the progress you've made in terms of noticing your toward and away moves and the difference between your five-senses experience and inner and mental experience.

Client: Yes, but I still get stuck when it comes to checking the stove before going to bed at night.

Therapist: Let's look at that now. Imagine that you, as you are sitting across from me right now, could somehow be teleported to meet you, as you will be in your kitchen tonight. Is there something you could tell yourself that may help you with the obsessions and compulsions? Take your time, and once you've found something to say, just say it as you would if you were in your kitchen, meeting the you who's having obsessions and the urge to check.

Client: Okay: "Don't be stupid! You know it's no use."

Therapist: How do you, in the kitchen, receive what you just said?

Client: Not well.

Therapist: Does it work?

Client: No.

Therapist: What tone of voice did you speak in?

Client: Harsh, I guess.

Therapist: Is that how you need to be spoken to when you're stuck in the kitchen?

Client: I need to be spoken to more gently.

Therapist: Could you, as you are here with me right now, speak more gently to the you that's stuck with your obsessions in the kitchen? What could you say?

Client: (*Pauses.*) I could say, "I know it's hard to have these thoughts and feel so much anxiety."

Therapist: How do you, in the kitchen, receive this?

Client: Better. I feel heard. It's like something is softening up a bit.

Therapist: What else could you, here with me, tell you in the kitchen?

Client: I could encourage myself to choose to do something important to me rather than my series of checks.

Therapist: How do you, in the kitchen, receive that?

Client: I can hear it. It feels like I could do it.

Therapist: What else could you do?

Client: I could go pet my cat and spend time with my partner.

Therapist: Would that be important to you?

Client: Yes, because checking the stove is about making sure my partner and my cat don't die in a house fire caused by me. So it's really about taking care of them.

Therapist: That sounds great. Would you now come back to this moment? It was touching to see this dialogue between you, here and now, and you, there and then in the kitchen. I was particularly touched by how you became kinder to yourself as the conversation went on and you turned toward what's important to you. What showed up for me is that it seems the more difficult the situation, the more you need to be spoken to gently and have your difficult emotions validated. Would that make sense to you?

Client: Yes, I guess that's true. I have had a tendency to treat myself harshly.

Therapist: So how about we continue practicing treating yourself more gently, the way we've been doing here?

Client: That would be nice.

Therapist: I wonder how you would rate the probability that you will be able to speak to yourself in the way you've just done when you're there in your kitchen.

Client: Maybe 70 percent.

Therapist: I'm looking forward to hearing what you notice.

Having established the therapeutic relationship as an experiential model of a more compassionate relationship in prior sessions, in this session the therapist invites Mike to generalize this ability through some perspective-taking work. Guiding Mike carefully through several shifts between here-now and there-then perspectives, the therapist helps him notice the functions of different ways of speaking to himself, particularly a harsh and judging stance versus a gentler stance. By the end of the exchange, Mike has been able to practice a kinder stance (CRB2) and notice its reinforcing functions. The therapist then concludes the exchange by asking Mike to assess the probability of engaging in a similar perspective-taking exercise when next besieged by obsessions. No matter what estimate the client provides, the therapist reinforces it, given that simply paying attention to whether or not one engages in the targeted behavior increases the probability of doing it.

Compassion in the Therapeutic Dyad

In summary, this chapter addressed how clinicians can maximize the benefits of the therapeutic relationship and use operant learning principles to aid clients in cultivating compassion and transforming their responses to self-critical thoughts and shameful self-directed emotions. We explored self-compassion as a condition for compassion and highlighted relevant behavioral principles. Among these, we examined positive reinforcement to cultivate compassion and self-compassion, applying FAP principles to cultivating compassion, using defusion with shame-based self-criticism, and specifically shaping compassion through in-session interactions. We also reviewed the therapeutic process of helping clients accept compassion from others and eventually turn that compassion toward themselves.

Using the principles of FAP, the therapeutic relationship can provide a context that is ideally suited to noticing self-criticism and shame in the moment and gently shaping kinder behavior toward self and others. From an ACT perspective, compassion and self-compassion are highly related and both are invaluable, and in this chapter we demonstrated different ways in which the therapeutic relationship can be used to foster more compassionate behaviors toward self and others. The components and processes that are emphasized in FAP expand the clinician's awareness and shape compassion and self-compassion in the moment, while also encouraging clients to incorporate these qualities and behaviors into daily life. This is done through training in flexible perspective taking, including extending compassion to oneself and others when faced with shame-eliciting situations or stimuli.

6

Initial Elements of a Compassion-Focused ACT

Practicing therapy with a compassionate focus means more than simply being especially kind or being mindful of the desire to help alleviate suffering. Furthermore, simply adding self-compassion meditations to an ACT protocol, while potentially beneficial, doesn't quite capture what becomes possible when we appreciate compassion as an evolved human capacity and an active, interacting array of psychological processes. In this chapter, we draw upon CFT theory and practice, and the science of compassion more broadly, to illustrate elements of an ACT approach specifically focused on generating and expanding compassionate flexibility.

Compassion involves a verbally mediated, embodied state of attention, affect, and arousal that facilitates flexible perspective taking, relaxed wakefulness, and preparedness to face the suffering we encounter in the world. We come to this state through our affiliative emotions, evoked through current and historical experience of safe, caring social connectedness. Bringing a compassionate focus to our work as therapists requires connecting with our own empathy, mindfulness, and openness. By becoming available to our compassionate mind as ACT therapists, we enhance our ability to experientially move these processes in the therapeutic relationship.

What this looks like during the flow of a psychotherapy session often includes a calm deceleration of our pacing, a deliberate focus on being grounded in the present moment, and a deeply caring engagement within a mindful conversation and authentic emotional exchange. Unlike much of how mindfulness is described today, compassion is not a state of bare attention and is not neutral. The meditations and visualizations involved in compassionate mind training provide a specific form of self-practice and neurobehavioral exercise for both client and therapist. Just as the practice of mindfulness training can help us bring a more focused and flexible quality of attention to our therapy sessions, practices that cultivate compassionate mind can provide us with a foundation for and facility in deepening compassion in our ACT practice, and in our lives.

Compassion and Freely Chosen Values

We have consistently highlighted the degree to which compassion is an emergent quality in humans. Importantly though, compassion involves making a decision. We decide to turn toward the suffering we encounter in the world and in ourselves, and we commit to working to do something about it. This decision then informs our state of being and what we extend into the world around us, including into the context of our therapeutic relationships. In this way, our movement toward compassion is a choice that has literal and practical extensions into everything we encounter. The world is filled with tragedies, loss, illness, and even death, but the choice to evoke and embody compassion is yours and yours alone. You can carry this decision with you, and it will guide your actions throughout the course of your life. You can bring this compassionate stance into your therapeutic relationships, and your clients, should they choose to do so, can bring compassionate action into their lives. With your example and guidance, they can choose to cultivate their compassionate mind.

From a place of mindful awareness and appreciation of just how patterned and painful our path through life can be, each of us can choose to be the compassionate person we wish to be, as much as we can. This is possible if we allow ourselves such a wish. Possessions, relationships, health, and even life itself can be swept away like a crowd of sorrows clearing our house of furniture, to paraphrase Rumi. And yet, waking up in this very moment and consciously choosing to be sensitive and responsive to the suffering we experience in ourselves and others—this is truly ours.

For our clients, this might mean consciously noticing and changing time-worn patterns of experiential avoidance. Choosing compassionate action may require that they access the courage and stillness of mind needed to find their feet and face the reality of destructive patterns in their lives. It might mean acknowledging ways that routinized self-blame and shame have implicitly been acting as safety behaviors. Though that pattern may sound counterintuitive, by heaping shame upon themselves and wrapping themselves in the false security blanket of a socially sanctioned control-and-avoidance agenda, clients can remain fixed, even in states of intense anxious avoidance, needless struggle, and ever-narrowing possibilities.

Clinical Example: Introducing a Client with Lifelong Struggles with Depression and Anxiety

Josh began therapy with one of the authors during his final year of college, at age twenty-four, as he was completing his BA in theater at a leading university. At the time, he was regularly experiencing panic attacks and pervasive worries. Despite the intensity of his anxiety symptoms, they weren't at the top of his list of problems. In his earliest sessions, Josh said he was depressed about what he harshly described as being a screw-up. As he approached completion of his BA, his self-attacking thoughts intensified, and at times he remained in bed for days on end, afraid to face the day and hating himself for his cowardice.

For years, Josh's friends and peers had regularly praised him for his good looks, sharp sense of humor, and exceptional social fluency. To many observers, Josh seemed to be one of the "beautiful people," going to all of the fashionable parties and apparently living it up. Although this may have been how things looked from the outside, Josh's experience looking out at the world was very different.

At the age of five, Josh's highly successful and status-conscious parents had him screened for attention deficit disorder, and he was prescribed stimulant medications. Nevertheless, his interest never remained focused on academics. Josh explained how it was nearly impossible for him to complete any homework because his family environment included consistent outbursts of rage and verbal abuse from his father, and his mother did not intervene to stop the abuse. Over many years, Josh's mother became dependent upon opiates and alcohol as she coped with the pain in her household. At the end of elementary school, Josh was sent to a military boarding school, and he continued in some form of boarding school until he went away to college.

The first time Josh was diagnosed with depression, he was only eleven years old, living miles away from family and having little contact with loved ones. When he began therapy, Josh described boarding school as "a cold environment at best." He remembered being verbally abused and beaten by peers—and the occasional enraged teacher—on a regular basis. He blamed himself and established a habit of extremely hostile self-talk. Because he often told himself that he was stupid and lazy, approaching his schoolwork became extremely anxiety provoking and depressing. More and more, Josh ignored his coursework, focusing on fashion, popularity, and any opportunity to be on stage and to perform. Although he had been medicated with relatively high doses of SSRIs and stimulant medication since childhood, he told his therapist that none of the drugs ever did any good.

Josh reported that the only time he felt relief was when he was losing himself in a theatrical role on stage, partying with friends (which included heavy binge drinking while using cocaine or other drugs), or hooking up with attractive women he barely knew. He regularly experienced blackouts due to drinking. This pattern of avoidance and addictive behaviors had begun as early as age twelve and continued through college and into his adult life. Following nights of substance abuse, Josh routinely awoke with panic attacks and dread.

He said that his relationship with his parents didn't really change from childhood into young adulthood. They provided him with a seemingly endless expense account, and he spent however much he felt like to, as he put it, "fill the hole and keep the dread away."

While he had been in therapy off and on since childhood, Josh never really considered himself to have been emotionally abused or neglected. Josh explained that he was just spoiled. As he told his therapist in his first session, and repeatedly throughout the course of his therapy, "I just want what I want when I want it. I'm a selfish piece of shit. I don't have any right to complain about anything. I'm spoiled."

By now, you have undoubtedly already begun to formulate a case conceptualization for this client and to imagine how you might help him. We will revisit Josh over the rest of this book to illustrate how a compassion-focused ACT practitioner might conceptualize his case and help him come to terms with his shame and emotional pain while moving toward a life of greater meaning, vitality, and joy.

Creative Hopelessness and the Wisdom of No Blame

Validation of an individual's unique experience and life context is key in compassion-focused ACT, as is an understanding of the universal human condition of vulnerability and suffering that connects us to one another. Rather than adopting the role of an emotionally distant and superior "expert," the ACT therapist acknowledges the universality of human suffering and the inherent equality we all share in the face of challenges in life. Rather than targeting direct change in clients' "negative" thoughts and feelings, the compassion-focused ACT therapist works to create conditions conducive to mindful, accepting, and compassionate experience. Working together, therapist and client create this context and facilitate the client in discovering new ways of seeing inner and outer experiences in the service of living with greater meaning, purpose, and vitality. By bringing a compassionate focus to ACT, we can teach clients to validate and to be compassionate toward all aspects of themselves, even aspects of their story, actions, or emotions that they are uncomfortable with.

Creative Hopelessness

An approach often used early in ACT is a technique known as *creative hopelessness*. The term "hopelessness" is, quite rightly, usually associated with desperation or giving up on life. When we are hopeless, we recognize that there is no way forward and that what we are trying to do simply will not work. However, the concept of creative hopelessness takes this in a different direction, referring to taking a clear and unvarnished look at the range of strategies and behaviors engaged in to try to get away from uncomfortable feelings through avoidance or excessive attempts at control. At the beginning of ACT, we often aim to draw out the system of control and avoidance and bring attention to where clients may be preoccupied with or stuck in unworkable patterns. This involves bringing attention to the following questions (Hayes et al., 2012):

1. What are the client's valued aims?

2. What has the client already tried to do to realize these aims?

3. How successful have these strategies been?

4. What has the pursuit of these strategies cost the client? Have these efforts led to the client's life growing bigger or smaller?

Through a process of successive open questions, clients can contact the impossibility of realizing their aims if they continue operating in the world as they have been. This realization is the core of creative hopelessness, and it can lead clients into a space of confusion and helplessness that is also rife with possibilities for change. Bringing a compassionate focus to these questions involves deliberately activating the attributes of the compassionate mind through the therapeutic discussion, as well as consciously activating various hexaflex processes throughout the dialogue.

Radical Blamelessness and Affiliative Emotions

Engaging in compassion-focused ACT creates an opportunity to expand on this position of openness and constructive confusion by grounding the client in the expansive reality of the human condition. In this way, the therapist explores how clients' life circumstances have been determined by their evolutionary and personal learning history. Although clients have not chosen either of these factors, they have been under their influence. They may not realize that much of their suffering has not been self-created and is not their fault.

As discussed, ACT posits that people often respond to aversive emotional experiences and painful mental events through attempts at avoidance or excessive control. One of the most common ways that people attempt to experience control in a situation that they actually cannot control is to blame themselves and imagine that they might be able to do something about it if they weren't bad, worthless, or inadequate in some key way.

In evolutionary terms, it makes sense that this tendency toward self-blame might be selected for across many iterations. If our evolutionary ancestors were on the savanna hunting and a stampede of buffalo suddenly thundered over the horizon at breakneck speed, the early human who thought *I'm never going to be able to outrun them* while freezing in place would be crushed. On the other hand, the early human who had the "irrational" thought *I can beat these guys* while running for his life would be that much more likely to survive. In another example, when some ancient civilizations were faced with incredibly difficult farming conditions, they hypothesized gods that must be placated. Imagining these gods to have desires similar to those of humans, the priests of such societies offered up sacrificial young virgins, killing their children as a gift to their gods and an act of submission. If the harvest still didn't go well, the priests might be more likely to blame themselves than their gods, believing that their sacrifice had been inadequate.

We humans depend upon one another for our very survival, and social isolation is therefore intensely threatening, even terrifying (Gilbert, 2000; Solomon, Greenberg, & Pyszczynski, 1991). In our evolutionary history, being abandoned by family and community would almost certainly result in death. As such, we have evolved to respond to social threats with intense attempts to avoid or control them. Poignantly, when people are abused, traumatized, or sexually assaulted, particularly as children, they often find themselves in a place of self-blame and deep-seated shame (Bennett, Sullivan, & Lewis, 2005). We can imagine how powerful and threatening the experience of an abusive parent might be for a child. To a great extent, children's lives depend upon their parents, who are, physically, like giants to them, and are also responsible for their feeding, protection, and very survival. It is no wonder, then, that so many children who experience patterns of abuse learn to shame themselves and fall into a shame-based control agenda, hoping that if they could just be good enough, they might finally get free from threats and emotional pain.

As mentioned, compassion-focused therapy places a great deal of emphasis on helping clients adopt a broad perspective on their evolutionary and personal history, recognizing that a great deal of their suffering has not been of their choosing and is simply not their fault. This is not just conceptual, but an attempt to make room for the activation of mindful compassion, which can facilitate psychological flexibility. While immersed and fused with self-focused shame, clients may experience life only through that lens, determining their behaviors and directions. By accepting what CFT therapists have termed *the wisdom of no blame,* and recognizing the creative hopelessness in patterns of persistent adherence to an agenda of avoidance and control, clients can begin to cultivate willingness to face difficult experiences in the service of meaningful behavior change. As they let go of clinging to shame as a safety behavior and recognize the futility of unworkable patterns, they can begin to take responsibility for their life direction and commit to action in service of their valued aims.

Clinical Example: Using Creative
Hopelessness and the Wisdom of No Blame

The clinical vignette below, from Josh's seventh session, illustrates how he and his therapist encountered and engaged with creative hopelessness, the wisdom of no blame, and psychological flexibility processes in session.

Explore Creative Hopelessness

Client: My life has just been a mess, you know? I'm not getting out of bed until late in the afternoon, and when I wake up I feel so much dread and anxiety. Then I stay out late and get messed up. I'm not functioning like a normal person.

Therapist: Josh, that really sounds dreadful. I feel sad to think of you stuck in that pattern, day in and day out. Is that how it is most of the time?

Client: Yeah, pretty much. I can't get my shit together.

Therapist: What do you think keeps you in bed in the morning? Are you exhausted from partying? Hungover?

Client: I guess that's part of it, but it's not the main thing. I just feel so depressed and ashamed of my life that I don't want to get up and face the day.

Therapist: So, you're feeling depressed and exhausted, and one way that you've dealt with that is by not getting out of bed at all?

(The therapist draws attention to present-moment contact with emotions, highlighting the avoidance function inherent in the client's pattern.)

Client: Yeah, I know it sounds crazy. It's gross.

Therapist: *(Pauses, makes eye contact, and smiles warmly.)* Well, maybe we can just slow down all of this business about how "crazy" or "gross" you are for a moment. *(Speaks more softly.)* We can come back to that in a little bit, okay? *(Picks up a notebook and places it on the coffee table between them.)* Let's imagine that all of your self-criticism is right here on the table for now, just sitting with us. We don't have to fight it, but our minds can focus on something else for the moment, can't they?

(The therapist slows to a more mindful, empathic conversational style. Using a physical metaphor of a notebook to represent the client's self-criticism, the therapist illustrates defusion, willingness, and flexible attention.)

Client: Yes. That's okay with me. The criticism isn't going anywhere anyway. *(Both laugh a bit about that.)*

Therapist: It sounds like one tactic you're using to deal with these uncomfortable feelings is just to stay in bed and avoid the day. Has that worked well for you so far?

Client: Absolutely not! If it did, we wouldn't be having this conversation.

Therapist: Of course! That makes a lot of sense. So staying in bed and hiding doesn't work for you...

Client: In fact, it makes things worse. I can't stop myself, so I just lie there, but it's like hell.

Therapist: Well, that sounds awful. You feel trapped there in that bed, and it's actually making things worse for you.

(The therapist again engages empathy and demonstrates flexible perspective taking while summarizing to draw out the system and point out a lack of workability in the current pattern.)

Client: Yes.

First Steps Toward Values Authorship

Therapist: If you weren't stuck in that bed, if you were getting up in the morning and pursuing the things that matter to you, what might you be doing?

Client: Oh, god....If that were happening, then I could go to auditions, I could go to the gym, I could make appointments with friends and agents....My life would be very different.

Therapist: All right, so there's a lot in your life that immediately rises to the surface in terms of what matters to you and what would make your life more meaningful. You have a sense of what you'd like your life to be about, and that's important. For now I want to focus on the fact that staying in bed is making your life smaller and isn't working. Do I have that right?

(Therapist and client are beginning to identify valued aims and to stimulate the client's potential motivation to care for his own well-being.)

Client: Exactly. Something has to change—I have to stop being such a disaster.

Therapist: And while talking about this to me, you're saying things like "I'm not normal," "I'm a disaster," and "I know I sound crazy." So this criticizing yourself and giving yourself a hard time about your actions—that's another strategy for dealing with your pain, isn't it?

Client: Somebody has to kick my ass into shape.

Therapist: Okay, so your mind tells you that somebody has to do that. But how is that working out? Is tearing into yourself making things better?

(Therapist and client continue to explore the unworkability of the patterns of avoidance in the client's life. Viewing thoughts as thoughts, the therapist explores the function of criticism as a safety behavior that is having unintended consequences.)

Client: My god, that might be the worst part of it. I feel disgusted with myself.

Therapist: "Disgusted." *(Slows and speaks in a warm and caring yet authoritative tone.)* That can be such a powerful feeling—to just feel sick about yourself. That's hard, Josh....No wonder you have such a struggle. Who wouldn't try to fight that? I hear the tone of disgust in your voice, and I can really appreciate how heavy all of this is for you. It really makes me want something to happen for you, you know? I feel like you could use some breathing room.

Client: *(Sighs and gets a bit teary-eyed.)* Thanks. I just feel like I need a break.

Therapist: Well, you've been pushing really hard to outrun your pain, and it feels exhausting. So far we've looked at how lying in bed and avoiding your life has worked out, and we've seen the effects of just viciously criticizing yourself, and neither has helped. You're going out every night, getting high and drunk and hanging out. What's that doing for you?

Client: Ha! Nothing. Maintaining. When I started, I could have a good time, be seen, feel like I was special at the clubs, basically because I got a lot of attention and getting messed up made me feel, you know, some euphoria. But now, honestly, I just kind of feel numb. In the morning it's sheer terror.

Therapist: I guess we have another approach here that has let you down. Hmm….Partying isn't working. The party is over. It just leaves you anxious and alone. Well, I know you've been through a lot of treatment. How has therapy or medication helped?

Client: You know that I've been to a ton of therapists, and nothing has changed. I still feel like I'm a piece of shit. If anybody could see the real me, they would know.

Therapist: After all of your experiences of therapy failing you, I'm kind of amazed, and honored, that you would be here at all, you know? So, therapy hasn't worked….Hmm….Has the medication helped?

Client: I've been on one thing or another my whole life, and it doesn't seem like medication has helped at all. Prozac, Zoloft, Adderall…you name it. Nothing makes a dent.

Therapist: You've tried just about anything you can think of…

Client: Oh, you can throw in yoga, weight lifting, Outward Bound, backpacking…a ton of other shit.

Therapist: Okay, so you've tried just about anything anybody has thought of to get a hold of this, to stop feeling anxious and ashamed, to stop believing that people will find out just how bad you are deep inside, and has anything worked?

Client: No. Nothing.

(Together, the client and therapist have identified the extent of the problem inherent in the client's struggle to avoid fundamental human experiences that can't be outrun, avoided, or suppressed.)

Bringing in Compassionate Defusion and Perspective Taking

Therapist: Nothing has worked. And what does that tell us?

Client: That I suck and need to do better.

Therapist: (*Picks up the notebook that serves as a physical metaphor for the client's self-criticism.*) And when all of the harsh correction and abusive criticism tells you to do better and work harder, what happens? Do you live a bigger life? Do you get out of bed in the morning?

(*The earlier physical metaphor is deployed to facilitate defusion and a clear-eyed functional analysis.*)

Client: No, nothing is working. It's hopeless.

Therapist: Yes, it is hopeless in a sense. That's a good starting point.

Client: What? I don't understand. Nothing works and that's somehow good? C'mon, dude…

Therapist: Let's just take a moment and play with this idea together. What do we have to lose? Nothing so far has done the trick. So maybe your old ways of doing things are, in fact, hopeless. That might be a good thing, because it allows us to begin where we are. You admitting that you don't understand what might help is a place for us to begin…an honest place. Our recognition that all of the things you've been taught about how to deal with your pain have been hopeless—well, that's just honest. This is where we find ourselves, Josh.

Client: Okay, but I'm scared. I don't know what to do, Doc.

(*The client has accessed an opening to the compassion available to him in the therapeutic relationship, building the potential for activation of his own capacity for self-compassion.*)

Therapist: I can really appreciate that—and I appreciate your courage in taking this kind of clear-eyed look at the situation. If you saw yourself through my eyes and heard your story through my ears, you would see and hear a young man who has been through a lot of pain and a lot of very harsh treatment. He's trying like hell to get away from that pain, and he's knocking himself out in the process. They say that when you're in a hole, it's time to stop digging. Do you think you might be ready to move toward something new? Can you stop digging?

(In response to the client's softening, the therapist uses his own affiliative emotions as a social reinforcer, creating a context for compassion. Flexible perspective taking is deployed.)

Client: That's why I'm here. I'm really hoping for something new.

Therapist: That's a good thing for our work together. Do you think you're willing—I mean—can you find it in yourself to be willing to take a very different look at all of this? It might even mean stopping the direct fight you've had with yourself, you know? It might mean having to carry some of these difficult feelings rather than wrestling with them.

Client: I'm not sure I know what you mean, but I think I'm willing. Can you give me an example?

Therapist: Sure. Let's imagine the life you told me you want in our first few meetings. You've told me you want to go to auditions and really hone your craft. You've said you'd like to be able to get out of bed in the morning, build stronger relationships, and begin to exercise and take better care of yourself. You'd like to feel loved by those close to you and to be a more loving person. Now, if feeling some anxiety and hearing your mind criticize you along the way were *necessary* parts of the journey to that life, would you be willing to carry those feelings and thoughts?

Client: If I could really do it…if I could really take those steps, then yes. Yes, I could get through the feelings.

Therapist: So you would choose to feel what you feel and move forward?

Client: Yes, but…I just can't freaking believe I did this to myself!

The Wisdom of No Blame

Therapist: Well, I want to take a look at that for a minute. I want us to sit here together and recognize what you have and have not chosen in your life.

Client: I've made a lot of bad choices.

Therapist: Perhaps you did. I don't know, really. But how did you get to those choices, Josh? What led you to where you are sitting right now?

Client: What do you mean?

Therapist: Did you choose your grandparents or your ancestors?

Client: No. I wasn't sitting on some cloud picking where to be born, like in a cartoon.

Therapist: Exactly. You didn't pick your place in the genetic lottery that determines what qualities we bring into the world. You didn't choose your parents, and you didn't choose what part of the world you grew up in, did you?

Client: No. That's all out of my hands. (*Appears less anxious and aggressive, but also appears to be about to cry.*)

(*The therapist is using a process of Socratic questioning and thinking with the client, not for him, to collaborate in taking a new perspective on the client's self-story while placing his choices in context.*)

Therapist: Even though we've only met a few times, you've trusted me enough to tell me some terrible things that were done to you. It matters a lot to me that you found the courage to talk about this with me. We've talked about how you were subjected to rageful abuse, bullying, and neglect. These are sad things. Would you have chosen any of those things for yourself?

Client: Of course not, it was awful. (*Both therapist and client are making direct eye contact in a nondefensive way, and both appear sad yet relaxed.*)

(*Empathic bridging and affect matching are blended into the therapeutic style, evoking an emotionally aware apprehension of the discussion and activating reciprocal empathy.*)

Therapist: And would you choose to have a brain that is set up to have a 24/7, always-on, threat-detection system, so that you feel anxiety and shame in response to the slightest sign of danger? No, of course you wouldn't.

Client:　All of that has hurt so much, and none of it is about me.

Therapist:　Exactly. So much of who we are and what we do has been set up by our learning history and our biology. All of us suffer, and we come into this crazy world doing our level best to survive and be happy. What you are facing, Josh, is not your fault.

Client:　Yes, I know.

Therapist:　I bet you do know that logically, but let's just sit for a moment together with that. *(Therapist and client remain in silence for a few moments, and the therapist makes very direct eye contact, with an upright yet relaxed body posture, then speaks with warmth and patience.)* It isn't your fault, Josh.

Client:　*(Appears calm and a bit tearful.)* I do think I get it. It's hard to even approach it. That all of this has been out of my control and not my choice or fault is a lot to get my head around. I don't know why, but it's kind of a relief. I don't want it to stay like this, though. I want to do something about it.

Therapist:　Well, that's why we're here together in this room right now, isn't it? It's an honor to work with you, and to take a look at things a bit differently.

Client:　Thanks, man. I'm glad I came in today. I almost didn't make it, you know?

Summary

The above example illustrates how the fundamental assumptions and techniques of CFT and ACT can come together to create a compassionate context for our work as clinicians. Much of the example involves helping the client discover new ways of understanding his situation, such as practicing willingness, adopting a broader perspective, defusing from content, and noticing and releasing the grip of the control and avoidance agenda. However, the key element in this session that resulted in new learning was establishing the therapeutic relationship as a compassionate, warm, and nonjudgmental context. Rather than training the compassionate mind through verbal instruction, the therapist moves the relevant psychological processes experientially. This approach requires that we, as therapists, be involved in our own compassionate mind training and become increasingly open to the presence of compassion in ourselves and others.

Compassion-Focused Defusion Techniques

Thus far, we have looked at the role of defusion in compassion from a variety of theoretical and applied dimensions. Below, we provide a couple of specific techniques adapted from ACT. While neither ACT nor CFT is a cookie-cutter or toolbox approach to therapy, the following exercises provide a starting point for breathing compassion into defusion. Both of these approaches can be used with clients in session or provided as homework practices. You might also consider using them yourself to cultivate your own compassion and psychological flexibility.

Intervention: Externalizing and Thanking the Mind

The following transcript introduces the practice of imagining thoughts and the workings of the mind as a process that one is disidentified from. Flexible perspective taking and defusion from self-narratives allow people to realize that they are more than just whatever thoughts pop into their minds. This practice capitalizes on that insight, allowing clients to see their mind as an external object and relate to it in new ways. There are many versions of this practice, as well as other defusion techniques, available on the Internet and in various publications. However, we have chosen this blend of externalizing and thanking the mind (Hayes, 2005) as a point of beginning compassion-focused work on defusion. As you'll note, the text includes examples that are quite specific. When using this approach with clients, it is, as always, important to be sensitive to the context of that particular client at that particular time, including choosing examples relevant to the client. (For a downloadable audio recording of this practice, please visit http://www.newharbinger.com/30550.)

> *Your foot is a part of you, but it isn't all of you. When you have a dream, that dream unfolds in your mind, but it isn't you. Similarly, our thinking and verbal minds are a part of who we are, but they aren't all of who we are. For*

this exercise, imagine that your mind is something outside of yourself, almost separate from who you are. For example, you might think, "My mind is telling me that I need to stay inside today" or "Oh, my mind is doing its old familiar pattern of worrying about my retirement."

It can also be helpful to talk through your emotional responses by describing them out loud or to yourself: for example, "My mind is telling me that I'm going to fail this test, and that's generating a flash of anxiety. This means my body has picked up a perceived threat. Now I'm sensing butterflies in my stomach. Let's see if I can just make space for this experience for a moment. I can notice how these thoughts are pulling my feelings around, but I'm going to return my focus to where I am and what I'm doing."

By learning to stand back from your experiences with nonjudgmental observation, you are gradually learning to defuse from the flow of mental events, rather than overidentifying with them and handing your life over to thinking, imagining, and emotions.

Now call to mind a physical sense of warmth and the strength and wisdom that emerges from self-kindness. Understand that you are not merely the thoughts that float across your mind. You are something much bigger and much more important. You are something that can contain this experience. Holding yourself in kindness, practice this defusion from the flow of your thoughts and explore what happens.

Next, let's see if we can take a compassionate view on the actions of the mind in this moment. Remember that our minds have evolved to warn us about potential dangers and problems, and that our minds hate unemployment. We're not surprised that our hearts keep beating or that our lungs keep breathing, so why should we be surprised that our minds keep thinking, moving back and forth in time and creating worries and ruminations? This mind of yours is doing all it knows how to do, and it thinks it's doing it on your behalf. By taking this moment to distance yourself from the activities of the mind, you can even come to thank the incessantly active mind for doing its job. As you breathe in and out, with a long, slow exhalation and feeling a sense of centeredness, you can say something like, "Thanks, mind. You're doing your best to keep me safe and on top of things. Buddy, I think you take your job a little too seriously, though. Why don't you take some time to rest and let me get on with my day? You can hang around, but I'm not handing my life over to you. Thanks, though. I've got this."

Intervention: The Children on the Bus

Before describing this exercise (adapted from Tirch, 2012) we have to admit that this defusion technique is an ACT author's equivalent of a guilty pleasure. It's a variation on the classic ACT metaphor Passengers on the Bus (Hayes et al., 1999), an ACT move that's wildly popular, and for good reasons. In our clinical work, the following defusion technique, which also helps people reconnect with their fundamental values, has had a way of sticking with clients. That might be because this technique brings in many of the hexaflex processes and blends them in a seamless way. Other variations sometimes call this the Monsters on the Bus, but we prefer to invoke children, rather than monsters, because this helps both therapist and client remember to be compassionate even with those parts of ourselves that we don't like. (For a downloadable audio recording of this practice, please visit http://www.newharbinger.com/30550.)

Let's begin this exercise by imagining that you're a bus driver. You have your uniform, your shiny dashboard, your comfortable seat, and a powerful bus at your command. This bus represents your life: all of your experiences, challenges, and strengths have brought you to this role. You will be driving this bus to a destination of your own choosing—a destination that represents the valued aims you wish to pursue and are willing to pursue. Arriving at your destination is deeply significant to you, and every inch that you travel toward this valued aim means you've been taking your life in the right direction. As you're driving, it's necessary for you to keep your course and follow the path you've chosen.

Like any bus driver, you're obliged to stop along the way to pick up passengers. However, some of these passengers are difficult to deal with; they are the most unruly and aggressive children you've ever encountered. Each one represents a difficult, anxiety-provoking thought or feeling that you've had to contend with over the course of your life. Some of the children might be self-criticism, others are panic and dread, and yet others represent worry and fear. Whatever has troubled you and distracted you from the rich possibilities of life is now hopping on your bus in the form of these unruly children who, because of their behavior, seem cruel and rude. They shout insults at you and throw rubbish all over the place. You can hear them calling, "You're a loser!

Why don't you just give up? It's hopeless. We'll never get there!" One even shouts, "Stop the bus! This will never work!"

You think about stopping the bus to scold and discipline the children or throw them out, but if you did that, you would no longer be moving in the direction that matters to you. You think that maybe if you made a left turn and tried a different route, the children would be appeased and become quiet. But this too is a detour from living your life in a way that takes you toward realizing your freely chosen, valued aims.

Then, all of a sudden you realize that while you were preoccupied with devising strategies and arguments for dealing with the unruly children on the bus, you missed a couple of turns and lost some time. You realize that in order to keep moving in the direction that you've chosen in life and get where you want to go, you need to continue driving, allowing the children to continue their catcalls, teasing, and nagging all the while. You can make the choice to take your life in the direction you've chosen while just making space for all of the noise the children generate. After all, you can't kick them off and you can't make them stop, because each child represents a part of your very tricky brain, a brain that has evolved over millions of years to respond in all sorts of anxious, angry, and confusing ways to a complicated environment.

So you decide to take a moment to pay attention to the road and rest in the rhythm of your breathing. When you do this, you can recognize that it isn't your fault that these painful thoughts, emotions, and experiences show up. Your compassionate self, driving the bus, can make room for them all: the anxious self, the angry self, the cruel self, the jealous self, and the entire range of different aspects of your experience, all of them carrying on and vying for your attention like so many restless and mischievous children. All of this can take place as you move toward your valued aims. Importantly, you are being kind to yourself and nonjudgmental as you keep your eyes on the road.

CFT Two-Chair Techniques for ACT Self-as-Process Work

Using two-chair techniques to help clients role-play different self-processes has its roots in Gestalt and experiential therapies and figures largely in emotion-focused therapy and process-experiential therapy, among other modalities. These methods have been integrated into CFT and other compassion-based disciplines, providing a context for the compassionate mind to interact with other self-experiences and stimulating an affiliative and warm self-to-self relationship.

In CFT, a great deal of our work involves helping clients bring mindful awareness to the ways in which the activation of different emotional systems can organize the mind and influence their experience. Drawing upon method acting techniques that allow the therapist to evoke emotional responses, in CFT therapists encourage clients to embody and enact different emotional selves, such as an angry self, a critical self, and other self-processes, while engaging in a dialogue, using different chairs from which to role-play different parts of the self. In chapter 7, on compassionate mind training, we will provide further exercises for noticing, defusing from, and working with these different aspects of the mind as if they were different selves.

Intervention: Two-Chair Technique for the Inner Critic and Compassionate Self

This technique (adapted from Tirch, 2012, and inspired by Gilbert, 2009a) allows therapists to facilitate defusion from self-as-content and also gives clients an opportunity to experience different emotions while grounded in contact with the present moment. Compassionate sensitivity, sympathy, and empathic responding on the part of the client are rehearsed as the client moves flexibly between different aspects of self-as-process. This example uses a dialogue between the compassionate mind and the self-critical mind; as always, adapt the example to the context of the particular client's struggles.

As with many of the exercises to come, this one uses the Soothing Rhythm Breathing practice from chapter 3 as a key component in invoking classical mindfulness and collecting attention in the present moment. The following script can be used to guide chair work in session or be provided as a homework practice. It can also be helpful for therapist self-reflection and self-work.

This exercise involves noticing the different parts of ourselves using a role-play between your self-critical mind and your compassionate mind and then drawing a contrast between the two. By using this form of role-play, you can feel what it's like when you're spoken to by your anxious or angry inner critic and then experience how dramatically different it is to speak with and from your compassionate self. In addition, this will help you practice activating compassionate flexibility in the face of challenges and distress.

Here we have two chairs, facing one another. To begin, sit in one chair and imagine that you're looking at a mirror image of yourself in the other chair. When seated in this chair, you are playing the role of your inner critic, with your compassionate self sitting in the opposite chair. In a moment, you're going to speak as your inner critic, so take a minute now to imagine yourself as that inner critic. Breathing into your physical sensations, connect with whatever emotions might arise and observe the formation of self-critical thoughts.

Now speak directly to your compassionate self in the other chair as if you were the personification of the aggressive, self-critical part of yourself. Your words will involve shaming and bullying yourself and creating worry. You might be familiar with this kind of dialogue already from prior experiences of similar thoughts. When you're ready, speak to the empty chair while continuing to imagine that you're facing yourself. Speak purely from your self-critical mind and give a voice to your threat-based emotional self. Speak your fears, your self-criticisms, and your worries out loud. Let yourself say things you typically might not be comfortable saying. Feel free to verbalize your anxiety, shame, and self-criticism as openly as you can. Continue doing this for a few minutes.

When you're ready, allow yourself to stop speaking. Take a moment to settle into your chair, letting some silence pass after you've spoken.

Next, and again when you're ready, rise up and take a seat in the opposite chair. Close your eyes and allow yourself to settle into a few mindful breaths, resting in your Soothing Rhythm Breathing. Bring to mind the image of your compassionate self and allow a gentle smile to form on your face. Make sure you're sitting in a grounded and dignified posture, and then call to mind thoughts of acceptance, forgiveness, openness, warmth, and kindness. Allow these thoughts to become physical sensations, perhaps a feeling of warmth around your heart or a broadening of your smile. If it's helpful, you can even place your hands over your heart for a few moments as you follow your breath and hold the image of your compassionate self in your mind.

Now open your eyes, look at the chair across from you, and begin to speak to your inner critic completely from your compassionate, mindful self. As you speak with your inner critic, you aren't chiding, bullying, or criticizing; instead, you're acknowledging and accepting the fears of that self sitting opposite you. You speak with wisdom, emotional strength, kindness, and the ability to tolerate the distress of your critical self. For example, you might say, "I understand how difficult this experience is for you. You are very distressed, and you aren't sure if this experience will be worthwhile. You feel you need to treat me harshly and beat me into performing better. Maybe you're trying to protect me or drive me forward, or maybe you're just being cruel. I really don't know, but it doesn't matter. You're in pain and feel threatened, and I get that. But please remember that it isn't your fault. Despite your criticism, I hold you in kindness and have a real wish for your happiness and well-being. It's okay for you to feel this way. If you can, remember that you're turning this criticism on all the different parts of us. What you're trying to do isn't working. I hope you can find some space to rest, and that you can be well. I'm moving forward with this life, even as you come along for the ride. Perhaps we can find a place to release this struggle together. May you be well, and may you be happy." Stay with this compassionate voice for a few minutes.

When it feels right, close your eyes, and with your next natural exhalation, let go of the exercise altogether. When you open your eyes, bring your attention back into the room and allow yourself some credit for courageously engaging with this practice.

This exercise can seem a bit strange or tricky at first, but with a little practice you can begin to learn what it's like to deliberately activate your compassionate mind, and to respond with compassion and self-correction when you feel fear, anxiety, and self-criticism begin to arise within you. With regular practice, compassionate self-correction will become automatic. Your range of possible responses to self-criticism will broaden, and you can find a new freedom to bring self-compassion into the present moment as you face your anxiety and self-criticism from a place of safety, strength, and wisdom.

Sensitivity to Client Suffering When in Contact with the Present Moment

Mindfulness begins with connection to the present moment, just as compassion arises from sensitivity to suffering encountered in the here and now. As we help clients cultivate mindfulness through meditative practices and the therapeutic relationship, it is important for them to take their mindful compassion out into the world and begin to extend present-moment sensitivity to their experiences of distress in real time. The following worksheet can assist clients with this by providing a routine practice of bringing mindful compassion to the range of experiences in life, broadening their repertoire of compassionate and psychologically flexible actions. Feel free to follow the format of this worksheet to use it in your practice. You can also download a blank version at http://www.newhar binger.com/30550 (see the last page of the book for more information on how to access it).

ABCs of Compassion Worksheet

Instructions for clients: Fill out the ABCs of Compassion form each day to record moments of mindful compassion throughout your day, whether through formal or informal practice or arising spontaneously. Use the annotated version provided as a guide. A filled-out sample form is also shown. Try to remember to use this worksheet whenever you notice and experience an opportunity for applying mindfulness and compassion during a stressful or challenging situation. You can then discuss these observations and any questions you may have with your therapist during your next meeting.

Awareness of the moment	Bring attention to responses	Cultivate compassion
Who? Who is with me or involved in this experience?	**Sensations:** Using my five senses, what am I experiencing in this moment? What is my body doing?	How can I direct compassion toward my physical being in this moment? What does my body need right now?
What? What is happening in this moment? What's activating my mind?	**Thoughts:** What am I thinking? How does this thought influence my actions?	Does this thought lead me in valued directions? How might I bring more compassion to my thinking here and now?
Where? Where am I right now?	**Emotions:** What emotions am I feeling now? What emotional space am I in?	Are other feelings or other parts of me present? How might I bring compassion to these feelings?
When? When is this happening? (Now?)	**Attention:** What am I focusing on? Is my attention focused on the present, the past, or the future?	How can I become as present as possible, with kindness to myself and others, in this moment? What is available to me right now?
How? How is this happening?	**Behaviors and urges:** How am I responding? How do I wish to respond?	How can I act skillfully to realize my valued aims? What compassionate action might I take?

Sample ABCs of Compassion Worksheet

Awareness of the moment	Bring attention to responses	Cultivate compassion
Who? Who is with me or involved in this experience? *My daughter*	**Sensations:** Using my five senses, what am I experiencing in this moment? What is my body doing? *Heart racing, butterflies in my stomach, feeling restless and fidgety*	How can I direct compassion toward my physical being in this moment? What does my body need right now? *I need to practice Soothing Rhythm Breathing and hold a warm cup of mint tea to sip and smell.*
What? What is happening in this moment? What's activating my mind? *She hasn't called and is very late getting home.*	**Thoughts:** What am I thinking? How does this thought influence my actions? *There's been an accident and she's hurt or worse.* *I should call her again.* *I can't stand not knowing where she is.*	Does this thought lead me in valued directions? How might I bring more compassion to my thinking here and now? *Of course I'm worried. I'm a mother and I love and care for my daughter. Just because my mind is trying to protect her and me doesn't mean something bad has happened. I can wait for there to be a problem before I solve it.*
Where? Where am I right now? *Home, sitting and waiting by the phone*	**Emotions:** What emotions am I feeling now? What emotional space am I in? *Fear. I'm anxious and panicky.*	Are other feelings or other parts of me present? How might I bring compassion to these feelings? *I'm sad that I get so anxious and angry when she doesn't call. I value being a mom, and so I guess it's worth it to me to deal with these situations in service of being the kind of mom I want to be, including being most helpful to my family.*

When? When is this happening? (Now?) *Saturday night*	**Attention:** What am I focusing on? Is my attention focused on the present, the past, or the future? *The future. I'm imagining my daughter in the hospital or me at her funeral.*	How can I become as present as possible, with kindness to myself and others, in this moment? What is available to me right now? *I can begin with three mindful breaths. I can focus on other ways of caring for my family and home, like caring for my plants or taking the dog for a walk.*
How? How is this happening? *I've been sitting by the phone and calling my daughter repeatedly.*	**Behaviors and urges:** How am I responding? *Impulsively calling her, and also calling hospitals, police stations, and her friends' houses* How do I wish to respond? *By calling once and then patiently waiting for half an hour before calling again. Reaching out to others, being compassionate toward myself, and mindfully focusing on the present moment.*	How can I act skillfully to realize my valued aims? What compassionate action might I take? *Breathe. Remind myself that I can be patient and that I am a loving mother who worries but is bigger than her worries. I'll have some tea and focus my caring on my home, pets, and plants while patiently awaiting the arrival of my daughter. If I need to, I can speak with my sister or even write her an e-mail. I can listen to my recording of Visualizing the Compassionate Self and practice being here for myself right now. I'll be okay.*

Cultivating Compassionate Willingness

Much of the wisdom of ACT and many of its methods emerge from the research on experiential avoidance (Hayes et al., 2012). Our clinical experience and critical reading of the behavioral science literature supports the idea that attempts at avoidance or suppression of distressing private events only compounds suffering. Therefore, acceptance is, in a sense, the alpha and omega of ACT. Furthermore, cultivating openness to distressing emotions and willingness to tolerate and remain in the presence of distress are key features of compassion.

In the words of an ancient Buddhist saying, "The lotus flower emerges from the mud." In terms of self-compassion, this means cultivating a noncondemning acceptance of even those parts of ourselves that we dislike or are ashamed of as we seek to liberate ourselves from the struggle with suffering. Generating compassion is not about suppressing unwanted experiences or fighting with parts of ourselves. While training our compassionate mind, we engage even with our least wanted thoughts and feelings, such as shame and self-criticism. As discussed, this engagement is not a war; it is a reconciliation and an extension of our innate wisdom, understanding, and loving-kindness.

In this way, compassion becomes a context for increased willingness to experience life just as it is, without needless defenses. Mindful awareness of our distress can be seen as the soil from which the flower of compassion grows. This compassion, in turn, creates space for resonant and enduring acceptance and the cultivation of courage.

Clearly, when people are under the influence of threat-based emotions and excessive aversive control, their behavioral repertoires and attention both become narrower. And conversely, with the engagement of mindful compassion, empathy, and willingness, people can build broader and more flexible patterns of responding to the challenges of life.

The following two exercises are both excellent techniques for helping clients bring compassion and willingness into contact with their difficult emotions and their struggle against their own experience.

Intervention: Compassionately Letting Go, or Dropping the Rope

This intervention is a classic physicalized ACT metaphor, Dropping the Rope (Hayes et al., 1999), recast with an emphasis on bringing compassion to clients' experience of shame and self-criticism. It uses an actual, if small-scale, tug-of-war with the client to illustrate the futility of the struggling to avoid or attempt to control unwanted mental experiences. Activating the compassionate mind in the middle of this struggle helps clients understand in an emotional and embodied way how they might naturally shift their focus to letting go of the struggle with shame and self-criticism.

To prepare for this exercise, you need to have a strong piece of soft rope or a towel to use for the physical or experiential demonstration of the tug-of-war. To begin, the client and therapist might discuss the various ways that the client has tried to get rid of patterns of shame and self-criticism. In this way, the therapist can elicit this unwanted material, allowing both therapist and client to make experiential contact with it in the context of an empathic and engaged conversation.

Next, the therapist asks the client to imagine his inner critic as a creature or animal that he will challenge to a tug-of-war. Together, the client and therapist can describe the size and shape of the creature, including the details of its appearance and expression. The following example illustrates the flow of the exercise using Josh, who has imagined his self-critic to be an evil monkey.

Therapist: So, we'll be imagining the struggle you're having with your self-critic as a tug-of-war, with you on one end and your evil monkey on the other. The more you argue and struggle with it, the more the evil monkey struggles back. (*Grabs one end of a rolled-up towel, holding it tightly, and hands the other end to the client.*) Now, you are your everyday self, who is subject to vicious self-criticism, and I am the evil monkey. We can pull back and forth, but we aren't really going anywhere. (*Both pull at the towel gently but firmly in a brief exchange.*)

Client: I get it. This is how it goes every morning when I wake up, back and forth with myself.

Therapist: Okay then, here we're imagining you're in a tug-of-war with the evil monkey, who can pull when you pull and can tell you all of the things you hate about yourself, everything you're ashamed of. Just like other thoughts and feelings, he can't touch you directly. However, he can meet you in this struggle. You're fighting this criticism, but the evil monkey is trying just as hard as you, so the harder you pull, the harder the monkey pulls. And so it goes, a seemingly unending struggle, with nothing else to do but keep pulling back. So both you and the critic are clenching this rope firmly, with your feet dug in, stuck in bracing yourself and pulling harder and harder. The self-critic doesn't seem to ever tire out, and like an evil monkey, it's very strong for its size. This seems like it would be an exhausting task, doesn't it?

Client: It is exhausting.

Therapist: Now bring your attention to how this experience feels for you—what it actually feels like to be in this struggle. Notice any tension in your muscles and changes in your breathing, body temperature, and facial expressions. What does it feel like to be in this struggle and hear things like "You've ruined everything" the entire time? Where is your attention focused? What thoughts show up? Perhaps you might notice the thought that maybe you'll win this time. Or you might notice the thought that you could be stuck in this struggle forever or that the critic will win. (*Pauses.*) What do you feel like doing?

Client: I could pull harder. (*Note that clients sometimes come up with the idea of dropping the rope on their own.*)

Therapist: Yes, you could try harder. You could fight back more. You could also get other people to help pull on your end. Have you ever succeeded in getting rid of the critic forever? And for that matter, have you ever been pulled in and gotten lost for a very long time?

Client: All of my attention is wrapped up in this. I'm totally focused right here on this damn towel. I can't win, and I can't stop, and I hate myself. Yep. This is like any weekday morning.

Therapist: Do you have any other choices? Do you have to win this tug-of-war? What would happen if you were to stop fighting with the monkey?

What if you decided to drop the rope and surrender the tug-of-war? And, come to think of it, what is this monkey doing anyway? Does *he* have any choice? Does your inner critic ever do anything but criticize you and point the finger? This struggle is kind of sad, isn't it? You're just digging in and fighting with a part of yourself that can do nothing else but fight. But you are so much more than that—so much more than this tension and this fighting. It's kind of sad that this absorbs you when you don't need to fight, this struggle with an adversary who isn't even really your enemy, and who will pull on you forever if you pull back.

(At some point, almost all clients indicate they feel like dropping the rope. When they do, be sure they drop it completely while bringing mindful awareness to the experience of physically letting it go.)

Therapist: Drop the rope. As you feel it falling away, let's slow our breathing with a long exhalation, like a deep sigh…resting in the breath and holding yourself in kindness. Let's recognize that you've had an experience of struggle—a struggle that's universal—and direct warm and accepting wishes inward. Let's direct kindness toward you and even toward your monkey.

What do you notice? What's different now? Allow yourself to notice how this experience feels. What does it feel like to drop the rope? Notice any changes in your muscles, breathing, body posture, and facial expressions. How do your hands and feet feel? You may notice that your hands and feet are no longer engaged in the battle. Now they're free. Now that you're no longer trapped in an impossible struggle, you're free to choose how you want to use your body and mind.

When you let go of the rope, it doesn't mean the monkey will flee, and it doesn't mean you've won. The monkey may still show up to taunt you. It may even judge you for dropping the rope in the first place. But now you can choose what you want to do. You can choose not to fight, not to pick up the rope, and instead do something perhaps more important to you. And consider this: When you make that choice, what becomes available? How much more of your life becomes yours to live?

Intervention: Stopping the War

This practice, inspired by an ancient Buddhist meditation that was popularized by Jack Kornfield (1993), blends mindfulness, self-as-context, and compassion in a way that is entirely consistent with compassion-focused ACT. (For a downloadable audio recording of this practice, please visit http://www.newharbinger .com/30550.)

Take a few moments to allow yourself to become comfortable where you're sitting, adopting a posture that's secure and grounded. Make any small adjustments to your position and posture that you may need so you can be at ease. Now allow your eyes to close... Without deliberately changing the pace of your breathing, begin to gently bring attention to the flow of the breath in and out of your body... Now bring part of your attention to the soles of your feet... Next, bring part of the attention to the top of your head... And now bring attention to everything in between... Now return your attention to your breathing and simply follow the breath. As you're breathing in, know that you are breathing in, and as you're breathing out, know that you are breathing out.

Begin to notice the sensations that are present in your body. If there are feelings of tension, pressure, or discomfort, bring your attention to these as well. As much as you can, bring an attitude of willingness to these experiences. As you breathe in, breathe attention especially into those areas of the body that present discomfort, tension, or resistance. Can you make space for these experiences? Bring part of your attention to any feelings of resistance, to any struggle that you're experiencing around these sensations. Notice the tension that's involved in fighting these experiences, moment by moment. When meeting each of these sensations, wherever it may arise in the body, open yourself to the experience. Let go of the fight. Bring gentle attention to your breath. Let yourself be exactly as you are in this moment.

As you exhale, completely let go of attention to physical sensations. Then, with your next natural inhalation, bring your attention to your thoughts and emotions. What thoughts are flowing through your mind? What feelings are moving in your heart? Bring an open, receiving attention especially to those thoughts and emotions that you would typically struggle against. As much as you can, allow yourself to soften around these thoughts and feelings in this moment. Can you make space for these events in your mind and heart? Can you let go of this war within yourself, if even just for this very moment?

Now return your attention to the flow of your breath, to your feet on the ground, to your seat in the chair, and to your back feeling upright and supported. As you breathe in, bring attention to the struggles in your life. What battles are you continuing to fight? See if you can feel the presence of these battles. If you struggle with your body, bring awareness to that. If you struggle against your emotions, notice that in this moment. If there are thoughts that intrude, thoughts that you wage war against, bring a gentle awareness to those struggles. For a moment, allow yourself to feel the weight of all of these struggles and battles. How long have these armies within you been fighting?

Softening around even this experience, allow yourself to bring open, compassionate attention to the struggles. Let go of these battles. As you exhale, allow yourself to feel a complete willingness to be exactly who you are, right here and right now. In this moment, allow yourself to accept the totality of everything that life has brought to you and all that you have brought to life. Isn't it time to stop the war you've been waging within yourself? Allow yourself again to choose to let this war go. With courage and commitment, allow yourself to fully accept who you are, right here and right now.

Now bring part of your attention to the soles of your feet… Next, bring part of your attention to the top of your head… And now bring attention to everything in between… Returning attention to breathing, simply follow your breath. As you're breathing in, know that you are breathing in, and as you're breathing out, know that you are breathing out.

When you're ready, open your eyes and allow yourself to let go of this exercise and resume your day.

Preparing the Body and Respecting the Practice

In CFT workshops and trainings, Paul Gilbert often says, "Prepare the body and respect the practice," using it much like the ringing of a mindfulness bell to signify the beginning of a meditation or imagery practice. This phrase holds a key to maintaining compassion-focused practice: an engaged stance. Our experience of cognition and emotion does not exist solely in the brain. We are bodies in motion, in constant interaction with our present-moment context, with behaviors that are informed and influenced by factors that extend millions of years into our ancestral past.

The elements of a compassion-focused ACT described in this chapter include mobilizing the foundational and interacting processes of compassion and psychological flexibility. These processes can be shaped in the context of the therapeutic relationship and developed through structured, interactive experiential exercises. Homework practices can also be useful for cultivating mindfulness, compassion, and commitment to valued aims. These practices may be as simple as a self-monitoring worksheet that reminds clients to return to their present-moment experience with acceptance and compassion, or they may be as complex as an extended meditation and visualization. Whatever form they take, these elements of compassion-focused ACT all are designed to foster psychological flexibility so that clients can bring more compassion into their lives and into the world.

7

Training the Compassionate Mind

Training the compassionate mind involves an interplay between skills development and cultivating characteristics of compassion, with a focus on what is workable. It has been demonstrated that compassion can be cultivated through specific forms of mental training, and can play a significant role in emotional healing (Harrington, 2001; Gilbert, 2010). We have discussed the many ways in which compassion, through CFT, FAP, ACT, and the development of psychological flexibility, can help transform the way people experience and respond to pain and suffering. In this chapter we will provide a series of experiential and meditative exercises and practices that can be used during psychotherapy sessions to help clients develop compassionate mind. They can be practiced by clients and therapists alike, and all can play an integral role in developing a personal compassion-focused practice.

Compassionate Mind Training in a Functional Contextual Framework

The exercises in this chapter are primarily derived from compassionate mind training (Gilbert & Irons, 2005), a method of systematically training compassion that served as a precursor for the more elaborate and comprehensive development of CFT. In this volume, in order to provide an introduction to compassion work for the ACT practitioner, we have sought to present training methods that can work well within a functional contextual framework, without the need for ACT practitioners to reinvent their entire clinical approach. As you have seen in earlier chapters, there is a great depth of theory and practice in CFT, and we hope that what you will learn in this chapter on training the compassionate mind will inspire you to look deeper into the CFT literature, community, and tradition. (And we provide details on avenues to further education in CFT in the Resources section at the end of the book.) Beyond the attention and imagery-based exercises below, further CFT education, supervision, and training includes a range of techniques for working with emotions, thinking, and overt behaviors that can in turn be applied to a range of problems from a contextualist point of view. Nevertheless, this entrée into the science of compassion is designed to fit within ACT-consistent interventions almost like a module, and each of the exercises mesh well with the target processes in the psychological flexibility model.

The practices in this chapter are aimed at cultivating new, compassionate ways to respond to suffering and associated urges for avoidance or resistance as they arise, creating alternatives to both internal and external aggression, ignorance, cruelty, avoidance, and suffering. When engaging in these practices, whether personally or with clients, it is important to keep in mind that it is easy to evoke compassion for people we like or the parts of ourselves we like. Therefore, some of the most important work in training the compassionate mind is developing or experiencing compassion for others and parts of ourselves that we intensely dislike. Compassion is not just reserved for ourselves or those we have positive emotions toward; it is extended to all living beings.

All of the exercises in this chapter involve guided meditation or imagery. As is the case with many guided techniques, when you are leading the experiential exercise, you will be engaging in the contemplative act together with the client. For this reason, having your own ongoing practice of mindfulness and compassion, preferably with a teacher, therapist, or group, is crucial for effectively developing the skill to help others to train their own compassionate mind. Furthermore, these practices are far more than just simple sets of instructions; they are cues for activating specific states of attention. Accordingly, the instructions should be delivered slowly, with periods of silence interspersed throughout, to facilitate deeper engagement. Ideally, you will have practiced each exercise sufficiently to have internalized it and, to some degree, memorized it. Audio recordings of these practices are available for download at http://www.newharbinger

.com/30550, and working with these recordings may serve as a good starting point in your own compassionate mind training. (See the very back of the book for instructions on how to access the downloadable recordings.)

In addition, many therapists have found that apps on mobile devices and notebook computers allow them to easily record personalized sessions with individual clients. In this way, both the stimulus properties and stimulus functions of a real-time interaction between the therapist and client, within the context of a compassionate therapeutic relationship, become accessible outside of session. We have taken that approach with many of our clients, and they have often told us that they value having such documentation of our shared work and compassionate journey. Our clients often use guided audio meditations and imagery practices as part of their daily practice of cultivating compassion, beginning with basic exercises and progressing to more complex imagery, engaging with the practices gradually on a path designed collaboratively in session.

The Importance of Practice

Training the compassionate mind involves deliberately targeting the attributes and skills of compassion elaborated in chapter 2. Through gradual practice, these processes and skills can become enduring characteristics, broadening people's everyday actions and enhancing valued living. In clinical settings, we sometimes metaphorically liken this training in both processes and skills to learning to play a musical instrument. To become a master guitarist, for example, a person must learn many skills, such as calisthenic exercises for the hands, how to play scales, and how to memorize and play various songs. These skills involve what is played. At a deeper level, the master musician learns about music theory, the relationships of intervals and arpeggios, how to improvise within a song's chord structure, how to compose to fit the music involved, and how to train the ear, body, and emotions to play the music in tune, in time, and with heart. These processes involve how the music is played.

Similarly, training the compassionate mind involves developing certain skills, but also developing broad and adaptive behavioral processes. In another parallel, when an individual practices a musical instrument for thousands of hours and masters her craft, there is evidence of new neural connections being formed—neuroplasticity and neurogenesis—resulting in the brain and body of the person coming to resemble and function similarly to the brain and body of a trained musician (Münte, Altenmüller, & Jäncke, 2002). And indeed, when we train the compassionate mind, changes in neural activity and structure do occur (Lutz et al., 2008). Hence, cultivating the attributes and skills of compassion can transform the mind and brain in demonstrable and lasting ways. So let us begin!

Compassionate Attention

When training compassionate attention in CFT, much of the work begins with mindfulness. This focus allows clients to deliberately develop their ability to pay attention in the present moment with acceptance and self-compassion. From this inherently defused perspective, they can intentionally bring a compassionate tone to the very fabric of their experiences: awareness itself. The early phases of compassionate mind training are often devoted to exercises that bring compassion to focusing, guiding, and modulating attention in a manner that is skillful, supportive, and helpful (Gilbert, 2009a). These practices blend appreciation, mindfulness, concentration, attention, and relaxation training and provide a foundation for the next steps in compassionate mind training (Gilbert, 2009a).

It is often helpful to begin attention training with mindfulness practice and other exercises for calming the mind and the body. In CFT we generally start with the Soothing Rhythm Breathing exercise in chapter 3. (As a reminder, an audio recording of that practice is available for download at http://www.newhar binger.com/30550.) Soothing Rhythm Breathing is the foundational mindfulness practice in CFT, and many of the other exercises used in compassionate mind training begin with this form of mindful breathing. As you read the rest of this chapter, you will notice that we often engage in a few minutes of Soothing Rhythm Breathing before proceeding to visualizations or practices that involve intentionally directing compassion toward oneself or others. Accordingly, compassionate mind training begins with clients learning Soothing Rhythm Breathing during the first or second session of therapy and then using it as part of a daily sitting practice. It is a key approach in engaging compassionate attention and centeredness and activating the parasympathetic "tend and befriend" system in response to arising threat reactions. Additionally, the range of mindfulness practices found throughout ACT, third-wave behavior therapies, and the host of Buddhist traditions can help prime the pump of attention necessary for the cultivation of compassion.

Before initiating formal mindfulness training, we often provide training in attention by helping clients explore what it is like to simply direct their attention to one part of the body, such as the right foot, and then to another, such as the right hand. Through guided discovery and Socratic questioning, clients are invited to notice how they can move their attention around the body and direct it to different sensory experiences. In this way, they might observe how they can use their attention like a spotlight, illuminating certain experiences and casting others into darkness. Then we gently broaden the scope of this attention work, perhaps by asking clients to close their eyes and bring to mind different memories, beginning with a memory of a quarrel or difficult time, then moving to a memory of a happy time with loved ones, and completing the series of observations by revisiting a memory of relaxing deeply, such as while resting on a beach on a vacation.

In this way, clients experience how they can direct their attention in potentially more interesting and meaningful ways than simply moving it around within the physical space of the body. Our attention can't be physically moved around the world of space and time, but psychologically, we can move our attention freely though space, time, and emotional landscapes. We can bring attention to an experience from the past and evoke the emotions of the self that was there and then. If this is a happy memory, we can trigger bodily sensations, emotions, and thoughts associated with that happiness. Similarly, we can turn toward a difficult or painful memory and elicit the emotions that this past self was grappling with there and then. Working with thoughts, physical sensations, and emotions in this way, from a place of mindful compassion, creates opportunities to enter into a new and more accepting relationship with painful memories and struggles.

When you train clients in compassionate attention as a part of a compassion-focused ACT intervention, it is best to begin with psychoeducation about the nature of mindfulness, compassion, and attention using examples and guided discovery. Training in Soothing Rhythm Breathing is the ideal next step and lays the groundwork for directing mindful and compassionate attention toward deeper emotional experiences, which serves the dual purposes of illustrating how the emotional self functions and enhancing willingness, openness, contact with the present moment, and flexible perspective taking. The following practice helps clients take that next step: turning mindful attention toward emotions.

Intervention: Compassionate Mindfulness of Emotions

Based in Buddhist training in the four foundations of mindfulness, this intervention blends compassionate mind training into a guided meditation that involves directing compassionate attention toward one's emotions in the present moment. It provides a useful introduction to working with attention and emotions, and it can also be practiced daily on a long-term basis. It aims to help people see how they can use mindfulness to make space for their experience of distress, and how they might use compassionate attention to help them tolerate and contend with difficult emotions. Intentionally practicing this exercise can help anyone manage instinctive mental and physical urges to resist or avoid stress and discomfort. Importantly, like all compassionate mind training, this exercise involves actively directing attention to the experience of warm affiliative emotions. In a sense, all of our work with compassion involves moving attention toward a valued aim of alleviating and preventing suffering and promoting well-being. (For a downloadable audio recording of this practice, please visit http://www.newharbinger.com/30550.)

> *After getting comfortable on your cushion or chair, allow your breath to settle into the naturally slow and even pace that emerges through Soothing Rhythm Breathing. When you're ready, take three mindful breaths in this way and feel the release of tension with each exhalation....On your next natural inhalation, bring part of your attention to the sensations that are present in your body. Whatever you notice, allow yourself to just rest in the breath, feeling the movement of your belly and bringing open, nonjudgmental attention to the presence of your breath in your heart center.*
>
> *With each inhalation, bring compassionate attention into your body. And with each exhalation, let go of tension, bringing awareness to any experience of emotions in your body. In this moment, what physical sensations feel related to your emotional experience? Perhaps you're having an experience of distress, as is so often the case in our lives. Whatever your emotional experience may be, in this moment allow yourself to feel where this emotional experience presents itself to you as physical sensations. For example, you may feel distress as tension in your chest or throat. Just notice what you feel and where you feel it, and then bring mindful and compassionate attention to that place with each inhalation.*

Once you've located where you feel this emotion in your body, release any unnecessary tension that may be present in that area. Without demanding anything of yourself, invite your muscles to relax around this experience. Imagine yourself willingly making space for the emotion and directing compassionate attention to your physical experience of the emotion in your body. Without physically forcing anything at all, label the emotion using a feeling word. For example, if you're feeling sad, you might softly, in your mind's inner voice, say the word "sadness." As you breathe compassion for yourself into your body and release any needless tension, make space for this experience. Remind yourself that whatever arrives in your emotional life, it's okay to experience it.

In this present moment, your intention to rest in compassionate attention is an invitation for your body and mind to soften into your experience. You aren't aiming to suppress or avoid any experience that is here. You're simply bringing mindful attention to your emotional and physical experience in this very moment. Stay with this process of softening for a few minutes.

Now deliberately and intentionally bring soothing attention to your experience. If you'd like, bring one of your hands to your chest, just over your heart center. Feel the warmth of your hand against your heart region and intentionally bring kindness and soothing to your experience. Bring part of your attention to the soles of your feet…part to your sit bones against your chair…and part to the top of your head. Feel the dignity and centeredness in your posture as you radiate compassionate attention from the center of your physical and emotional being. In this moment, you are awake, alert, and alive.

Recognize any distress or struggle you're facing and direct soothing warmth and self-acceptance toward your experience. Bring mindfulness and compassion into contact with your emotions in this moment. Breathing in, notice that you are breathing in, and breathing out, notice that you are breathing out. Remain with this process of soothing for a few minutes.

As much as you can, let go of any urge to get rid of your emotional experience. With each exhalation, let go of any effort to avoid or suppress emotions. Stay with the breath for as long as you need or like, resting in the soothing rhythm of your breath and directing mindful, compassionate attention to your emotions.

Now begin to form an intention to let go of this practice, taking a moment to acknowledge and appreciate your courage and self-kindness in moving *toward greater mindfulness and compassion in your everyday experience. Thank yourself for engaging in this practice, then gradually let go of the exercise entirely, exhaling and bringing your attention back to the flow of everyday life.*

The Power of Imagery

Compassionate mind training begins with cultivating mindfulness and compassion in the way attention is deployed, and then proceeds to include the use of imagery. In this way, we can directly train the mind to activate its capacity for compassion, calm, and courageous acceptance steeped in warmth and inner strength. This takes time and involves working directly with one's experience of distress.

In fact, the human capacity for imagery is one of the most powerful tools in cultivating compassionate mind, as it can be used to help activate different emotions and physical sensations. What we focus our attention on can affect how we feel. When our minds begin to imagine things, our entire being can respond as though this mental event were actually happening. If we are hungry and imagine a meal, we can stimulate our salivary glands. Similarly, if we imagine scenes of a sexual nature, we may feel aroused. This power of imagination often gets us into trouble through fusion and experiential avoidance. For example, we might imagine a potential disaster, become fearful, and then avoid the situation we worry about. Yet this basic human ability for the imagination to stimulate systems in our brains and bodies can also be harnessed to stimulate the compassionate mind and, in turn, our soothing systems. And, crucially, if we engage with compassionate imagery, we can activate brain systems that will help us tolerate and cope with the experience of suffering.

Helping Clients Overcome Perceived Deficits in Imagery Skills

Imagery work with clients often begins with an inquiry into any deficits in imagery skills clients may believe they have. Possible obstacles to engaging in imagery include clients' beliefs that they are not good at imagery or cannot come up with the right images. This is where mindfulness and attention training are useful. We recommend helping clients develop mindfulness skills before doing imagery exercises and then reminding clients to remain nonjudgmental and open to the experience of imagery. You can also explain that imagery is imperfect and may change and shift over the course of a given exercise. This encourages clients to remain open to any natural changes in imagery within a particular practice and between different practices. When it comes to perceived deficits in imagery skills, some individuals are, of course, better or worse at imagery. However, there are a few interventions and questions you can use to help such clients access their imagination, as suggested in the following clinical example.

Clinical Example: Helping a Client Access Imagination Skills

The following dialogue provides an example of how the therapist helped Josh overcome his initial belief that he wasn't capable of doing imagery exercises.

Client: I can't do imagery. My brain just won't do it. I suck.

Therapist: So, you feel you can't do imagery. That's not an uncommon belief. However, imagery is a skill, and as with many skills, we can get better at it with practice. Ever go to the gym?

Client: Sure. I don't go as much as I'd like, but I'm putting my time in these days.

Therapist: Great! Practicing imagery is like going to the gym: keep at it and you'll get stronger and better at it.

Client: Okay. Got it.

Therapist: Also, we may not know how good we are at a skill until we begin to practice. So, in a moment I'm going to ask you a series of questions, and I'd like you to just notice what shows up for you. Okay, here we go: What does a pencil look like? (*Pauses.*) Where is your refrigerator in your home? (*Pauses.*) Where do you keep your keys? (*Pauses.*) What did you have for breakfast this morning? (*Pauses.*) So, what did you notice? How did your mind respond to these questions?

Client: I saw where I put my keys, what my breakfast looked like, and all that other stuff.

Therapist: Ah, so you pictured these items?

Client: Yes.

Therapist: This is imagery, and you're doing it already.

Client: Cool. That was easy. Why didn't you say it was so easy?

Therapist: I think I did, didn't I?

Client: Yes, sir, you did. (Laughs.)

This might seem like a very simple way to address clients' perceived difficulties with imagery, but it is actually a very direct, efficient way to tackle this problem with clients in session, through a straightforward practice. Then you can proceed with the following series of compassionate imagery exercises, which can be used over a period of several sessions as in-session illustrations of key concepts, and as central elements in helping clients develop a personal compassion-focused practice.

Safe Place Visualization

Safe place visualizations, which are widely used in various modes of therapy, have two primary functions. First, they help direct clients' attention toward feeling a sense of safeness. Sometimes when people are feeling stressed-out, taking time to just imagine a safe place can give them somewhere to rest. Second, creating a safe place helps them imagine being somewhere that gives them a sense of joy.

Intervention: Creating a Safe Place

This specific safe place visualization (adapted with permission from Tirch, 2012, and inspired by Gilbert, 2009a) begins with Soothing Rhythm Breathing, as is typical in CFT meditations and visualizations. Because each client's safe place is an individual creation and springs from the individual's imagination, it is a place that welcomes and appreciates the client. Emphasize to clients that it is important to make the place their own and find their own ways of thinking about it. Explain that the place they create is meant to embody compassionate warmth and safety. In this exercise, they are allowing themselves to experience feelings of being safe already, here and now, abiding in a place where they are at peace, relaxed, and confident about their well-being. When they feel distressed, a sense of contentment and security may seem very far away. If need be, explain that our minds respond to our imaginations as though what they produce is or may be real, giving us an inborn capacity to cultivate feelings of safety and activate our self-soothing system. (For a downloadable audio recording of this practice, please visit http://www.newharbinger.com/30550.)

Begin this exercise as you might begin Soothing Rhythm Breathing, lying comfortably on a mat or sitting in a comfortable, secure posture on a chair or meditation cushion. Take some time to allow a few mindful breaths to move in and out of your body.

Now turn your attention to your imagination and begin to think about a happy, secure place that surrounds you. Perhaps it's a place you've visited in the past, or maybe it's a place you've only thought about visiting. It's important that this place be calm, such as in a shady picnic spot, on a seaside balcony, or in a cozy chair by the fireside in winter. Whatever it may be, this place is just for you, and you are free to imagine anywhere that feels right to you.

If you imagine a serene sandy beach, feel the smooth, soft sand beneath your feet and the warmth of the sunlight. Do you hear the waves lapping against the shoreline? Do you hear seagulls calling? If you imagine somewhere secure, cozy, and warm indoors, such as a comfortable chair beside the fire, can you feel the heat radiating out to warm you? What does the room smell like? Can you hear the fire crackling?

You may remember somewhere you've walked among ancient trees and greenery, or somewhere else that holds fond memories for you—a place where you felt supported and loved and were able to experience a sense of playfulness. In order to vividly evoke images from that place, recall what it was like, or what it might be like if you were actually there right now. Notice the quality of the light, the texture of the sand, the fabric of the chair, and the bark of the tree. Notice the sounds, smells, and temperature.

Remain with this visualization for a few minutes, and from time to time, note the natural rhythm of your breathing, feeling your diaphragm expanding and your belly rising and falling with the even pace of your breath. Whenever your mind wanders, draw your attention back to the image of your safe space on your next natural inhalation.

As you're ready, allow the image to fade. With your next natural inhalation, let go of the exercise entirely and return your awareness to your actual surroundings.

Using Images from Personal Experiences to Cultivate Compassion

The following two exercises (adapted with permission from Tirch, 2012, and inspired by Gilbert, 2009a) allow clients to begin to access the compassionate mind by deliberately focusing on memories and personal images that evoke an experience of warmth and affiliation. Therapists may choose to begin with either an experience of compassion flowing in (of receiving it from someone else) or the experience of compassion flowing out (of extending it to someone else), based upon discussions with the client and an appreciation of the client's learning history. Compassionate mind training is meant to be challenging yet not overwhelming, so begin with whichever approach would seem to be less demanding for the individual client and build from there. In essence, this is a form of gradual exposure to the emotions involved in secure attachment; and, as such, it is particularly helpful for people whose experiences, potential traumas, and attachment memories have resulted in difficulties with distress tolerance and aversion to self-soothing.

Intervention: Experiencing Compassion Flowing In

Before beginning this practice, explain to clients that this exercise will build upon their practice of mindful, compassionate attention and help them activate affiliative emotions by using imagery of an experience of receiving compassion. When suggesting or assigning this exercise for home practice, recommend that clients find a quiet space where they won't be disturbed to do the exercise, and that they set aside ten to twenty minutes for it. (For a downloadable audio recording of this practice, please visit http://www.newharbinger.com/30550.)

Sit with your back upright and supported, either in a comfortable chair or on a meditation cushion. Begin by bringing attention to your breathing, observing its flow and rhythm and allowing it to find its own pace. Observe and remain with this flow for a few minutes, engaging in Soothing Rhythm Breathing.

Now bring part of your attention into your body and feel the strength and compassion that is available to you in your posture. Feel your feet on the floor, your sit bones connected to your cushion or chair, and your spine upright and supported. Your posture is grounded and dignified and reflects your sense of calm and self-compassion. Allow your face to form a gentle smile.

Now, with part of your attention staying with the flow of your breath, begin to remember a pleasant day in your past when someone was compassionate and supportive toward you. This person wasn't judgmental and didn't condemn you; rather, this person was empathic and cared about you and your happiness. As much as you can, remember the sensory details of this experience: Can you remember what you were wearing? Where were you? Was it hot or cold? Was it raining or was the wind blowing through the trees? Was the radio on in the background?

Now, bringing part of your attention back to the flow of your breath, inhale and exhale and, for a few moments, stay with this imagery of an experience of receiving compassion. By remembering receiving such help and kindness, you can focus your attention on and increase your desire to be kind and helpful, including toward yourself.

Whenever your mind is inevitably distracted and wanders away from this memory, gather your attention with your next natural inhalation and make space for whatever is arising; then, with your next natural exhalation, simply return your attention to your breath and to the image of this compassionate person. As you breathe in again, with your next natural inhalation, bring your attention to the facial expression of this person from your past. Allow yourself to remember, as much as you can, this person's body language and movements. What did this person say to you? How did the person say it? Pay particular attention to tone of voice. Stay with this experience for a little while, breathing in and out.

Next, bring your attention to the quality of the emotion this person seemed to display toward you. How did the person feel toward you? And how does this make you feel? Do you have any physical sensations as a result of your emotion? Take a few minutes to remain in the presence of that emotion.

You may feel safe and protected or feel as if your body is grounded and stronger. However this emotion shows up, see if you can welcome it, identify it as mindful compassion, and invite yourself to make space for it. This is a time to bring attention to the experience of compassion flowing into you.

Now bring your attention back to the flow of your breath, inhaling and exhaling smoothly, and take a few moments to stay with the way this experience feels. As much as you can, connect with the emotions of appreciation, gratitude, and happiness that arrived with this person's care. For as long as it feels right to you, perhaps a few minutes more, remain in the presence of this memory and this feeling.

When it feels right, let this experience go with your next natural exhalation, allowing the memory and images to fade away. After a few more slow and even breaths, exhale and completely let go of this exercise. Before you open your eyes, take a moment to give yourself credit for engaging with your practice of self-compassion, recognizing that you have made a conscious decision to take care of yourself and move toward alleviation of your suffering.

Intervention: Experiencing Compassion Flowing Out

Again, before beginning this practice, explain to clients that this exercise builds upon their practice of mindful, compassionate attention and helps them activate self-compassion by using images of extending compassion to others. When suggesting or assigning this exercise for home practice, recommend that clients find a quiet space to practice where they won't be disturbed, and that they set aside ten to twenty minutes for the practice. (For a downloadable audio recording of this practice, please visit http://www.newharbinger.com/30550.)

Adopt a dignified, meditative posture, with the soles of your feet connected to the floor, your sit bones on your chair or cushion, and your back upright and supported. Start by following the breath in and out of your body, and become aware of your physical presence, just as it is, in this very moment. Allow your breath to find its own rhythm and pace. Whenever your attention wanders, gently and consistently draw your attention back to this moment by focusing on the breath once again.

After a few minutes, once you've gathered and collected your awareness in a mindful and compassionate way, bring your attention to a time when you felt compassionate toward another person—someone who was in need of a helping hand. Alternatively, you can bring your attention toward compassion you felt for an animal, perhaps a pet. Fully remember that time of relative peace and happiness. Although we often direct compassion toward loved ones during times of distress, this exercise involves using imagery to evoke a feeling that's separate from difficult emotions.

As you imagine feeling kindness and compassion toward this other person or being, see if you can imagine yourself expanding as the warmth and care of your intention grows. Imagine that you're becoming wiser, emotionally stronger, and warmer with each inhalation and exhalation. As you become more attuned and resilient with every breath, recognize this means that, with each breath you have more to give, and with each moment you are becoming more helpful, open, and wise. How does this feel? What physical sensations are you experiencing?

Now bring your attention back to the flow of your breath and, for a moment longer, focus on these feelings and the images associated with your experience of extending compassion to another. All the while, observe your desire for this person or being to be happy, filled with compassion, peaceful, at ease, and well. What is your tone of voice like? What is the expression on your face? How is your body moving and reacting to your feelings and to the feelings of the other person? Take some time to enjoy the sense of pleasure you may feel as a result of being helpful and caring.

Smile gently, and as you breathe in and out, allow yourself to notice the sensation of compassion flowing out of you so that it reaches this person or being whom you care so deeply about. Imagine your compassion touching the other's heart. Imagine that the burden of the other's suffering is lifted, little by little, with every breath. With your next natural exhalation, once again sense the compassion flowing out of you and joy and peace flowing into the person or being to whom you're extending kindness.

With your next natural exhalation, let go of this representation of the other person or being and draw your attention to the experience of compassion in yourself. Recognize where in your body your open and heartfelt desire to share kindness and helpfulness presents itself. Allow yourself to rest in this feeling of loving-kindness for others, feeling the presence of compassion for others as it flows through you. Stay with this sensation for a few moments.

If your attention wanders at any point, simply notice where it has gone and then refocus by bringing part of your attention to your next natural inhalation and the exercise at hand. Remain in the presence of this warmth and kindness for several minutes.

As you're ready to end this visualization, return your awareness to your feet on the floor…then to your position in the chair…then to your back, upright and supported…and ultimately to the top of your head. When you feel you're ready, exhale and completely let go of this exercise. Before you open your eyes, take a moment to give yourself some credit for having engaged in this practice, recognizing that you have made a conscious decision to take care of yourself and move toward alleviation of your suffering.

Developing a Compassionate Self-Identity Through Visualization

The exercise Visualizing the Compassionate Self is a foundational CFT practice that harnesses the power of imagery to cultivate compassionate responding. It involves first using imagination to develop a personalized image of the compassionate self, and then using this image in a visualization practice. As is the case with most of the contextual compassion work in this book, and particularly the visualizations in this chapter, this one can be used as a daily meditation or coping tool for clients, or as part of your own self-reflection and practice.

Intervention: Visualizing the Compassionate Self

As usual, please adjust the following script to fit your own therapeutic style and vernacular, and also adapt it as necessary to meet individual clients' needs. However, the guided imagery below (adapted from Tirch, 2012, and inspired by Gilbert, 2009a, and Gilbert & Choden, 2013) proceeds in a way that's essential to this practice, so do follow the spirit and intent as closely as possible. (For a downloadable audio recording of this practice, please visit http://www.newharbinger.com/30550.)

As you'll see, the first portion of the script isn't a visualization per se. Rather, clients are initially guided in identifying the qualities they would wish to have in a compassionate self, providing a basis for the visualization.

This exercise will help you imagine yourself in a very different way than you might be accustomed to. It's like being an actor who's rehearsing a role in a play or a film. It involves creating a personification of your compassionate self, whom you will meet and who will be happy to see you.

Take a moment to think about the qualities of your compassionate self and write down the qualities you would ideally like to have if you were calm, confident, and compassionate. Would you be wise? Would you be strong and able to tolerate discomfort? Would you have warm feelings toward others and toward yourself? Would you feel empathy for other people's suffering and more insight into their behavior? Would you be understanding of others' faults and foibles and therefore be nonjudgmental, accepting, kind, or forgiving? Would you have courage? Ask yourself how you would picture your most compassionate self. Perhaps you might imagine yourself older and wiser, or maybe younger and more innocent. This is your personal exploration, so please feel free to design an image of your compassionate self and embellish it as you wish.

Now we'll do a visualization utilizing the compassionate self you've identified and described. Allow your eyes to close, then bring part of your attention to the soles of your feet as they connect with the floor and to your sit bones on the chair or cushion. Allow your back to be upright and supported. Next, partly direct your attention to the flow of your breath in and out of your body, then allow it to find a slow, soothing rhythm and pace. Feel yourself breathing in and breathing out. Continue breathing in this way until you've gathered your attention and feel focused on the present moment.

Now recall the qualities of your compassionate self that you wrote down and imagine that you already have those qualities. Breathe in as you experience yourself having that wisdom, and breathe out knowing that you're part of the flow of life on earth, with a brain and life history that weren't of your design or your choosing. Breathe in and imagine yourself as strong and able to tolerate distress while confronting your fears, then breathe out. Each time you breathe in, feel yourself having the qualities you wrote down. Experience yourself as committed, with a calm and completely dedicated intention to alleviate the suffering you encounter.

As you follow the breath in and out of your body, feel yourself heavy in your chair and rooted to the earth. Your wisdom, strength, and commitment are all present. Imagine yourself as a completely nonjudgmental person who doesn't condemn yourself or others for their faults. Allow yourself to bring to mind the sensory details you'd notice as your compassionate self. What are you wearing? Is your body relaxed and receptive? Does your body language signal openness and kindness? Are you smiling? If not, smile now, and at the same time imagine the warmth you feel when you carefully hold an infant. As you breathe in, bring attention into your body, imagine yourself expanding, and welcome your ability to be wise, warm, and resilient.

For the next few moments, as you're breathing in and out, continue to imagine being the compassionate self you described. How would your compassion manifest? What would your tone of voice be if you were this compassionate self? How would you behave? What sort of expression would you have on your face? Allow yourself to take pleasure in your capacity to share kindness with and care for those around you and yourself. If your mind wanders, as it so often does for all of us, use your next natural inhalation to gently bring the attention back to this image of your compassionate self. For the next several minutes, continue to give mindful attention to this compassionate self, returning and refocusing as needed.

When you feel ready, and with your next natural exhalation, allow any attachment to this exercise to simply melt away. Breathe in again, and with your next natural exhalation, allow yourself to become aware of your surroundings once again. Take a moment to recognize and acknowledge the effort you have invested in this exercise. Then fully return your attention to your surroundings.

Compassionate Contact with the Many Parts of the Self

The next two exercises involve contacting different parts of the self as a way of gaining more understanding of the various parts of emotional experiences and how they impact behavior. Much like the two-chair technique described in chapter 6, this approach helps develop flexible perspective taking, defusion from self-narratives, and willingness to engage with and tolerate distress.

Intervention: Contacting the Many Different Selves

Before conducting the following visualization with clients, take a moment to explain that there are many different parts of each of us: our compassionate self, our angry self, our anxious self, our joyful self, and so on. In the script below (adapted from Tirch, 2012, and inspired by Gilbert & Choden, 2013), we focus on contacting the angry self and the anxious self and examining how they interact. You may wish to focus on different aspects of the self depending on the difficulties individual clients are facing. Whichever aspects of self are targeted, after invoking them and perhaps bringing them into contact, the compassionate self from the previous visualization is summoned to help cultivate compassion for these other parts of the self. (For a downloadable audio recording of this practice, please visit http://www.newharbinger.com/30550.)

After taking a comfortable and supported posture, close your eyes. Begin by grounding yourself in your body and breath. After settling your awareness and focusing your attention on your breath, slow your breathing and even out your inhalations and exhalations, briefly practicing Soothing Rhythm Breathing.

When you're ready, with your next natural inhalation, imagine that you're having an argument with someone you know to be harsh and critical. What does the angry side of your personality think about this situation? What sensations arise in your body when you feel criticized or attacked? What behavioral urges does this angry part of yourself feel? And if this angry part of your personality were to seize control of things, what would it do? Allow yourself to step back and observe this frustrated or angry part of you and see what it looks like.

Now bring your attention back to the flow of your breath. With your next natural exhalation, let go of this image of the angry self. Then, with your next natural inhalation, focus on your anxious self and how it might deal with the same argument. What does the anxious part of you think? What physical sensations arise? What would this anxious part of your personality do if it were to seize control of your behavior? See if you can picture your anxious self in front of you or have a felt sense of being in the presence of your anxious self.

Once again bring your attention back to the flow of your breath. With your next natural exhalation, let go of this image of the anxious self. Then, with your next natural inhalation, focus on the interaction between your angry self and your anxious self. Do they like one another? Does your angry self approve of your anxious self and how it behaves? Does it feel threatened or stifled by the anxious self? And what does your anxious self think about your angry self? Is it frightened of it? Does the anxious part feel protected by your angry self?

Now bring your attention back to the flow of your breath. Again, with your next natural exhalation, let go of imagining these two parts of your personality. These, and all of the other different parts of yourself, are really just the way you deal with events as they unfold. Sometimes these different parts are in conflict with one another, making us feel in conflict with ourselves. However, activating and connecting with the compassionate self can change this dynamic quite dramatically. So now, rather than focusing on the anxious or angry aspects of yourself, turn your focus to the wise, calm, and authoritative compassionate part you've worked with in the exercise Visualizing the Compassionate Self.

Resting in the flow of your breath, spend a few moments focusing on your compassionate self. See yourself from the outside. See a gentle smile on your face, and see other people relating to you as someone who is calm, kind, and wise. Once you have a sense of this aspect of yourself, imagine your compassionate self dealing with that argument you visualized at the beginning of this practice. What are your thoughts about the argument now? How does your calm, wise, and compassionate self feel? What does your compassionate self do when it takes control of your behavior? How does this differ from the ways in which your angry and anxious selves behave?

Now bring your attention back to the flow of your breath. Then exhale and completely let go of all of these images and the exercise. Return your attention to the room around you and open your eyes.

Intervention: Cultivating Compassion for the Anxious Self and Angry Self

This exercise builds on the previous practice by asking clients to have their compassionate self make contact with and cultivate compassion for the anxious self and then the angry self. Again, it may be appropriate to work with different aspects of the self depending on the needs of the individual client, so adapt this exercise accordingly. (For a downloadable audio recording of this practice, please visit http://www.newharbinger.com/30550.)

After taking a comfortable and supported posture, close your eyes. Begin by grounding yourself in your body and breath. After settling your awareness and focusing your attention on your breath, slow your breathing and even out your inhalations and exhalations, briefly practicing Soothing Rhythm Breathing.

When you're ready, bring to mind an image of your compassionate self. Focus on the qualities of this self, perhaps contacting compassionate warmth, wisdom, and strength. You may want to adopt a friendly facial expression of a half smile as you imagine the characteristics of your compassionate self. If you're willing, place one or both hands over your heart and remain in this position throughout the visualizations that follow, bringing mindful attention to the warmth and physical sensations of this gesture while imagining your compassionate self.

When you feel connected to your compassionate self, and as you're ready, bring to mind your anxious self in the context of the argument you imagined in the previous exercise. See if you can look upon this part of yourself from the perspective of your compassionate self, making room for the tension and fear in the anxious self and connecting with the anxious experience while remaining rooted in the qualities of your compassionate self. Allow your compassionate strength to support the aggravated, scared, or uncertain anxious self. Let your wisdom witness the impermanence of anxiety and how it's impacted by thoughts and memories.

Next, bring warmth to the scared and anxious part of yourself, showing it kindness and caring. As you bring to mind your desire to be there for your anxious self in a way that's helpful and caring, consider what this part of you that is struggling with fear and anxiety needs most. How does your compassionate self want to be with your anxious self? How might you validate and support this anxious part of you? What does your compassionate self want to offer to this part of yourself?

After spending some time experiencing these compassionate intentions for your anxious self, allow yourself to let go of these images. Expand your awareness to your breathing and the feeling of your hand over your heart.

Now bring your attention back to the flow of your breath. With your next natural exhalation, and while remaining connected to your compassionate self, bring to mind your angry self in the context of the argument you imagined in the previous exercise. Allow yourself to step back and look at this frustrated or angry part of yourself. Observe what your angry self is doing. What facial expression does it have? What tone of voice does it use? Who is the angry self mad at? What is the angry self most irritated about? What does this angry self need most right now? What would help it find peace? How does your compassionate self want to be with your angry self? How might you validate and support this part of you? What does your compassionate self want to offer to your angry self?

After spending some time experiencing these intentions for your angry self, allow yourself to let go of these images. Let your awareness settle on your breathing and the feeling of your hands over your heart. Resting in this way, allow yourself to notice other feelings or experiences that may have arisen during this visualization. Bring attention to how you feel physically and emotionally, or to anything particularly important or meaningful that has shown up.

Now bring your attention back to the flow of your breath once again. With your next natural exhalation, allow your hands to rest comfortably in your lap. Then exhale and completely let go of this practice. Return your attention to the room around you, open your eyes, and adjust your posture or gently stretch as needed.

Revisiting the Importance of Practice

Previously, we've mentioned the importance of practice. All of the visualizations in this chapter, and many of the other exercises in the book, are suitable for home practice by clients. Some, such as the final two, may require some modification to be more suited to ongoing practice. You can recommend variations as you see fit depending on the client's needs, perhaps engaging the client in a discussion about this. To help encourage ongoing practice, you may wish to ask clients to fill out the following Compassion Practice Log. Feel free to copy it for use in your practice. For a downloadable version, please visit http://www .newharbinger.com/30550 (see the last page of the book for more information about how to access it).

Compassion Practice Log

Instructions to client: Fill out the Compassion Practice Log each day to record your compassion practices. Try to remember to use this form each time you practice, indicating the date, the time you began, the time you ended, the type of practice, your observations, and anything you'd like to remember about that particular practice experience. You can then discuss these observations and any questions you may have with your therapist during your next session.

Day and date	Time started	Time ended	Practice (Guided? Formal? Informal?)	Observations (What did you notice?)	Learning (What would you like to remember?)
Monday __/__/__					
Tuesday __/__/__					
Wednesday __/__/__					
Thursday __/__/__					
Friday __/__/__					
Saturday __/__/__					
Sunday __/__/__					

The Emphasis of Compassionate Mind Training

While the range of practices for cultivating compassion within CFT, FAP, and ACT—and beyond—is truly vast, the visualization exercises in this chapter are sufficient, in and of themselves, to provide a foundation for training the compassionate mind. When folded into the course of a compassion-focused ACT intervention, these approaches to working with imagery and attention also target the capacities and skills involved in psychological flexibility. Importantly, each therapist and each client will bring individual intuitive wisdom to these practices and travel a unique path to create a deeply personal relationship with the compassionate self.

When we reference the compassionate self, we are both speaking metaphorically and referring to an essential component of embodied human experience. Of course, the reification of any aspect of self, in regarding it as a solid, stable, and enduring structural entity, generally isn't in keeping with ACT interventions. This is hardly a new approach. For several thousand years, most of the world's wisdom traditions have recognized that what we experience as a self is more of an action of a human being engaging with the wider world. So, when we speak of the experience of any sense of self, including the compassionate self, we are more accurately referring to an experience or quality of "selfing," if you will. In this way, the compassionate self is metaphorical. However, the experience of the compassionate self is something characteristically human. It correlates with a distinct neural signature and a pattern of activation that spreads throughout the body, and it's an essential part of how our species has preserved itself and flourished. Accessing a conscious awareness of this part of our being is a deliberate, healing, and perhaps even sacred type of work.

8

Case Formulation, Assessment, and Treatment Planning

Historically, Buddhist philosophy has described compassion as being one of the four immeasurables, which represent wholesome states of mind that are key components to liberation from suffering: loving-kindness (*metta*), compassion (*karuna*), empathetic joy (*mudita*), and equanimity (*upekkha*). Prescientific traditions might have found it sufficient to view such experiences as being outside the realm of quantitative analysis. However, Western psychology is less comfortable with things that can't be measured and places a great deal of emphasis upon assessment and evidence-based conceptualizations of dimensions of human functioning. As might be inferred from the term "immeasurable," though, compassion has proven somewhat difficult to assess using modern psychometric tools. Although a range of different evidence-based assessments of compassion exists (with several being described in this chapter), each reveals only part of the picture of the compassionate mind as it is understood in contextual compassion-focused therapy. Nonetheless, a thorough case conceptualization, grounded in evidence-based principles and processes, is possible—and also crucial for helping clients cultivate a capacity for compassion.

This chapter provides in-depth guidance on case conceptualization, assessment, and treatment planning with a compassionate focus. The techniques and concepts we review can be used by practitioners in any modality, not solely ACT, CFT, or FAP. Bringing compassion into the equation as we come to know our clients' aims and personal histories in detail can enhance the therapeutic relationship and uncover important pieces of the puzzle. Compassion creates a context for calming, soothing, and grounding in the face of difficult emotions, and for the treatment planning approach we advocate. Furthermore, the case conceptualization approach and assessment tools outlined here offer clear benefits in cultivating greater psychological flexibility.

In order to best illustrate the concepts and techniques in this chapter, we will return to Josh's case example, examining how his learning history, safety behaviors, and efforts at experiential avoidance were related to his experiences of trauma and threatening experiences in key attachment relationships. We will also present a semistructured clinical interview designed to assess the degree to which the attributes and skills of compassion are available to clients, again using Josh's case to exemplify use of this interview. While this is not an empirically validated assessment tool, it can provide a road map for client and therapist to collaboratively formulate targets for treatment and identify blocks to self-compassion.

The Self-Compassionate Mind Interview

The processes involved in the two psychologies of compassion (engagement and alleviation) are key targets of compassionate mind training, CFT, and compassion-focused ACT. As such, it is important to identify how available these aspects of compassion are to our clients. As we start shaping these attributes and skills through the therapy process, it is a good idea to know where we are beginning. Furthermore, it is important to understand the patterns of avoidance, control, or needless defense that might be blocking or inhibiting clients' ability to access their capacity for self-compassion and growth in acceptance, courage, and commitment to valued aims.

Several researchers are currently developing measures of various dimensions of compassion in a self-report format. While this work is underway, we have collaborated with CFT researchers to develop a semistructured interview aimed at helping clients gain insight into their strengths and areas of potential growth in regard to compassion. This interview is designed to help formulate aims for interventions and inform treatment planning and is meant to be used in the course of one of the earlier sessions in therapy. The best time is probably as soon as the client has developed a validating and engaged relationship with the therapist, framed some preliminary aims for therapy, and been introduced to some of the assumptions of a compassion-focused ACT via methods such as evoking creative hopelessness, engaging in the Reality Check from chapter 3, and exploring the wisdom of no blame. All of this will serve as a foundation of understanding from which the client can more effectively engage with the kinds of questions posed in the interview. Ideally, the client will also have an understanding of the two psychologies of compassion or will have learned some basics about how compassion can be trained and how it can aid in tolerating difficult experiences in the service of living a life of greater meaning and purpose. The interview also allows for assessing psychological flexibility processes due to the natural relationship between aspects of compassion and hexaflex processes, as described in chapter 2.

While the guidelines within the interview offer suggestions about what therapists might say to their clients, it is highly important that the interview proceed as a mindful and compassionate conversation within the context of the client's nature and struggles. Furthermore, the tone of validation and connectedness discussed and illustrated throughout chapters 4 through 6 should inform your therapeutic stance as you meet clients where they are and build on the conversational style, rapport, and empathic bridging they have displayed thus far in therapy.

Clinical Example: Using the Self-Compassionate Mind Interview in Session

Later in this chapter, we present a blank template for conducting the Self-Compassionate Mind Interview. However, to help you visualize and genuinely feel the process, we first present it in the context of Josh's case example.

Therapist: Now that we've gotten our minds around what is meant by "compassion" and have seen how strong of a hold your self-criticism has on you, I'd like to see if we can take a closer look at how we might help you build up some new ways of responding.

Client: New ways of dealing—of coping with this? That's good, because I'm sick of feeling like this.

Therapist: Well, we're going to do something *like* that. Honestly, we're not so much going to be finding out how to best get rid of what you've been feeling. We're going to see where your strengths lie in being better able to hold the tough stuff and keep going. We'll look at how you can get out of bed in the morning, take good care of yourself, and get moving with some kindness and strength. Is that good with you?

Client: It sounds a lot better than lying in bed with a hangover and cable news in the background to drown out my brain.

Therapist: I imagine so.

Client: So when do we start?

Therapist: You sound ready, so let's begin now. I'm going to ask you about how able and willing you believe you are to engage in specific types of compassionate action. Our compassionate minds can guide us to take specific steps in our lives, and I'd like to know how able you believe you are to engage these aspects of your compassionate mind.

Client: Aspects of what?

Therapist: Do you remember how we took a look at the different capabilities we can work with to grow in mindful compassion?

Client: To be present, and to be more able to take things on?

Therapist: Exactly. Spot on.

Client: Okay, I know what you mean. Fire away.

The therapist then proceeded to walk Josh through the Self-Compassionate Mind Interview, recording Josh's responses as indicated in the example below. To orient you to the form, for many items the therapist asks the client to rate a given experience or capacity on a scale of 0 to 6, with 0 being absent or completely lacking and 6 being very high. (And as you'll note, in Josh's case, the therapist actually began the first step of this formal interview a few exchanges earlier in the dialogue.)

Self-Compassionate Mind Interview Worksheet

Now I'm going to ask you about how able and willing you believe you are to engage in specific types of compassionate action. Our compassionate minds can guide us to take specific steps in our lives, and I'd like to know how able you believe you are to engage these aspects of your compassionate mind.

Attributes of the Psychology of Engagement

1. Sensitivity

How sensitive do you feel you are to your experience of distress as it occurs, in the present moment? Can you notice your experience of suffering as it arises in you? Please rate this on a scale of 0 to 6, where 0 means you aren't at all sensitive to your experience and 6 means you're highly sensitive to it.

0 Absent	1	2	3	4	5	6 Very high
			X			

What experiences and emotions might block or hinder your compassionate sensitivity to your own distress?

> *I can notice how much distress I'm in when I'm sober or not zoned out. My anxiety makes me want to check out or get messed up. Also, I hate myself!*

Can we think of one way in which we can address that block or obstacle together?

> *Based on what we've been talking about, I think I need to be able to just deal with these feelings without hiding anymore.*

2. Motivation to care for well-being

Using the same scale of 0 to 6, how motivated are you to take care of yourself and ensure your own well-being? To what degree are you motivated to alleviate or prevent the suffering you witness within yourself?

0 Absent	1	2	3	4	5	6 Very high
				X		

What experiences and emotions might block or hinder your motivation to care for your well-being?

When I'm hung up on all the ways that I've failed or how I'm too scared to talk to women, I feel like I just don't give a damn anymore. When I procrastinate too much, I also start to give up.

Can we think of one way in which we can address that block or obstacle together?

I can plan to take one mindful action each day, like making coffee, as a way of doing something in my own interest. That sounds weird, but I can do one thing. This is another thing, but I could call my old sponsor from my 12-step work in Austin.

3. Sympathy

Using the same scale of 0 to 6, how much can you extend sympathy toward yourself during difficult experiences? When you notice your own distress, to what degree do you feel spontaneously sympathetically moved?

0 Absent	1	2	3	4	5	6 Very high
X						

What experiences and emotions might block or hinder your sympathy toward yourself?

I know this is probably wrong, but I feel pretty numb about my own pain. Sometimes I don't even see it until it's too late.

Can we think of one way in which we can address that block or obstacle together?

When I think of my mother being caught up in her addiction and waking up from a blackout, it makes me want to cry. If I could feel that way about me, it would be better.

4. Empathy

Using the same scale of 0 to 6, to what degree do you feel able to reflect upon your own suffering and understand your experience? How much would you say you're able to look upon your own experience with the empathy you might feel toward another person in distress?

0 Absent	1	2	3	4	5	6 Very high
					X	

What experiences and emotions might block or hinder your empathy for yourself?

I think I get it intellectually. I can see the big picture and how I'm screwing up. I know the patterns are killing me, but I just don't seem to be able to care because I'm so full of hate for myself.

Can we think of one way in which we can address that block or obstacle together?

Just noticing that all of the self-hate talk was stories in my head started to help last week. I might not be able to stop thinking like that—sorry! But I can notice that it's an old story.

5. Nonjudgment

Using the same scale of 0 to 6, how much do you believe you're able to adopt a nonjudgmental stance toward your own suffering? To what extent do you feel you can unlock yourself from the influence of judgmental and condemning thoughts and attitudes?

0 Absent	1	2	3	4	5	6 Very high
	X					

What experiences and emotions might block or hinder you in being nonjudgmental with yourself?

I think you must be joking here! Really, I think that if I stopped running and getting high, maybe I could give myself a break. If I put together a few days of sobriety, maybe something could happen.

Can we think of one way in which we can address that block or obstacle together?

I could get to a meeting again. Maybe if I go to one meeting I could give myself a small break.

6. Distress tolerance

Using the same scale of 0 to 6, to what extent do you think you can tolerate distress when you experience difficult emotions? How able are you to adopt an accepting and open attitude toward your distress?

0 Absent	1	2	3	4	5	6 Very high
				X		

What experiences and emotions might block or hinder you in tolerating your distress?

> *This question is funny because I can take a lot of pain and distress except for feeling disgust for who I am. When I feel like I look good or just crush a performance, I feel on top. Most kinds of pain I can handle, but I hate how angry and scared I've been.*

Can we think of one way in which we can address that block or obstacle together?

> *It's starting to sound like I need to stop taking myself so seriously. Maybe I could lighten up for, like, an hour or two?*

Attributes of the Psychology of Alleviation, or Compassionate Mind Skills

Now I'm going to ask you how capable you believe you are of engaging in various compassionate mind skills. For all of these questions, use the same scale of 0 to 6 that we've been using.

1. How would you rate your ability to engage in self-compassionate thinking or reasoning?

0 Absent	1	2	3	4	5	6 Very high
	X					

2. How would you rate your ability to bring self-compassionate attention to your present-moment experience?

0 Absent	1	2	3	4	5	6 Very high
	X					

3. How would you rate your ability to use imagery that evokes warmth, wisdom, strength, and commitment to your well-being?

0 Absent	1	2	3	4	5	6 Very high
				X		

4. How would you rate your ability to remain open to sensory experiences that are soothing to you?

0 Absent	1	2	3	4	5	6 Very high
						X

5. How would you rate your ability to access or contact self-compassionate feelings, such as contentment, connectedness, and safeness?

0 Absent	1	2	3	4	5	6 Very high
	X					

6. How would you rate your ability to behave in a self-compassionate way that's intended to care for and protect your well-being?

0 Absent	1	2	3	4	5	6 Very high
	X					

Clinical Example: Summarizing What Josh's Self-Compassionate Mind Interview Revealed

Given the tone and style of Josh's pervasively shaming self-talk, it should come as no surprise that he said he had little capacity for self-compassion. However, some of the details he offered point the way to areas his therapist might want to emphasize in treatment. These responses can be treated as hypotheses and held lightly, but they do offer more precise information about how Josh experiences himself:

- Josh says he can contact the present moment with sensitivity to his suffering when he isn't intoxicated or semidissociative. He believes that he responds to anxiety by checking out from sensitivity to his experience.

- He has more motivation to care for himself as a valued aim than we might have thought, but he's blocked from acting on that motivation by fusion with shaming self-stories.

- Josh feels numb to his pain and completely lacking in sympathy for himself. However, he is able to experience empathy for himself cognitively and can make sense of his experience. When he relates his suffering to the way his mother's addiction has harmed her, he's more feeling.

- Josh feels very judgmental toward himself and wishes he could give himself a break and not take himself so seriously.

- He believes that he is tough and can handle a lot of pain and distress. However, social threats, shame, and fear are very hard for him to sit with.

- He reports that he has a very limited ability to use compassionate mind skills. However, he reports that he can self-soothe through sensory experiences.

- Josh is already aware that he can benefit from seeking sobriety and that this might be an act of kindness toward himself.

All of this information might have been generated in the course of a few regular sessions, but with the structured interview, it was gathered in just half of a single session. In the process, several avenues for developing the client's capacity for self-compassion were clearly identified.

Self-Compassionate Mind Interview Worksheet

This worksheet is intended for use by therapists, to be completed with clients. The structured interview and its rating scale provide a format for assessing the attributes and skills of compassion. We have provided preliminary questions for you to engage with your client around each of the attributes and skills of the two psychologies of compassion; however, allow your own compassionate wisdom to guide you through the assessment. When conducting the interview, briefly reflect on each question together, then rate the client's skills or attributes of compassion using a scale of 0 to 6, in which 0 means the skill or attribute is absent, and 6 means it is present to a very high degree. All of the information gathered in the course of this interview may guide your case formulation and treatment planning, helping determine the direction and course of a compassion-focused intervention. Feel free to copy this worksheet for use in your practice. For a downloadable version, please visit http://www.newharbinger.com/30550 (see the last page of the book for more information on how to access it).

Begin by orienting the client to the process along these lines: *Now I'm going to ask you about how able and willing you believe you are to engage in specific types of compassionate action. Our compassionate minds can guide us to take specific steps in our lives, and I'd like to know how able you believe you are to engage these aspects of your compassionate mind.*

Attributes of the Psychology of Engagement

1. Sensitivity

How sensitive do you feel you are to your experience of distress as it occurs, in the present moment? Can you notice your experience of suffering as it arises in you? Please rate this on a scale of 0 to 6, where 0 means you aren't at all sensitive to your experience and 6 means you're highly sensitive to it.

0 Absent	1	2	3	4	5	6 Very high

What experiences and emotions might block or hinder your compassionate sensitivity to your own distress?

_____

_____

_____

Can we think of one way in which we can address that block or obstacle together?

_____

_____

_____

2. Motivation to care for well-being

Using the same scale of 0 to 6, how motivated are you to take care of yourself and ensure your own well-being? To what degree are you motivated to alleviate or prevent the suffering you witness within yourself?

0 Absent	1	2	3	4	5	6 Very high

What experiences and emotions might block or hinder your motivation to care for your well-being?

_____

_____

_____

Can we think of one way in which we can address that block or obstacle together?

_____

_____

_____

3. Sympathy

Using the same scale of 0 to 6, how much can you extend sympathy toward yourself during difficult experiences? When you notice your own distress, to what degree do you feel spontaneously sympathetically moved?

0 Absent	1	2	3	4	5	6 Very high

What experiences and emotions might block or hinder your sympathy toward yourself?

_____

_____

_____

Can we think of one way in which we can address that block or obstacle together?

_____

_____

_____

4. Empathy

Using the same scale of 0 to 6, to what degree do you feel able to reflect upon your own suffering and understand your experience? How much would you say you're able to look upon your own experience with the empathy you might feel toward another person in distress?

0 Absent	1	2	3	4	5	6 Very high

What experiences and emotions might block or hinder your empathy for yourself?

_____

_____

_____

Can we think of one way in which we can address that block or obstacle together?

_____

_____

_____

5. Nonjudgment

Using the same scale of 0 to 6, how much do you believe you're able to adopt a nonjudgmental stance toward your own suffering? To what extent do you feel you can unlock yourself from the influence of judgmental and condemning thoughts and attitudes?

0 Absent	1	2	3	4	5	6 Very high

What experiences and emotions might block or hinder you in being nonjudgmental with yourself?

_____

_____

_____

Can we think of one way in which we can address that block or obstacle together?

_____

_____

_____

6. Distress tolerance

Using the same scale of 0 to 6, to what extent do you think you can tolerate distress when you experience difficult emotions? How able are you to adopt an accepting and open attitude toward yourself when you are in distress?

0 Absent	1	2	3	4	5	6 Very high

What experiences and emotions might block or hinder you in tolerating your distress?

_____

_____

_____

Can we think of one way in which we can address that block or obstacle together?

_____

_____

_____

Attributes of the Psychology of Alleviation, or Compassionate Mind Skills

Now I'm going to ask you how capable you believe you are of engaging in various compassionate mind skills. For all of these questions, use the same scale of 0 to 6 that we've been using.

1. How would you rate your ability to engage in self-compassionate thinking or reasoning?

0 Absent	1	2	3	4	5	6 Very high

2. How would you rate your ability to bring self-compassionate attention to your present-moment experience?

0 Absent	1	2	3	4	5	6 Very high

3. How would you rate your ability to use imagery that evokes warmth, wisdom, strength, and commitment to your well-being?

0 Absent	1	2	3	4	5	6 Very high

4. How would you rate your ability to remain open to sensory experiences that are soothing to you?

0 Absent	1	2	3	4	5	6 Very high

5. How would you rate your ability to access or contact self-compassionate feelings, such as contentment, connectedness, and safeness?

0 Absent	1	2	3	4	5	6 Very high

6. How would you rate your ability to behave in a self-compassionate way that's intended to care for and protect your well-being?

0 Absent	1	2	3	4	5	6 Very high

Compassion-Focused Case Formulation

Compassion-focused case formulation is designed to provide an understanding of the specific nature, history, and context of clients' lives. By understanding this highly individualized learning history and the functional relationships among patterns of reinforcement, avoidance, and emotion regulation, we can more effectively address the suffering and struggle that have led a client to seek psychotherapy. Therefore, in case formulation it is important to distinguish between the intended and inadvertent functions of the client's thoughts, feelings, and behaviors. The aim in a compassion-focused approach to formulation is to provide an individualized case conceptualization, establish treatment goals and targets, provide validation, and elicit the client's freely chosen values (Gilbert, 2007; Tirch, 2012). This type of compassion-focused formulation must include four essential elements:

- The client's biological and environmental contexts, both past and present, which must be understood in light of the antecedents, behaviors, and consequences that have shaped the client's patterns of action and coping

- What the client fears most and is least willing to experience, such as fears around themes of abandonment, rejection, shame, abuse, or harm

- The client's internally and externally focused "protective" safety strategies and behaviors

- The intended and unintended consequences of those safety strategies (both public and private) for the client, such as shame-based self-criticism, beliefs about coping, or views on the nature of the client's own suffering, including depression and anxiety

To guide the process of compassion-focused formulation, we have created a case-formulation worksheet (inspired by principles in Gilbert, 2009b), which we will provide shortly. Of course, such formulation is an ongoing endeavor that occurs in stages, beginning with the initial assessment and formulation, in which the therapist interviews the client and collects information regarding current difficulties, symptoms, and problems. The therapist also provides validation and psychoeducation regarding the client's struggles and current coping.

This is done through collaborative perspective taking and by acknowledging the universal need for compassion. The therapist also helps the client recognize that, given the client's context and experiences thus far, her approach to her problems is understandable, even though it probably isn't functional. Another focus of this initial stage of compassion-based formulation is the establishment of rapport and a working therapeutic relationship. While using empathy, compassionate listening, and reflecting, the therapist looks for any potential difficulties in establishing such a relationship, including any obstacles to compassion.

Next, therapist and client survey the client's cultural context and learning history, in general as well as in relation to experiences of compassion and related processes. This allows the client to share her life narrative and gives the therapist insight into the client's emotional memories of self and others. The therapist may inquire about the client's early experiences of feeling cared for, neglected, or not having needs met. Furthermore, the therapist looks for significant experiences surrounding early development, attachment, and feeling safe or threatened and, as always, assesses for a history of significant trauma or abuse. These early experiences often relate to certain emotional memories that can be central to the client's experience of the self and can be activated by current contexts and experiences. The therapist listens to the client's content, as well as tone and other nonverbal communication, in order to identify the client's felt sense surrounding important emotional memories and impressions of self and others. For example, repeated early experiences of being sent to her room alone when upset and crying might lead a client to associate the experience of distress with the feeling or felt sense of being all alone.

Repeated early experiences of feeling unsafe or uncared for can lead to feeling easily threatened or impair an individual's ability to take perspective, experience compassion, or remember early or trauma-related events (Gilbert, 2009b; Mikulincer & Shaver, 2007a). Thus, it is important to be sensitive to clients and recognize any difficulty they may have in recalling their history, including the possible activation of threat-response systems when retelling their narrative. Each client will have a different pace and sequence of stages during this formulation process. Therefore, the therapist is encouraged to meet each client wherever she may be in ability and willingness. In any case, a comprehensive compassion-focused assessment of early experiences and learning allows the therapist to utilize compassionate empathy and validation for both the client's historical and current struggles, and provides the client with the chance (perhaps for the first time) to tell her story in the presence of someone who is attentive, nonjudgmental, empathic, safe, and warm (Gilbert, 2009b).

Next, the therapist helps the client identify particularly problematic behaviors or strategies adopted in response to fears and perceived threats. These personally significant threats often relate to public and private events the client fears most and is least willing to experience. Thus, the client tries to avoid or control these things in an effort to feel safe and ultimately protect herself. These are natural defense responses or strategies, and they often vary between people and between internal and external threats (Gilbert, 2007). Examples of these "protective" or coping strategies include avoidance, rumination, substance abuse, and reassurance seeking. Together, therapist and client might review the costs and benefits of these safety behaviors. In addition, the therapist provides information regarding the nature and principles of behavioral reinforcement, and about the various functions of these strategies and why employing them is understandable. However, the therapist also illustrates how certain forms of these seemingly protective safety behaviors can often create more difficulties, rather than solving problems. Examples of unintended consequences of these responses are impeding new learning, eliminating opportunities to test the workability of beliefs about the threat, and reducing the client's range of behaviors (Tirch, 2012). Thus, the therapist helps the client develop awareness of these behaviors and extend compassion to herself regarding unintended difficulties or consequences. Metaphors, inventories, and experiential exercises can be used in session to illustrate this point.

Based on everything outlined above, the therapist has the information and insights necessary for completing a structured compassion-focused formulation addressing the four domains as listed above (historical influences, significant threats and fears, safety strategies, and unintended consequences). This formulation emphasizes de-shaming, with the therapist providing an open and safe context and not using judgmental language or terms like "distortion" or "maladaptive" (Gilbert, 2007, 2009b). Therapists guide clients through this formulation and to the understanding that their struggles and difficulties are not their fault and not of their choosing. Engaging in this careful assessment and formulation allows clients to adopt new perspectives and find new ways of taking responsibility and gaining the freedom to choose how they want to respond to both perceived and actual threats.

As you can see, this formulation involves a fluid, collaborative process of functional analysis and reflective listening (Gilbert, 2009a). Therapists support clients in developing their own formulation, an approach that continues throughout therapy. As necessary, therapist and client may identify new therapeutic targets, goals, and interventions or revise old ones. The therapist keeps this formulation in mind while moving through therapy with the client, consistently tracking progress and developments, using functional and solution analysis, and assessing for deficits, integration, and generalization of skills. In addition to periodically reviewing and reexamining earlier formulations based on progress, the therapist persistently keeps an eye out for new or previously overlooked obstacles to compassion or other events or behaviors that interfere with treatment in order to keep the formulation as comprehensive and up-to-date as possible.

Clinical Example: Developing a Compassion-Focused Case Formulation

As with the Self-Compassionate Mind Interview Worksheet earlier in this chapter, we provide an example of the Compassion-Focused Case Formulation Worksheet in clinical practice, once again with Josh, to help illustrate its use.

Compassion-Focused Case Formulation Worksheet

1. Presenting symptoms and problems

Binge drinking and chronic shame, anxiety, depression, and behavioral avoidance. "I hate myself and am only happy when I'm partying, looking good, and the center of attention. Doesn't that make me a bad person?"

2. Current context of problems

Client is in college completing a degree in theater and beginning a career as an actor. He is living on family wealth, neglecting his own needs and responsibilities, and becoming increasingly avoidant. A cycle of substance abuse and "crashing" and "hiding from the world" has resulted in psychological inflexibility, a constricted life, and low levels of self-compassion and positive emotions except for brief periods during intoxication.

3. Background and historical influences

What do you see as important background experiences to the struggles the client is experiencing today?

The client experienced prolonged periods of verbal and physical abuse in childhood at the hands of his father, and severe bullying and emotional abuse from students and teachers in boarding schools. He was socially neglected by loved ones, who exhibited lack of care and sometimes hostility.

How did others show affection or caring?

The client's attachment relationships involved a great deal of hostility, abuse, and neglect. Threat-based emotions and emotional memories have become associated with and related to affiliative emotions and interpersonal relationships.

When the client was distressed, how did caregivers provide comfort or soothing?

The client describes an absence of comforting and connection.

How did caregivers and important others respond to the client's achievements?

Josh reports that his achievements were ignored until he began to be praised for his good looks and acting ability, but only by peers. He was also praised for being "the life of the party."

Significant biological or developmental events

Academic difficulties, diagnoses of ADHD and depression, and subsequent "overmedication." Isolation and social struggles until physical maturity.

Significant emotional memories

Rejection, shame, sadness, fear of being alone.

Questions for the client

When you think about these events and memories, how do you feel in your body? What emotions show up?

"I don't like to think about them. I feel disgusted with myself."

Where is your attention drawn?

"I want to go to bed. I want to get out of here."

What were your experiences of your emotions growing up?

"Being screamed at, being beaten until I was black-and-blue, being rejected, and being left alone. I might as well have been left for dead."

What were your experiences of the emotions of close others or caregivers as you were growing up?

"Rage, anger, and craziness."

What is your felt sense of yourself?

"I feel like I'm lower than low. I've been given all the opportunities and money in the world and I've messed up."

What is your felt sense of others?

"Other people have it worse than me. I got picked on and had a drunk dad— so what. I don't have anything to complain about. Other people scare me, too."

4. Key threats and resulting fears

Questions for the client

What significant fears and concerns do you think these experiences influenced for you?

> *"I can't stand being seen by people unless they're really impressed or I'm really drunk."*

What significant fears do you have about what others might do or what might happen in your environment?

> *"Rejection! That and more punishment."*

What significant fears or concerns do you have about what you might do?

> *"Letting people see how weak and messed up I am."*

Are there particular themes or connections in these fears, such as rejection, abandonment, shame, or physical harm?

> *"All of the above!"*

Therapist summarization of client's external threats

> *Social rejection, death from drugs and alcohol, failure.*

Therapist summarization of client's internal threats

> *Living in perpetual state of shame and isolation. Feeling overwhelmed by rage and fear.*

5. Safety strategies

Questions for the client

What do you do to cope when faced with these threats and fears?

> *"Stay in bed or get really high and drunk. Charm the pants off of everyone."*

Looking back, how do you think your mind has tried to protect you from these threats and fears?

"By being a fucking rock star."

How did your mind try to protect you from external threats, such as aggression from others?

"Hiding from everyone. Seeming very cool and on point."

How did your mind try to protect you from internal threats, such as the experience of intense emotions or physical sensations?

"Being numb, checking out, and getting high."

Therapist summarization of external safety behaviors

Taking drugs, drinking, "being fake," and isolating during the day.

Therapist summarization of internal safety behaviors

"Attacking myself so I can kick my ass into shape."

6. Unintended consequences

Questions for the client

What unintended costs or disadvantages have these strategies had?

"Making embarrassing scenes, wasting my money, losing relationships, hurting good people, seeming like a jerk, losing acting roles, bad academic performance, horrible panic attacks, and crushing depression—that and constant self-loathing. Is that enough for you, Doc?"

What do you think about yourself when these fears, behaviors, or consequences come up?

"Like I said, I'm full of self-hate."

Therapist summarization of external consequences

Compromised functioning across many domains, lack of clear valued directions, difficulty in commitment to responsibilities and "things that matter," diminishing rewards, alienation from more and more peers.

Therapist summarization of internal consequences

Depression, anxiety, pervasive shame and dread, "fierce" cravings for intoxication, high levels of reported stress, recurrent emotional reexperiencing of abuse, absence of joy, and fusion with hostile self-criticism.

As you can see, repetitive themes of avoidance, control, and self-destructive behaviors in response to a pervasive history of trauma are present in this case. Josh's history of abuse and neglect in the context of key attachment relationships, his safety strategies, and the fact that he did not learn to experience emotional soothing in stressful situations have all contributed to a rigid and inflexible pattern of responding, with minimal mindfulness, acceptance, compassion, or committed action. This case formulation reveals a painful history and a young man who has experienced a great deal of shame. From a CFT point of view, the therapist can recognize that little of Josh's suffering was of his choice or his fault, and be sensitive to Josh's suffering based on a precise and nuanced understanding of the patterns that are keeping him stuck. By building on this compassion-focused case conceptualization, the therapist can help Josh experience the value inherent in caring for himself and moving toward a place of freedom, choice, and perhaps even joy. Josh has a long road ahead—in therapy, in his recovery, and in his life. Within CFT, the hope is that compassion can serve as a foundation for acceptance and help him find his feet, perhaps for the first time in his life.

To facilitate the approach to case formulation with your own clients, we offer the following blank worksheet. Feel free to copy it for use in your practice. For a downloadable version, please visit http://www.newharbinger.com/30550 (see the last page of the book for instructions on how to access it).

Compassion-Focused Case Formulation Worksheet

1. Presenting symptoms and problems

_____

_____

_____

_____

_____

_____

_____

_____

2. Current context of problems

_____

_____

_____

_____

_____

_____

_____

_____

3. Background and historical influences

What do you see as important background experiences to the struggles the client is experiencing today?

_____

_____

_____

How did others show affection or caring?

_____

_____

_____

When the client was distressed, how did caregivers provide comfort or soothing?

_____

_____

_____

How did caregivers and important others respond to the client's achievements?

_____

_____

_____

Significant biological or developmental events:

_____

_____

_____

Significant emotional memories:

_____

_____

_____

Questions for the client

When you think about these events and memories, how do you feel in your body? What emotions show up?

_____

_____

Where is your attention drawn?

_____

_____

What were your experiences of your emotions growing up?

_____

_____

_____

What were your experiences of the emotions of close others or caregivers as you were growing up?

_____

_____

_____

What is your felt sense of yourself?

_____

_____

_____

What is your felt sense of others?

_____

_____

_____

4. Key threats and resulting fears

Questions for the client

What significant fears and concerns do you think these experiences influenced for you?

_____

_____

_____

What significant fears do you have about what others might do or what might happen in your environment?

_____

_____

_____

What significant fears or concerns do you have about what you might do?

_____

_____

_____

Are there particular themes or connections in these fears, such as rejection, abandonment, shame, or physical harm?

_____

_____

_____

Therapist summarization of client's external threats

_____

_____

_____

Therapist summarization of client's internal threats

_____

_____

_____

5. Safety strategies

Questions for the client

What do you do to cope when faced with these threats and fears?

_____

_____

_____

Looking back, how do you think your mind has tried to protect you from these threats and fears?

_____

_____

_____

How did your mind try to protect you from external threats, such as aggression from others?

_____

_____

_____

How did your mind try to protect you from internal threats, such as the experience of intense emotions or physical sensations?

_____

_____

_____

Therapist summarization of external safety behaviors

_____

_____

_____

Therapist summarization of internal safety behaviors

_____

_____

_____

6. Unintended consequences

Questions for the client

What unintended costs or disadvantages have these strategies had?

_____

_____

_____

What do you think about yourself when these fears, behaviors, or consequences come up?

_____

_____

_____

Therapist summarization of external consequences

_____

_____

_____

Therapist summarization of internal consequences

_____

_____

_____

Compassion-Focused Assessment Instruments

Like many human experiences, compassion is a process that is very tricky to measure scientifically. By its very definition and the multimodal approaches to its training, compassion requires assessment tools that are more closely aligned with its dynamic nature (MacBeth & Gumley, 2012). Thus far, empirical science and research have mostly relied on self-report measures of compassion and self-compassion. A significant need remains for further development and investigation of instruments for assessing and measuring compassion. The Western science of compassion is young, and self-report measures are limited. However, there are a few measures that we would like to introduce to you as you begin to implement compassion-focused techniques into your work.

Self-Report Measures of Compassion

The Self-Compassion Scale (SCS) is a self-report measure of beliefs and attitudes toward compassionate self-responding (Neff, 2003a). This twenty-six-item self-report questionnaire aims to assess overall self-compassion as reflected in the total score and the score for each component of self-compassion outlined by Neff (2003a):

- Self-kindness (SCS-SK)

- Common humanity (SCS-CH)

- Mindfulness (SCS-M)

In the development of this scale, factor analysis suggested six subscales to represent a positive and negative aspect of each facet (Neff, 2003b). Thus, the SCS has six subscales that reflect opposing pairs of its components: self-kindness (SK) versus self-judgment (SJ), common humanity (CM) versus isolation (I), and mindfulness (M) versus over-identification (OI) (Neff, 2003a, 2003b). Using a five-point Likert scale ranging from 1 (almost never) to 5 (almost always), participants respond to items that are intended to reflect how they perceive their responses toward themselves in challenging times. The negative aspects of each component are reverse-coded. Here are some example items:

- **Self-kindness** ("I try to be understanding and patient toward aspects of my personality I don't like") versus **self-judgment** (reverse-coded; "I'm disapproving and judgmental about my own flaws and inadequacies")

- **Common humanity** ("I try to see my failings as part of the human condition") versus **isolation** (reverse-coded; "When I think about my inadequacies, it tends to make me feel more separate and cut off from the rest of the world")

- **Mindfulness** ("When something painful happens, I try to take a balanced view of the situation") versus **over-identification** (reverse-coded; "When I'm feeling down, I tend to obsess and fixate on everything that's wrong")

The SCS has been reported to have good reliability and validity cross-culturally (Neff, 2003b; Neff, Pisitsungkagarn, & Hsieh, 2008). This research supports appropriate factor structure of the SCS, with a single higher-order factor of self-compassion explaining the strong intercorrelations among the subscales (Neff, 2003a). The internal consistency reliability of the subscales were reported as 0.78 (SK), 0.77 (SJ), 0.80 (CH), 0.79 (I), 0.75 (M), and 0.81 (OI).

The scale demonstrates convergent validity (i.e., correlates with therapist ratings), discriminate validity (i.e., no correlation with social desirability), and test-retest reliability ($\alpha = 0.93$; Neff, 2003a; Neff, Kirkpatrick, et al., 2007).

The psychometric properties of the SCS have been examined in college and graduate student samples (Neff, 2003a), as well as with adults who practice meditation, an unspecified community sample of adults, and adults in remission from recurrent depressive disorder who were recruited to participate in mindfulness-based cognitive therapy (Kuyken et al., 2010; Van Dam et al., 2011). Overall SCS scores correlated negatively with self-criticism, depression, anxiety, and rumination, and positively with social connectedness and emotional intelligence (Neff, 2003a). In their meta-analysis of the association between self-compassion and psychopathology, MacBeth and Gumley (2012) examined studies that used the SCS, using only the total score in their analysis. They found significant associations between higher self-compassion and lower psychopathology and emotional distress and noted significant effect sizes. However, the authors of this book do note the limitations of this self-report scale and assert that the results of these analyses cannot distinguish whether results are due to high levels of self-compassion or due to low levels of self-judgment and self-isolation.

Fears of Compassion Scales

Gilbert, McEwan, Matos, and Rivis (2011) developed a series of scales measuring fears of compassion that examine three distinct processes. The first examines fears of feeling or expressing compassion for others, or compassion flowing out. The second looks at fears of receiving compassion from others, or compassion flowing in. The third assesses fears of compassion for oneself, or the experience of self-compassion (Gilbert et al., 2011). On all three scales, respondents use a four-point Likert scale to rate how much they agree with each statement. In a student sample, the Cronbach's alphas were 0.72 for fears of expressing compassion for others, 0.80 for fears of receiving compassion from others, and 0.83 for fears of compassion for oneself (Gilbert et al., 2011). In a therapist sample, the Cronbach's alphas for this scale were 0.76 for fear of compassion for others, 0.85 for fear of compassion from others, and 0.86 for fear of compassion for oneself (Gilbert et al., 2011). Clinically, these three scales are quite useful in distinguishing capacities for the different flows of compassion in clients and allow for exploration of client experiences of fear and active resistance to engaging in compassionate experiences or behaviors. They also provide information on possible fears related to affiliative emotions in general (Gilbert et al., 2011). This has important implications for compassion-focused interventions and the therapeutic relationship due to the significant role affiliative emotions play in effectively addressing experiences of fear and threat. The measure may be found at http://www.compassionatemind.co.uk/downloads/scales/Fear_of_Compassion _Scale.pdf.

Compassionate Love Scale

The Compassionate Love Scale (CLS) was developed by Sprecher and Fehr (2005) to measure the dispositional tendency to engage in compassionate or altruistic love toward various targets. There are three original versions of the CLS, targeting compassionate love toward family or friends, toward people in general ("stranger-humanity"), or toward a "specific close other," with each item of the latter version including the specific target's name (Sprecher & Fehr, 2005). The authors define compassionate love as an "attitude toward other(s), either close others or strangers of all of humanity; containing feelings, cognitions, and behaviors that are focused on caring, concern, tenderness, and an orientation toward supporting, helping, and understanding the other(s)" (Sprecher & Fehr, 2005, p. 630). Each version has twenty-one statements or items rated with a seven-point Likert scale that ranges from "not at all true of me" to "very true of me." All three versions have similarly worded items (e.g., beginning with "I spend a lot of time concerned about the well-being of"), modified as appropriate for each scale (e.g., ending with "those people close to me," "humankind," or the specific target's name). The three CLS versions have a unifactorial structure and good internal reliability, with a reported Cronbach's alpha of 0.95 (Sprecher & Fehr, 2005).

Santa Clara Brief Compassion Scale

The Santa Clara Brief Compassion Scale (SCBCS) was developed from the CLS for large epidemiological studies (Hwang, Plante, & Lackey, 2008). The five items of this scale were selected based on a factor analysis of the longer instrument. Respondents are asked to rate themselves on each of the five items using a five-point Likert scale ranging from 1 (does not describe me well) to 5 (describes me very well). Scores on this scale are an average rating across all five questions. The correlation between the original and the brief version is 0.96 (Hwang et al., 2008). A study comparing the SCS with the CLS (Gilbert et al., 2011) found a significant correlation of $r = 0.31$ ($p \{ 0.01$) for the association between self-compassion and compassionate love for others in a student sample. However, there was not a significant correlation between self-compassion and compassionate love in a sample of therapists ($r = 0.21$, $p = $ n.s.).

Self-Other Four Immeasurables Scale

The Self-Other Four Immeasurables Scale (SOFI) is a self-administered scale that assesses four qualities at the core of Buddhist teachings known as the four immeasurables (Kraus & Sears, 2009): loving-kindness, compassion, empathetic joy, and equanimity. It uses a five-point Likert scale for items consisting of adjectives chosen by the authors to embody or represent the theoretical qualities of the four immeasurables from Buddhist psychology and their opposing processes. The final version of the scale after factor analyses yielded eight pairs of adjectives (totaling sixteen items) with four proposed subscales. The adjectives of opposing processes are friendly versus hateful, joyful versus angry, accepting versus cruel, and compassionate versus mean. The subscales are positive self, negative self, positive other, and negative other. Participants are instructed to mark the appropriate answer on each item to indicate to what extent they have thought, felt, or acted this way toward themselves and others during the past week. The measure's authors calculated Cronbach's alphas for the four proposed subscales and the entire measure. Internal consistency when measured across all items was 0.60. For the positive self, internal consistency was 0.86; for the negative self, 0.85; for the positive other, 0.80; and for the negative other, 0.82 (Kraus & Sears, 2009).

The Experiences of Compassion Interview

Researchers are beginning to explore different approaches to the measurement and assessment of compassion. These new measures of compassion are intended to examine the specific variants of the intentional and behavioral components and processes of compassion that are the foundation of the theory and science of compassion as discussed thus far (Gilbert, 2010; Goetz, Keltner, & Simon-Thomas, 2010; Neff, 2003a, 2003b). One example of such an attempt is the development of an interview-based rating scale of compassion (Gumley, 2013). The development of this assessment is intended to complement and enhance the research and data on compassion, particularly in clinical populations (Gumley, 2013; MacBeth & Gumley, 2012).

In 2013, at the Second International Conference on Compassion-Focused Therapy, organized by the Compassionate Mind Foundation, Gumley described this narrative-based approach to the assessment of compassion, specifically the Experiences of Compassion Interview. This interview is proposed as a way to engage individuals in the evaluation of compassion from self to others, from others to self, and from self to self. The inspiration for this assessment came from clinical and theoretical observations of apparent contradictions between semantic and episodic memory in regard to compassionate experiences of self and others. This approach to assessing compassion is derived from the coding of individuals' narratives, and the measure includes four subscales of compassion that reflect wisdom and compassion in four realms (Gumley, 2013):

- Understanding of compassion

- Compassion for self

- Compassion from others

- Compassion for others

This interview uses semantic portrayal, via a card-sorting task, and episodic portrayal of three scenarios: a time when respondents expressed compassion to another, a time when another expressed compassion to the respondents, and a time when the respondents expressed compassion toward themselves. Gumley (2013) asserts that this measure is sensitive to the effects of CFT, is associated with the process of mentalization, and can facilitate the experience of compassion.

Cultivating Compassionate Behavior

While our human need for compassion is not freely chosen, compassion-based behavior and values are. In other words, the ways in which we embody compassionate behavior and commitment to such behavior are up to us. In this section, we will discuss several approaches that can help clients cultivate a broader repertoire of compassionate behavior, with a specific orientation toward alleviating suffering and allowing for growth and well-being. This involves exploring behaviors that embody the experience of wisdom by doing what works, gaining strength and courage through facing feared experiences, and coming into contact with an awareness of suffering. These approaches rely on the intentional use of behavioral experiments, behavioral activation, and exposure in a manner that is consistent with the individual's values and willingness (Tirch, 2012). To begin this work, therapist and client collaboratively arrive at an agreement as to what these new behaviors are, what they look like, and how they would feel to the client. Throughout, compassion-focused behavioral activation and exposure also emphasize compassion and values through the use of warmth, courage, strength, and kindness to facilitate engaging in more frightening or challenging activities (Gilbert, 2010).

What is truly helpful in easing the suffering of clients is to provide them with opportunities to learn new ways to behave in relationship to their suffering. To this end, therapists remind clients of things that have happened in the past as a result of changing their relationship and response to distress. An example might be not obeying the orders of the anxious self and instead going out on a date, despite anticipatory worry or stress. Compassionate behavior is about choosing to go out, even if doing so is difficult. Thus, compassionate behavior comprises not just what to do but how to do it.

Why ask clients to engage in these challenging actions? Because it helps them get unstuck from habitual patterns of fusion and avoidance that lead to increasingly constricted lives. Therefore, we often develop interventions and series of behavioral practices that are flexible and challenging but not overwhelming, where, step-by-step, clients begin to engage in successive (and successful) approximations of their desired compassionate behavior. For example, with clients who are suffering from agoraphobia, it isn't truly compassionate to advise them to just stay inside, where it feels less scary. That much is obvious. But teleporting them into the middle of a Rolling Stones concert without warning wouldn't be truly compassionate either. So we might begin encouraging them to go to the door and look down the road; then, next time, by encouraging them to take a few steps down the sidewalk or to the mailbox, and so on. This gradual exposure is a form of self-compassionate action by virtue of its pace and intention, and it can also serve as a form of compassionate exposure as both client and therapist actively recruit the client's previously trained capacity for mindful compassion and flexible responding in the presence of feared stimuli.

The more we can help clients create an understanding, supportive, and warm inner voice for themselves—a perspective that validates and recognizes how unpleasant suffering can be—the better able they may be to find a secure base from which to explore and face challenges. Compassionate mind training can help keep them in touch with their compassionate wisdom: the part of the self that has learned suffering is impermanent and that can make room for distress rather than fuse with it or avoid it. This kind of compassionate self-perspective allows clients to more easily recall new, intended responses and coach themselves through engaging in those responses. All behavioral changes are important, as they all help clients build courage and confidence.

Clarifying Valued Aims and Choosing to Care for Well-Being

When clients begin to engage with their suffering, they will be deliberately moving toward difficult things that they have historically avoided. This experience is likely to be uncomfortable. Therefore, as therapists we hear clients asking, "Why bother?" In response, we must remain flexible, bearing in mind that there are no absolute rules in terms of which exposure practices or compassionate actions matter to a given client. In chapter 6, we noted how creative hopelessness and the wisdom of no blame could create a context to begin the process of moving toward a life of meaning and vitality, even in the presence of difficult emotions. However, clarification and authorship of personally meaningful values also plays a crucial role in compassion-focused ACT. Therefore, some issues may be relevant to compassion-based exposure work, while others may not, depending on values and workability. For example, a client may have a fear of giraffes and not see any reason to overcome it because it does not interfere with mindfulness, compassion, and values-based living. Therefore, it is important to work with clients to explore and clarify their values-based aims and goals. This will inform decisions about whether and how to work with particular difficulties or treatment goals and illuminate which parts of their distress are most relevant to focus on.

For example, one client might wish to address his chronic but mild depression because he wants to move to a new city and begin a new job, whereas another client may want to stop compulsively seeking reassurance from her friends and relatives that she is able to face the anxiety of commuting to her job. Clearly, it is important to clarify with our clients specifically what they would like to achieve and why they would like to achieve it. In other words, why does a given aim matter to a person, and what makes it worth it to overcome habitual patterns of avoidance and excessive attempts at control? This becomes especially useful when obstacles or resistance appear in therapy, allowing therapists to help clients keep in mind what their aims are and why the work is worthwhile. Otherwise, clients may lose both motivation and perspective when suffering arises, making it all too easy for them to slip back into patterns of avoidance and feelings of unwillingness.

As you are undoubtedly well aware, valued aims or valued directions are behaviors that are intrinsically rewarding across time and across situations, reflecting clients' true intentions for how they want to behave in the world. This means choosing the version of themselves that they most wish to be. Therefore, a key goal for therapist and client alike is to discover what, specifically, seems to light a fire in the client. This will reveal the client's values and reflect the degree to which certain behaviors are reinforcing. So in order to help clients engage in truly compassionate behavior and take good care of themselves, it is important to explore their values and help them find effective ways to move in the direction of their valued aims.

Through guided discovery, therapists can aid clients in discovering what aims and directions are most meaningful and worthwhile to them. All of the following questions can be helpful in exploring clients' values and goals for compassionate behavior:

- Given that facing our suffering is difficult, what in life is worth suffering for?

- What would you have to give up caring about in order to not wish to avoid this experience?

- In the service of what valued aim would you be willing to face these difficult emotions?

- What behaviors are intrinsically rewarding for you?

- If you were to be compassionate toward yourself and courageous in your pursuit of your valued aims, where would you be headed?

- What do you want to be about in this life? What matters most to you? What would you be willing to face in order to realize these values?

Additionally therapists can assist clients in authoring their own valued directions and beginning to pursue valued aims by using the following worksheet (adapted from Tirch, 2012, and inspired by Hayes et al., 1999). Feel free to make copies of this worksheet for use in your practice. For a downloadable version, please visit http://www.newharbinger.com/30550 (see the last page of the book for instructions on how to access it). The worksheet can be used in session or be completed by clients as homework between sessions.

Becoming the Author of My Valued Aims and Directions

This worksheet is intended to give you space to write down some observations about the patterns of valued behavior you'd like to pursue in different areas of your life, such as career, family, and intimate relationships. Before completing each section, please take a few moments to reflect upon what aims you might pursue in your life that would be meaningful, rewarding, and filled with a sense of vitality and purpose for you. If you aren't filling out this worksheet in session, please find a place that feels safe to you and where you will be free from interruptions. Allow yourself sufficient time to complete it. Also schedule a time a day or two later to look over the worksheet and reflect upon your answers.

1. Career or work life

How important is this area of my life to me? (0–10): _____

What would my compassionate and values-based intention be in this area?

_____

_____

_____

What obstacles might I face in realizing this intention?

_____

_____

_____

How might I overcome these obstacles with strength, compassion, and wisdom?

_____

_____

_____

2. Family

How important is this area of my life to me? (0–10): _____

What would my compassionate and values-based intention be in this area?

_____

_____

_____

What obstacles might I face in realizing this intention?

_____

_____

_____

How might I overcome these obstacles with strength, compassion, and wisdom?

_____

_____

_____

3. Intimate relationships

How important is this area of my life to me? (0–10): _____

What would my compassionate and values-based intention be in this area?

_____

_____

_____

What obstacles might I face in realizing this intention?

_____

_____

_____

How might I overcome these obstacles with strength, compassion, and wisdom?

_____

_____

_____

4. Social life

How important is this area of my life to me? (0–10): _____

What would my compassionate and values-based intention be in this area?

_____

_____

_____

What obstacles might I face in realizing this intention?

_____

_____

_____

How might I overcome these obstacles with strength, compassion, and wisdom?

_____

_____

_____

5. Education

How important is this area of my life to me? (0–10): _____

What would my compassionate and values-based intention be in this area?

_____

_____

_____

What obstacles might I face in realizing this intention?

_____

_____

_____

How might I overcome these obstacles with strength, compassion, and wisdom?

_____

_____

_____

6. Physical well-being

How important is this area of my life to me? (0–10): _____

What would my compassionate and values-based intention be in this area?

_____

_____

_____

What obstacles might I face in realizing this intention?

_____

_____

_____

How might I overcome these obstacles with strength, compassion, and wisdom?

_____

_____

_____

7. Spirituality

How important is this area of my life to me? (0–10): _____

What would my compassionate and values-based intention be in this area?

_____

_____

_____

What obstacles might I face in realizing this intention?

_____

_____

_____

How might I overcome these obstacles with strength, compassion, and wisdom?

_____

_____

_____

8. Community involvement

How important is this area of my life to me? (0–10): _____

What would my compassionate and values-based intention be in this area?

_____

_____

_____

What obstacles might I face in realizing this intention?

_____

_____

_____

How might I overcome these obstacles with strength, compassion, and wisdom?

_____

_____

_____

9. Hobbies and recreation

How important is this area of my life to me? (0–10): _____

What would my compassionate and values-based intention be in this area?

_____

_____

_____

What obstacles might I face in realizing this intention?

_____

_____

_____

How might I overcome these obstacles with strength, compassion, and wisdom?

_____

_____

_____

Encouraging Compassionate Behavior

After clients have completed the worksheet, you may want to take some time to help them reflect upon what they learned and how this might relate to their development of compassionate behavior and mindfulness. It may be worthwhile to explain that when people's behavior becomes consistent with what they value, they are that much closer to living a life of compassion. They are also truly on the way to being better able to face challenges and overcome unnecessary suffering in the service of a life well lived.

Together, therapist and client should take a close look at how the client might cultivate compassionate behavior that fits with his freely chosen values and compassionate self, jointly discussing the process, acknowledging that it requires courage, discipline, and sacrifice and that it affords opportunities for joy and warmth as well. Therapists should encourage clients to remain open to whatever shows up in the present moment when pursuing valued aims, including shame, anger, sadness, fear of the unknown, and other challenging emotions. Compassionate and self-compassionate behavior involves perseverance and moving toward what matters most, even in the presence of distress, ultimately expanding clients' behavioral repertoires and choices. Therapists can also highlight compassionate behaviors that clients might already be engaging in, such as the following:

- Taking care of themselves, whether by having a relaxing massage or spending time with people they love

- Taking care of their health by visiting the doctor or exercising regularly

- Taking a break from a stressful situation to relax and enjoy other activities that bring them pleasure

In addition, therapists can point out that facing suffering through self-compassionate behavior may also take less obvious yet very important forms. Here are some examples:

- Dedication to moving in valued life directions, like studying for exams or pursuing a career, even when doing so is uncomfortable and involves sacrifices of time or energy

- Facing things that are frightening in order to engage in more values-based action, even though doing so involves experiencing distress

- Refraining from taking part in "pleasurable" activities that might be harmful, such as drinking a lot of wine at a party to "take the edge off" or "calm the nerves," when they know this behavior will have negative results in the long run

Clearly, after engaging in values clarification and authorship, clients are likely to face some difficult decisions. An example would be choosing to refrain from eating unhealthy foods that taste good in the short term but move the client away from his values around physical well-being. As always, it is important to keep in mind that each individual is different, with a unique learning history, set of values, and physical and emotional strengths. However, as human beings we all have the capacity to cultivate our compassion through the many skills and attributes of the compassionate mind. To that end, an important part of helping clients engage in compassionate action is looking at which fears or difficulties they would ideally face and how to face them.

Developing the Motivation to Engage in Compassionate Action

ACT involves a balance of mindfulness and acceptance processes and direct behavioral change processes, enacted in the service of living lives of meaning, purpose, and vitality. Part of working as an ACT therapist involves tracking the client's present-moment experience and emphasizing mindfulness and willingness, or specific steps toward change, based upon the client's needs and the opportunities in the moment. The process of values authorship and commitment to action involves evoking the motivation to move toward greater well-being, and this is a touchstone of compassionate motivation. Together, therapist and client can move through a specific behavioral change program, with the client gradually moving toward valued aims and overcoming patterns of avoidance, such as social isolation or addictive behaviors. In the process, the client commits to and then willingly enters experiences and situations she might prefer to avoid, doing so with clarity and purpose. To prepare for this, the therapist should help the client enhance her compassionate motivation.

There are many reasons clients may experience problems. Sometimes the experience of suffering seems clearly related to an ongoing psychological problem, or a DSM "disorder" or cluster of symptoms. Other sources of suffering might be external, such as stressful life events or environmental disasters. From the perspective of the compassion-focused therapist, it is important to remind clients that the suffering they experience is not their fault and that they didn't choose to have such an active threat-detection system. It may also be helpful to revisit the many reasons for their struggle with suffering. By conveying and reiterating this wisdom—that suffering is a fundamental part of being human— therapists can help clients experience more compassion for themselves and greater acceptance of their current experience of suffering. Our suffering, and our ability to recognize it, is part of our essential humanity, and being sensitive to that may increase clients' motivation to engage in compassionate action and move toward the life they wish to live.

Throughout this book, we have elaborated many ways that compassionate motivation can be stimulated through mindfulness, imagery, compassionate thinking, hexaflex process work, the therapeutic relationship, and a range of other methods. In a very simple and direct way, therapists can also use the process of guided discovery to help clarify the focus of compassionate action and increase clients' motivation to approach challenging situations. As an example, consider a client who suffers from anxiety. The therapist may first allude to how the client may have given up because of anxiety and avoiding feared situations. Then the therapist might ask about specific costs of avoidance behaviors and have the client reflect on or even write out the answers. Here are a few questions a therapist might ask in this situation:

- *How much has your struggle with unwanted emotions cost you in terms of your personal relationships? Have you avoided relationships, or have they become strained due to the limits your attempts to avoid or control your emotions have placed upon you?*

- *Have you avoided situations because of the feelings you thought you might have, and as a result missed out on meaningful opportunities? Have you made decisions that had a negative impact on your work life or finances due to avoidance?*

- *Has your struggle with your experience limited the amount of freedom you have to pursue the things you enjoy? Have you given up recreational activities, travel, or hobbies due to avoidance behaviors? How much time and energy have been absorbed by negative emotions involved with your struggle?*

- *What has your struggle with unwanted experiences and emotions cost you overall in your life?*

After exploring these kinds of questions, it's important to provide encouragement and hope by reminding clients that they are now taking steps to change this dynamic and to get their life back. Help them remember their aims: to reclaim their life and free themselves to experience life with kindness, courage, and authority.

Keeping sight of these aims is of paramount importance, especially when engaging in compassionate practices, wherein therapists ask clients to accept the fact that they are likely to feel more distress at first. In this way, therapists can help clients cultivate the willingness to experience some distress in the short term so that they might better overcome these struggles in the long term.

The threat-detection system can activate suddenly, and due to the accompanying physical sensations, emotions, and thoughts, the resulting reaction is not easily controlled or suppressed. Thus, it is important for therapists to emphasize to clients that the key is to approach this work with courage and an ever-growing ability to tolerate distress, which will build skill in meeting similar situations in the future. In CFT, this gradual approach to compassionate exposure is sometimes referred to as "challenging but not overwhelming."

During or after the work of guided discovery outlined above, therapists can work with clients to record and examine the costs and benefits of engaging in compassionate gradual exposure, perhaps using a formal worksheet such as the one we provide below. For a downloadable version, please visit http://www.newharbinger.com/30550 (see the last page of the book for instructions on how to access it).

Costs and Benefits of Facing My Feared Emotions and Experiences

Use this worksheet to list the specific costs and benefits that you might face.

Costs of facing my fears	Benefits of facing my fears

After reviewing the costs and benefits for the client, you might want to follow up with some questions along these lines:

- *What have you discovered after reviewing and listing the costs and benefits of facing challenging situations?*

- *Have you created a clear mental vision of how your life would be improved by coping with your difficulties?*

- *How might you describe the ways in which your life would be improved by being able to cope with distressing situations in a more mindful and compassionate way?*

Seeing One Another Through Compassionate Eyes

As we bring a compassionate focus to case conceptualization, we may discover aspects of our clients' lives and suffering that would otherwise have remained hidden. And as we engage in a systematic process of assessment and case conceptualization from a compassion-focused, ACT-consistent perspective, our sensitivity to the suffering we see in our clients may grow, as may our deep motivation to alleviate and prevent the suffering they experience. As we connect with their struggle and realize that so much of their pain truly is not about them and not their fault, our motivation to see them flourish and live larger and more fulfilling lives may deepen. This cycle, in which one person's pain awakens another's compassion and this compassion in turn gives rise to a shared, deep desire to alleviate suffering for all beings, is perhaps uniquely human. And it may very well represent the best of what we can see in ourselves and in each other.

9

Completion and New Beginnings

Some Eastern wisdom traditions, such as certain forms of Sufism, place a great deal of emphasis on how to draw a creative act to a close. If a process is allowed to unfold fully before it finally ceases to be, it is said to reach completion. Rather than coming to an abrupt end, where something is lost, or just fading out, which can feel like a zero-sum game, organically completing a series of actions creates new possibilities. It is said that with every completion a new beginning becomes possible. This is reminiscent of the processes involved in evolution and in life. Selection and variation result in adaptation, and as one generation of a species fades, new and more adaptive iterations may arise. Therefore, we have chosen not to provide a formal conclusion to this book in the hopes that as we complete this book together, with you the reader, we might generate new possibilities and new beginnings. As this book has demonstrated, bringing a focus on compassion to our ACT work is, in a way, a point of departure, and therefore can spark the creation of new directions and interventions. Integrating approaches such as CFT and FAP into the ACT context allows us to expand what is possible for us as therapists, and will hopefully spark creativity and innovation regarding research questions, theory, and specific interventions. Rather than concluding, we are aiming to begin. We hope that we have raised more questions than we have answered, and that our community carries these questions forward.

And how might we all move forward in exploring the applied science of compassion as psychotherapists? Certain key elements of ongoing education present themselves, and in this chapter we will address how to bring a compassion focus to each: supervision, training, and research and knowledge development. So before we come to the end of our journey together, let's discuss these dimensions and reflect upon how we might forward the mission of integrating CFT into contextual behavioral approaches.

Compassion-Focused Contextual Supervision

Psychotherapy, especially for the private therapist, is often a lonely pursuit. Many therapists have few people with whom they can share their professional difficulties. Compassion-focused supervision can be an important step toward not feeling isolated. It can also provide a context in which therapists at all levels of expertise can hone their skills and grow, both professionally and personally. Furthermore, while therapists are generally adept at validating other people's feelings and pain and responding with compassion to their clients' suffering, they often struggle when it comes to applying these skills to their own difficult situations and judgments. The compassion-focused supervision relationship thus offers a perfect arena in which therapists can train their compassion and self-compassion repertoires.

In addition to helping therapists develop new skills and deepen their knowledge, effective supervision also allows them to contact resources they already have. Even highly skilled therapists can get stuck at times and will benefit from the fresh perspective a supervision session can afford. In this way, the supervision relationship holds the same sort of central position as the therapeutic relationship does.

In our view, cultivating compassionate flexibility in supervision involves both supervisor and supervisee collaboratively engaging in a variety of processes:

- Being sensitive to emotional distress in the supervision relationship and, through a parallel process, in the clients discussed

- Extending sympathy and automatically engaging emotionally with the distress encountered

- Developing a capacity to tolerate distress in the service of alleviating and preventing human suffering

- Getting unhooked from judgmental, condemning, and shame-based thinking

- Creating conditions to further develop and hone empathic responding

- Working to develop specific therapeutic skills and capacities essential to ACT and compassion-focused work

The supervision relationship mirrors, in many aspects, the therapeutic relationship. There is an implied hierarchy between supervisor and supervisee. Supervisees often come to supervisors seeking to solve difficult problems, often as a result of having faced emotions of helplessness and quite possibly negative self-judgments about their professional abilities and perhaps self-worth. And at times, supervision issues are "problems to solve" in the sense that there may be an exercise or particular intervention the supervisee could use to help therapy move along. The more the supervisee is familiar with and skilled in the approach, the fewer such "problems" there are to solve. As skill level increases, supervision questions become more about how supervisees can receive their clients' emotions, and their own, from a stance of compassion.

Supervisees differ in their needs depending on skill level, so a wise supervisor assesses both supervisee needs and level of skill. Supervisees who are new to ACT and the functional contextual approach may need to be oriented toward specific techniques and exercises. Therefore, a supervisor may suggest that a supervisee who struggles with defusion try a range of techniques, such as inviting clients to preface thoughts with "I have the thought that…"; noticing hooks and what they do next; doing the Leaves on the Stream exercise (Hayes, 2005); noticing the different thoughts and sensations that make up their aversive experience in the moment; and so on. Suggesting metaphors, such as the Man in the Hole, the Children on the Bus (originally Passengers on the Bus), and the Tin Can Monster (all in Hayes et al., 1999), may also be useful. When it comes to training compassion, evocative exercises such as Visualizing the Compassionate Self, compassion-focused chair work, or systematic perspective-taking exercises may prove useful. At this stage, role-playing clients, first with the supervisor playing the therapist, then, increasingly, with the supervisee playing the therapist, is helpful.

Supervisees who are familiar with the approach and well-read in the techniques need fewer such technical suggestions and may be better served by guidance that helps them identify functions of behaviors that play out for their clients. Identifying antecedents, whether physical or verbal, and the verbal and physical consequences of both problematic and improved behavior, comes into more acute focus. The aim is to help supervisees better identify with clients' experience as it happens and have a better sense for what could help. For example, identifying that a particular thought, such as "I'm not interesting," serves as an antecedent for withdrawal in unfamiliar social situations can help the supervisee tailor interventions as needed. The supervisee might then elect to deal with the antecedent, perhaps by defusing from the thought by noticing it as hook, or to change the consequences of speaking to strangers, perhaps by linking this behavior, through values, to the kind of person the client wants to be.

An important part of this phase is to help supervisees notice the antecedents and consequences of their own therapist behaviors. This can be done by modeling, with the supervisor asking the supervisees what effect supervisor behavior has on them. This can help supervisees learn to recognize and receive emotions as they show up in the moment in session. In this way, the supervisor makes use of processes parallel to those showing up in the supervisees' therapeutic relationships with clients. This type of intervention is illustrated by the dialogue below.

Supervisor: So what do you imagine the antecedents to your client withdrawing were?

Supervisee: I'm not sure. We were talking about homework and he just shut down.

Supervisor: Had he done it?

Supervisee: No, he hadn't even made a start.

Supervisor: So a bit like my suggestion that you make a note of client antecedents and consequences?

Supervisee: (Remains silent.)

Supervisor:	What happened just now? I'm getting a sense that you just shut down on me.
Supervisee:	I feel guilty, as if I was at school and hadn't done my homework.
Supervisor:	Ouch! That must be painful. So what showed up?
Supervisee:	I felt judged and a bit ashamed.
Supervisor:	I'm sorry you felt this. Was that a hook for you?
Supervisee:	Uh-huh.
Supervisor:	And what did you do next?
Supervisee:	I shut down, I guess.
Supervisor:	Yes, I felt that. Would you say you bit the hook? And is that how the person you want to be would have acted?
Supervisee:	No, I wish I could have just said that I noticed those thoughts and feelings showing up and that I could even see them as antecedents to my withdrawal.
Supervisor:	Right. And as you say that, I don't feel you shutting down. Do you think something similar might have been at play with your client?
Supervisee:	That makes sense. I guess I got bogged down in trying to explain how important the exercises were for the client's progress.
Supervisor:	And what happened?
Supervisee:	He stayed shut down.
Supervisor:	So we're doing good noticing all of these antecedents and consequences…
Supervisee:	I guess if I'd asked him what was showing up for him, we then could have more easily done something with it. Right?
Supervisor:	See what happens when you do it.

Whether therapists are seeking supervisors who might help them better create a context of acceptance, wisdom, and flexibility, or are developing their own ability to serve as supervisors with openness, courage, and empathy and oriented to the needs and experiences of supervisees, compassion and the ability to shift perspective on emotional experiencing remains central. Within the realm of a therapist's emotional responses we can find a host of important information about clients' valued aims and experience of suffering. By remaining open and defusing from our habitual responses to our own emotions, we can draw these experiences closer. Our characteristically human capacity for perspective taking, and our ability to cultivate an emotional tone of warmth and care, can foster insight into what is going on in the mind of the other. We can imagine the function of the client's or trainee's emotional response and bring this information into case formulation and intervention with clinical wisdom and solid technique.

The Workshops and Further Training

The early twenty-first-century culture of training in mindfulness-, acceptance-, and compassion-focused behavior therapies typically involves psychotherapists attending workshops, reading background material, and hopefully seeking further training and supervision in order to deepen and apply their knowledge. As many of us know, workshop experiences can be intensely emotional and sometimes revelatory. When exploring ACT, CFT, and FAP with qualified trainers in a safe environment, many psychotherapists are able to take risks, look at their inner life through a new lens, and open themselves to strong emotions that they may have been avoiding or blocking. As therapists, we discover new possibilities through these experiences, and we come away with the challenge of how to build on that learning.

Several factors can help us build on the experience of participating in a workshop, attending a conference, or even reading a book, this one included:

• Developing a regular personal practice of mindfulness and compassion meditation

• Using the techniques we learn on ourselves, including role-playing, as part of a process of self-reflection

- Seeking qualified trainers and supervisors and establishing ongoing educational relationships with them

- Connecting to communities, professional organizations, and local peer groups to create conditions that can further our education and capacities

- Using online resources, recordings, social media, and e-mail discussion groups to facilitate and enhance our personal practice and education

All of these experiences become possible as you connect with fellow travelers on your journey into compassion-focused ACT. At the end of this book, we have provided a list of resources that will allow you to pursue these paths. Hopefully this will elucidate ways in which you might choose to take your work further or in new directions.

After workshop and training experiences, it can be easy to let new learning slip away as we are pulled back into the flow of life, and get caught up in habitual patterns. Sometimes, this might be just what we need. However, for our professional and personal growth, it is important to continue the journey, to keep on asking questions and assimilating new learning. All of the information in the Resources section is aimed at making it easier for you to pursue training and enrichment in ACT and compassion psychology if you wish to do so.

Research and Knowledge Development

While there is sufficient science to support the approach outlined in this book, many important directions for research in contextual psychology and the science of compassion remain, and endeavors in these fields will further the work. There is already a considerable amount of research supporting the fundamental processes of compassion and psychological flexibility, drawn from experimental behavioral science, affective neuroscience, developmental psychology, and psychotherapy outcome research. However, much work remains to be done. More research and randomized controlled trials regarding the efficacy of compassion-focused interventions, and compassion-focused ACT in particular, will be important for enhancing understanding and treatment methods. New and exciting directions that are beginning to emerge in research include more specific and conceptually focused assessment tools for compassion, such as the examination of implicit cognition (Ferroni Bast & Barnes-Holmes, 2014), qualitative interviews involving compassion and attachment (Gumley, 2013), and assessment of the two psychologies of compassion in the therapeutic dyad. How compassion might be trained at the level of organizations, communities, and societies also is important, and this is actively being explored at the Stanford University Center for Compassion and Altruism Research and Education, the Compassionate Mind Foundation, and the Charter for Compassion, as well as by members of the Association for Contextual Behavioral Science.

By reading and engaging with this book, you are already playing a part in the emergence of compassion in the ACT community and in the world. Should you choose, you can expand on this, framing the ideas and questions that have arisen for you during your reading. If it suits your aims, perhaps you might organize these questions around hypotheses for research or ideas for interventions, or as open questions in an online discussion group.

The Path Forward

Compassion emerges from a heartfelt recognition of the interconnection between all living things. As we are sensitive to the suffering we encounter and are moved to respond to do something about it, we naturally turn to one another for support, companionship, and collaboration. At this point in our evolution and history, there is far less distance than ever before between us, whether we are authors, readers, or researchers. Our communities and the vast networks of dedicated fellow travelers are ever more closely knit together. We hope that as we have shared this journey with you, you will share your journey with us. We are all joined in our common humanity, resting in kindness with the knowledge that we all wish to be happy, to be well, and to find peace and joy, including—and especially—in the face of great challenges.

May you become available to your compassionate mind as it becomes available to you. May the conditions that cultivate compassion and well-being organize themselves around you and your clients. And may you flourish and continue to share your own wisdom, strength, and commitment with those who have come to you for care, with your loved ones, and with yourself.

What matters most is how well you walk through the fire.

—Charles Bukowski

Love and compassion are necessities, not luxuries.
Without them, humanity cannot survive.

—Tenzin Gyatso, Fourteenth Dalai Lama

Resources

This is a time of exponential growth in the study and practice of the science of compassion within contextual science and cognitive and behavioral therapies. There are many channels that you can begin to explore to further your knowledge beyond what you have learned from this book. In order to present a focused and manageable path through the ever-expanding world of compassion psychology, we have included a brief list of Internet links below. Most of the links will bring you to websites that can serve as portals to further information and training about how to use compassion in an ACT or psychotherapy practice. Video recordings of lectures, documents of relevant readings, and guided audio recordings of compassionate imagery exercises are all available at these sites.

Importantly, several of the websites also have training and events calendars that outline opportunities for further training in ACT, CFT, FAP, and the integration of a compassionate focus into a range of psychological applications. Many opportunities for workshops, individual supervision, online consultation groups, and blended learning are emerging as mindfulness, acceptance, and compassion evolve in our Western psychological tradition. We hope that each link below serves as an inroad to other resources, and that you avail yourself of these in your own way and in your own time, crafting your own path for yourself as you continue your compassionate journey. Please feel free to connect with us and our community as you wish.

- The Association for Contextual Behavioral Science (ACBS): http://www.contextualscience.org

- The Compassionate Mind Foundation USA:
  http://www.compassionfocusedtherapy.com

- The Compassionate Mind Foundation UK:
  http://www.compassionatemind.co.uk

- Functional Analytic Psychotherapy (FAP):
  http://www.functionalanalyticpsychotherapy.com

- The Compassion Focused Special Interest Group of the Association for Contextual Behavioral Science:
  http://www.contextualscience.org/compassion_focused_sig

- The FAP Special Interest Group of the Association for Contextual Behavioral Science:
  http://www.contextualscience.org/fap_sig

- The Center for Mindfulness and Compassion Focused Therapy:
  http://www.mindfulcompassion.com

- The Contextual Psychology Institute:
  http://www.guidecliniqueact.com

References

Ashworth, F., Gracey, F., & Gilbert, P. (2011). Compassion focused therapy after traumatic brain injury: Theoretical foundations and a case illustration. *Brain Impairment 12*, 128–139.

Baer, R. A. (2003). Mindfulness training as a clinical intervention: A conceptual and empirical review. *Clinical Psychology: Science and Practice 10*, 125–143.

Barlow, D. H. (2002). *Anxiety and its disorders: The nature and treatment of anxiety and panic.* New York: Guilford.

Barnes-Holmes, D., Hayes, S. C., & Dymond, S. (2001). Self and self-directed rules. In S. C. Hayes, D. Barnes-Holmes, & B. Roche (Eds.), *Relational frame theory: A post-Skinnerian account of human language and cognition* (pp. 119–139). New York: Springer.

Barnes-Holmes, Y., Foody, M., & Barnes-Holmes, D. (2013). Advances in research on deictic relations and perspective taking. In S. Dymond & B. Roche (Eds.), *Advances in relational frame theory: Research and application* (pp. 5–26). Oakland, CA: New Harbinger.

Beaumont, E., Galpin, A., & Jenkins, P. (2012). "Being kinder to myself": A prospective comparative study, exploring post-trauma therapy outcome measures, for two groups of clients, receiving either cognitive behaviour therapy or cognitive behaviour therapy and compassionate mind training. *Counseling Psychology Review 27*, 31–43.

Bennett, D. S., Sullivan, M. W., & Lewis, M. (2005). Young children's adjustment as a function of maltreatment, shame, and anger. *Child Maltreatment 10*, 311–323.

Blackledge, J. T., & Drake, C. E. (2013). Acceptance and commitment therapy: Empirical and theoretical considerations. In S. Dymond & B. Roche (Eds.), *Advances in relational frame theory: Research and application* (pp. 219–252). Oakland, CA: New Harbinger.

Bowlby, J. (1968). Effects on behaviour of disruption of an affectional bond. *Eugenics Society Symposia 4*, 94–108.

Bowlby, J. (1969). *Attachment and loss. Vol. 1: Attachment.* New York: Random House.

Bowlby, J. (1973). *Attachment and loss. Vol. 2: Separation.* New York: Basic Books.

Braehler, C., Harper, I., & Gilbert, P. (2012). Compassion focused group therapy for recovery after psychosis. In C. Steel (Ed.), *CBT for schizophrenia: Evidence-based interventions and future directions* (pp. 235–266). Chichester, West Sussex, UK: John Wiley and Sons.

Brown, R. P., & Gerbarg, P. (2012). *The healing power of the breath: Simple techniques to reduce stress and anxiety, enhance concentration, and balance your emotions.* Boston: Shambhala.

Brune, M., Belsky, J., Fabrega, H., Feierman, J. R., Gilbert, P., Glantz, K., et al. (2012). The crisis of psychiatry: Insights and prospects from evolutionary theory. *World Psychiatry 11*, 55–57.

Bulmash, E., Harkness, K. L., Stewart, J. G., & Bagby, R. M. (2009). Personality, stressful life events, and treatment response in major depression. *Journal of Consulting and Clinical Psychology 77*, 1067.

Busch, F. N. (2009). Anger and depression. *Advances in Psychiatric Treatment 15*, 271–276.

Byrne, R. (1995). *The thinking ape: Evolutionary origins of intelligence.* Oxford, UK: Oxford University Press.

Cacioppo, J. T., & Patrick, W. (2008) *Loneliness: Human nature and the need for social connection.* New York: Norton.

Call, J., & Tomasello, M. (1999). A nonverbal false belief task: The performance of children and great apes. *Child Development 70*, 381–395.

Carter, S. C. (1998). Neuroendocrine perspectives on social attachment and love. *Psychoneuroendocrinology 23*, 779–818.

Clayton, N. S., Dally, J. M., & Emery, N. J. (2007). Social cognition by food-caching corvids: The western scrub-jay as a natural psychologist. *Philosophical Transactions of the Royal Society of London: Biological Sciences 362*, 507–522.

Cordova, J. V., & Scott, R. L. (2001). Intimacy: A behavioral interpretation. *Behavior Analyst 24*, 75.

Cozolino, L. (2007). *The neuroscience of human relationships: Attachment and the developing brain.* New York: Norton.

Cozolino, L. (2010). *The neuroscience of psychotherapy: Healing the social brain.* New York: Norton.

Dahl, J., Plumb, J., Stewart, I., & Lundgren, T. (2009). *The art and science of valuing in psychotherapy: Helping patients discover, explore, and commit to valued action using acceptance and commitment therapy.* Oakland, CA: New Harbinger.

Davidson, R. J. (2003). Affective neuroscience and psychophysiology: Toward a synthesis. *Psychophysiology 40*, 655–665.

Davidson, R. J., & Harrington, A. (2001). A science of compassion or a compassionate science? What do we expect from a cross-cultural dialogue with Buddhism? In R. J. Davidson & A. Harrington (Eds.), *Visions of compassion: Western scientists and Tibetan Buddhists examine human nature* (pp. 18–30). New York: Oxford University Press.

Decety, J., & Ickes, W. (2011). *The social neuroscience of empathy.* Cambridge, MA: MIT Press.

Depue, R. A., & Morrone-Strupinsky, J. V. (2005). A neurobehavioral model of affiliative bonding: Implications for conceptualizing a human trait of affiliation. *Behavioral and Brain Sciences 28*, 313–395.

De Waal, F. (2009). *Primates and philosophers: How morality evolved.* Princeton, NJ: Princeton University Press.

Dymond, S., May, R. J., Munnelly, A., & Hoon, A. E. (2010). Evaluating the evidence base for relational frame theory: A citation analysis. *Behavior Analyst 33*, 97–117.

Dymond, S., Schlund, M. W., Roche, B., & Whelan, R. (2013). The spread of fear: Symbolic generalization mediates graded threat-avoidance in specific phobia. *Quarterly Journal of Experimental Psychology 67*, 1–13.

Eifert, G. H., & Forsyth, J. P. (2005). *Acceptance and commitment therapy for anxiety disorders: A practitioner's treatment guide to using mindfulness, acceptance, and values-based behavior change strategies.* Oakland, CA: New Harbinger.

Ekman, P. (1992). An argument for basic emotions. *Cognition and Emotion 6*, 169–200.

Ekman, P. (1994). All emotions are basic. In P. Ekman & R. J. Davidson (Eds.), *The nature of emotion: Fundamental questions* (pp. 15–19). Oxford, UK: Oxford University Press.

Farb, N. A., Segal, Z. V., Mayberg, H., Bean, J., McKeon, D., Fatima, Z., & Anderson, A. K. (2007). Attending to the present: Mindfulness meditation reveals distinct neural modes of self-reference. *Social Cognitive and Affective Neuroscience 2*, 313–322.

Fehr, B., Sprecher, S., & Underwood, L. G. (Eds.). (2008). *The science of compassionate love: Theory, research, and applications.* Chichester, West Sussex, UK: John Wiley and Sons.

Ferroni Bast, D., & Barnes-Holmes, D. (2014). A first test of the implicit relational assessment procedure as a measure of forgiveness of self and others. *Psychological Record 64*, 253–260.

Fonagy, P., & Target, M. (2007). The rooting of the mind in the body: New links between attachment theory and psychoanalytic thought. *Journal of the American Psychoanalytic Association 55*, 411–456.

Fonagy, P., Target, M., Cottrell, D., Phillips, J., & Kurtz, Z. (2002). *What works for whom? A critical review of treatments for children and adolescents.* New York: Guilford.

Forsyth, J. P., & Eifert, G. H. (2007). *The mindfulness and acceptance workbook for anxiety: A guide to breaking free from anxiety, phobias, and worry using acceptance and commitment therapy.* Oakland, CA: New Harbinger.

Foster, K. R., & Ratnieks, F. L. (2005). A new eusocial vertebrate? *Trends in Ecology and Evolution 20*, 363–364.

Fredrickson, B. L. (2001). The role of positive emotions in positive psychology: The broaden-and-build theory of positive emotions. *American Psychologist 56*, 218–226.

Fredrickson, B. L., Cohn, M. A., Coffey, K. A., Pek, J., & Finkel, S. M. (2008). Open hearts build lives: Positive emotions, induced through loving-kindness meditation, build consequential personal resources. *Journal of Personality and Social Psychology 95*, 1045–1062.

Gale, C., Gilbert, P., Read, N., & Goss, K. (2012). An evaluation of the impact of introducing compassion focused therapy to a standard treatment programme for people with eating disorders. *Clinical Psychology and Psychotherapy 21*, 1–12.

Garland, E. L., Fredrickson, B., Kring, A. M., Johnson, D. P., Meyer, P. S., & Penn, D. L. (2010). Upward spirals of positive emotions counter downward spirals of negativity: Insights from the broaden-and-build theory and affective neuroscience on the treatment of emotion dysfunctions and deficits in psychopathology. *Clinical Psychology Review 30*, 849–864.

Germer, C. K. (2012). Cultivating compassion in psychotherapy. In C. Germer & R. Siegel (Eds.), *Wisdom and compassion in psychotherapy: Deepening mindfulness in clinical practice* (pp. 93–110). New York: Guilford.

Germer, C. K., Seigel, R. D., & Fulton, P. R. (Eds.). (2005). *Mindfulness and psychotherapy.* New York: Guilford.

Gilbert, P. (1989). *Human nature and suffering.* London: Psychology Press.

Gilbert, P. (1998). The evolved basis and adaptive functions of cognitive distortions. *British Journal of Medical Psychology 71,* 447–464.

Gilbert, P. (2000). Social mentalities: Internal "social" conflicts and the role of inner warmth and compassion in cognitive therapy. In P. Gilbert & K. G. Bailey (Eds.), *Genes on the couch: Explorations in evolutionary psychotherapy* (pp. 118–150). Philadelphia, PA: Taylor and Francis.

Gilbert, P. (2001). Evolutionary approaches to psychopathology: The role of natural defenses. *Australian and New Zealand Journal of Psychiatry 35*, 17–27.

Gilbert, P. (Ed.). (2005). *Compassion: Conceptualisations, research, and use in psychotherapy*. New York: Routledge.

Gilbert, P. (2007). Evolved minds and compassion in the therapeutic relationship. In P. Gilbert & R. Leahy (Eds.), *The therapeutic relationship in the cognitive behavioral psychotherapies* (pp. 106–142). New York: Routledge.

Gilbert, P. (2009a). *The compassionate mind: A new approach to life's challenges*. London: Constable and Robinson.

Gilbert, P. (2009b). Introducing compassion-focused therapy. *Advances in Psychiatric Treatment 15*, 199–209.

Gilbert, P. (2009c). Evolved minds and compassion-focused imagery in depression. In L. Stopa (Ed.). *Imagery and the threatened self: Perspectives on mental imagery in cognitive therapy* (pp.206–231). London: Routledge.

Gilbert, P. (2010). *Compassion focused therapy: Distinctive features*. London: Routledge.

Gilbert, P., & Choden. (2013). *Mindful compassion*. London: Constable and Robinson.

Gilbert, P., & Irons, C. (2005). Focused therapies and compassionate mind training for shame and self-attacking. In P. Gilbert (Ed.), *Compassion: Conceptualisations, research, and use in psychotherapy* (pp. 263–325). London: Routledge.

Gilbert, P., & Leahy, R. (2007). *The therapeutic relationship in the cognitive behavioral psychotherapies*. New York: Routledge.

Gilbert, P., McEwan, K., Gibbons, L., Chotai, S., Duarte, J., & Matos, M. (2012). Fears of compassion and happiness in relation to alexithymia, mindfulness, and self-criticism. *Psychology and Psychotherapy: Theory, Research and Practice 85*, 374–390.

Gilbert, P., McEwan, K., Matos, M., & Rivis, A. (2011). Fears of compassion: Development of three self-report measures. *Psychology and Psychotherapy: Theory, Research, and Practice 84*, 239–255.

Gilbert, P., & Procter, S. (2006). Compassionate mind training for people with high shame and self-criticism: Overview and pilot study of a group therapy approach. *Clinical Psychology and Psychotherapy 13*, 353–379.

Goetz, J. L., Keltner, D., & Simon-Thomas, E. (2010). Compassion: An evolutionary analysis and empirical review. *Psychological Bulletin 136*, 351.

Greenberg, L. S., & Paivio, S. C. (1997). *Working with emotions in psychotherapy*. New York: Guilford.

Greene, D. J., Barnea, A., Herzberg, K., Rassis, A., Neta, M., Raz, A., & Zaidel, E. (2008). Measuring attention in the hemispheres: The lateralized attention network test (LANT). *Brain and Cognition 66*, 21–31.

Gumley, A. (2013, December). So you think you're funny? Developing an attachment based understanding of compassion and its assessments. Presented at the International Conference on Compassion Focused Therapy, London.

Gumley, A., Braehler, C., Laithwaite, H., MacBeth, A., & Gilbert, P. (2010). A compassion focused model of recovery after psychosis. *International Journal of Cognitive Therapy 3*, 186–201.

Hackmann, A., Bennett-Levy, J., & Holmes, E. A. (Eds.). (2011). *Oxford guide to imagery in cognitive therapy*. Oxford, UK: Oxford University Press.

Hayes, S. C. (1984). Making sense of spirituality. *Behaviorism 12*, 99–110.

Hayes, S. C. (with Smith, S.). (2005). *Get out of your mind and into your life: The new acceptance and commitment therapy*. Oakland, CA: New Harbinger.

Hayes, S. C. (2008a). Avoiding the mistakes of the past. *Behavior Therapist 31*, 150.

Hayes, S. C. (2008b). Climbing our hills: A beginning conversation on the comparison of acceptance and commitment therapy and traditional cognitive behavioral therapy. *Clinical Psychology: Science and Practice 15*, 286–295.

Hayes, S. C. (2008c). The roots of compassion. Keynote address presented at the fourth Acceptance and Commitment Therapy Summer Institute, Chicago, IL.

Hayes, S. C., Barnes-Holmes, D., & Roche, B. (Eds.). (2001). *Relational frame theory: A post-Skinnerian account of human language and cognition*. New York: Springer.

Hayes, S. C., & Long, D. M. (2013). Contextual behavioral science, evolution, and scientific epistemology. In S. Dymond & B. Roche (Eds.), *Advances in relational frame theory: Research and application* (pp. 5–26). Oakland, CA: New Harbinger.

Hayes, S. C., Luoma, J., Bond, F., Masuda, A., & Lillis, J. (2006). Acceptance and commitment therapy: Model, processes, and outcomes. *Behaviour Research and Therapy 44*, 1–25.

Hayes, S. C., & Shenk, C. (2004). Operationalizing mindfulness without unnecessary attachments. *Clinical Psychology Science and Practice 11*, 249–254.

Hayes, S. C., Strosahl, K. D., & Wilson, K. G. (1999). *Acceptance and commitment therapy: An experiential approach to behavior change*. New York: Guilford.

Hayes, S. C., Strosahl, K. D., & Wilson, K. G. (2012). *Acceptance and commitment therapy: The process and practice of mindful change* (2nd edition). New York: Guilford.

Hofmann, S. G., Grossman, P., & Hinton, D. E. (2011). Loving-kindness and compassion meditation: Potential for psychological interventions. *Clinical Psychology Review 31*, 1126–1132.

Hume, D. (2000). *A treatise of human nature.* Oxford, UK: Oxford University Press.

Hutcherson, C. A., Seppala, E. M., & Gross, J. J. (2008). Loving-kindness meditation increases social connectedness. *Emotion 8,* 720.

Hwang, J. Y., Plante, T., & Lackey, K. (2008). The development of the Santa Clara Brief Compassion Scale: An abbreviation of Sprecher and Fehr's Compassionate Love Scale. *Pastoral Psychology 56,* 421–428.

Judge, L., Cleghorn, A., McEwan, K., & Gilbert, P. (2012). An exploration of group-based compassion focused therapy for a heterogeneous range of clients presenting to a community mental health team. *International Journal of Cognitive Therapy 5,* 420–429.

Kabat-Zinn, J. (2009). Foreword. In F. Didonna (Ed.), *Clinical handbook of mindfulness* (pp. xxv–xxxiii). New York: Springer.

Kannan, D., & Levitt, H. M. (2013). A review of client self-criticism in psychotherapy. *Journal of Psychotherapy Integration 23,* 166–178.

Kashdan, T. B., & Rottenberg, J. (2010). Psychological flexibility as a fundamental aspect of health. *Clinical Psychology Review 30,* 865–878.

Kirsch, P., Esslinger, C., Chen, Q., Mier, D., Lis, S., Siddanti, S., Gruppe, H., Mattay, V. S., Gallhofer, B., & Meyer-Lindenberg, A. (2005). Oxytocin modulates neural circuitry for social cognition and fear in humans. *Journal of Neuroscience 25,* 11489–11493.

Kohlenberg, R. J., & Tsai, M. (1991). *Functional analytic psychotherapy.* New York: Springer.

Kolts, R. L. (2012). *The Compassionate mind approach to working with your anger: Using compassion-focused therapy.* London: Constable and Robinson.

Kornfield. J. (1993). *A path with heart.* New York: Bantam.

Kraus, S., & Sears, S. (2009). Measuring the immeasurables: Development and initial validation of the Self-Other Four Immeasurables (SOFI) scale based on Buddhist teachings on loving kindness, compassion, joy, and equanimity. *Social Indicators Research 92,* 169–181.

Kriegman, D. (1990). Compassion and altruism in psychoanalytic theory and evolutionary analysis of self psychology. *Journal of the American Academy Psychoanalysis 18,* 342–367.

Kriegman, D. (2000). Evolutionary psychoanalysis: Toward an adaptive, biological perspective on the clinical process in psychoanalytic psychotherapy. In P. Gilbert & K. Bailey (Eds.), *Genes on the couch: Explorations in evolutionary psychotherapy* (pp.71–92). London: Routledge.

Kuyken, W., Watkins, E., Holden, E., White, K., Taylor, R. S., Byford, S., Evans, A., Radford, S., Teasdale, J. D., & Dalgleish, T. (2010). How does mindfulness-based cognitive therapy work? *Behaviour Research and Therapy 48*, 1105–1112.

Laithwaite, H., O'Hanlon, M., Collins, P., Doyle, P., Abraham, L., & Porter, S. (2009). Recovery after psychosis (RAP): A compassion focused programme for individuals residing in high security settings. *Behavioural and Cognitive Psychotherapy 37*, 511–526.

Leary, M. R., Tate, E. B., Adams, C. E., Allen, A. B., & Hancock, J. (2007). Self-compassion and reactions to unpleasant self-relevant events: The implications of treating oneself kindly. *Journal of Personality and Social Psychology 92*, 887–904.

LeDoux, J. (1998). *The emotional brain: The mysterious underpinnings of emotional life.* New York: Simon and Schuster.

Levenson, R. W. (1994). Human emotion: A functional view. In P. Ekman & R. J. Davidson (Eds.), *The nature of emotion: Fundamental questions* (pp. 123–126). Oxford, UK: Oxford University Press.

Loewenstein, G., & Small, D. A. (2007). The scarecrow and the tin man: The vicissitudes of human sympathy and caring. *Review of General Psychology 11*, 112–126.

Lucre, K. M., & Corten, N. (2012). An exploration of group compassion-focused therapy for personality disorder. *Psychology and Psychotherapy: Theory, Research, and Practice 86*, 387–400.

Luoma, J., Drake, C. E., Kohlenberg, B. S., & Hayes, S. C. (2011). Substance abuse and psychological flexibility: The development of a new measure. *Addiction Research and Theory 19*, 3–13.

Lutz, A., Brefczynski-Lewis, J., Johnstone, T., & Davidson, R. J. (2008). Regulation of the neural circuitry of emotion by compassion meditation: Effects of meditative expertise. *PloS One 3*, e1897.

MacBeth, A., & Gumley, A. (2012). Exploring compassion: A meta-analysis of the association between self-compassion and psychopathology. *Clinical Psychology Review 32*, 545–552.

Mansfield, A. K., & Cordova, J. V. (2007). A behavioral perspective on adult attachment style, intimacy, and relationship health. In D. Woods & J. Kanter (Eds.), *Understanding behavior disorders: A contemporary behavioral perspective* (pp. 389–416). Reno, NV: Context Press.

McHugh, L., & Stewart, I. (2012). *The self and perspective taking: Contributions and applications from modern behavioral science.* Oakland, CA: New Harbinger.

McKay, M., & Fanning, P. (2000). *Self-esteem: A proven program of cognitive techniques for assessing, improving, and maintaining your self-esteem* (3rd edition). Oakland, CA: New Harbinger.

Mikulincer, M., & Shaver, P. R. (2007a). Boosting attachment security to promote mental health, prosocial values, and inter-group tolerance. *Psychological Inquiry 18*, 139–156.

Mikulincer, M., & Shaver, P. R. (2007b). *Attachment in adulthood: Structure, dynamics, and change.* New York: Guilford.

Morf, C. C., & Rhodewalt, F. (2001). Unraveling the paradoxes of narcissism: A dynamic self-regulatory processing model. *Psychological Inquiry 12*, 177–196.

Münte, T. F., Altenmüller, E., & Jäncke, L. (2002). The musician's brain as a model of neuroplasticity. *Nature Reviews Neuroscience 3*, 473–478.

Neff, K. D. (2003a). The development and validation of a scale to measure self-compassion. *Self and Identity 2*, 223–250.

Neff, K. D. (2003b). Self-compassion: An alternative conceptualization of a healthy attitude toward oneself. *Self and Identity 2*, 85–101.

Neff, K. D. (2009a). The role of self-compassion in development: A healthier way to relate to oneself. *Human Development 52*, 211–214.

Neff, K. D. (2009b). Self-compassion. In M. R. Leary & R. H. Hoyle (Eds.), *Handbook of individual differences in social behavior* (pp. 561–573). New York: Guilford.

Neff, K. D. (2011). Self-compassion, self-esteem, and well-being. *Social and Personality Psychology Compass 5*, 1–12.

Neff, K. D., Hsieh, Y., & Dejitterat, K. (2005). Self-compassion, achievement goals, and coping with academic failure. *Self and Identity 4*, 263–287.

Neff, K. D., Kirkpatrick, K., & Rude, S. S. (2007). Self-compassion and its link to adaptive psychological functioning. *Journal of Research in Personality 41*, 139–154.

Neff, K. D., Pisitsungkagarn, K., & Hsieh, Y. (2008). Self-compassion and self-construal in the United States, Thailand, and Taiwan. *Journal of Cross-Cultural Psychology 39*, 267–285.

Neff, K. D., Rude, S. S., & Kirkpatrick, K. (2007). An examination of self-compassion in relation to positive psychological functioning and personality traits. *Journal of Research in Personality 41*, 908–916.

Neff, K. D., & Tirch, D. (2013). Self-compassion and ACT. In T. B. Kashdan & J. Ciarrochi (Eds.), *Mindfulness, acceptance, and positive psychology: The seven foundations of well-being* (pp. 78–106). Oakland, CA: New Harbinger.

Neff, K. D., & Vonk, R. (2009). Self-compassion versus global self-esteem: Two different ways of relating to oneself. *Journal of Personality 77*, 23–50.

Negd, M., Mallan, K. M., & Lipp, O. V. (2011). The role of anxiety and perspective-taking strategy on affective empathic responses. *Behaviour Research and Therapy 49*, 852–857.

Nesse, R. (1998). Emotional disorders in evolutionary perspective. *British Journal of Medical Psychology 71*, 397–415.

Nhat Hanh, T. (1998). *The heart of the Buddha's teaching.* Berkeley, CA: Parallax Press.

Nowak, M., & Highfield, R. (2011). *SuperCooperators: Altruism, evolution, and why we need each other to succeed.* New York: Simon and Schuster.

Pace, T. W., Negi, L. T., Adame, D. D., Cole, S. P., Sivilli, T. I., Brown, T. D., Issa, M. J., & Raison, C. L. (2009). Effect of compassion meditation on neuroendocrine, innate immune, and behavioral responses to psychosocial stress. *Psychoneuroendocrinology 34*, 87–98.

Panksepp, J. (1994). The basics of basic emotion. In P. Ekman & R. J. Davidson (Eds.), *The nature of emotion: Fundamental questions* (pp. 237–242). Oxford, UK: Oxford University Press.

Pierson, H., & Hayes, S. (2007). Using acceptance and commitment therapy to empower the therapeutic relationship. In, P. Gilbert & R. Leahy (Eds.), *The therapeutic relationship in the cognitive behaviour therapies* (pp.205–228). London: Routledge.

Polk, K., & Schoendorff, B. (2014). Going viral. In K. Polk & B. Schoendorff (eds.), *The ACT matrix: A new approach to building psychological flexibility across settings and populations* (pp. 251–253). Oakland, CA: New Harbinger.

Porges, S. W. (2003). Social engagement and attachment. *Annals of the New York Academy of Sciences 1008*, 31–47.

Porges, S. W. (2007). The polyvagal perspective. *Biological Psychology 74*, 116–143.

Porter, R. (2002). *Madness: A Brief History.* New York: Oxford University Press.

Premack, D., & Woodruff, G. (1978). Does the chimpanzee have a theory of mind? *Behavioral and Brain Sciences 1*, 515–526.

Pryor, K. (2009). *Reaching the animal mind: Clicker training and what it teaches us about all animals.* New York: Simon and Schuster.

Rapgay, L. (2010). Classical mindfulness: Its theory and potential for clinical application. In M. G. T. Kwee (Ed.), *New horizons in Buddhist psychology* (pp. 333–352). Chagrin Falls, OH: Taos Institute Publications.

Rapgay, L., & Bystrisky, A. (2009). Classical mindfulness: An introduction to its theory and practice for clinical application. *Annals of the New York Academy of Sciences 1172*, 148–162.

Rector, N. A., Bagby, R. M., Segal, Z. V., Joffe, R. T., & Levitt, A. (2000). Self-criticism and dependency in depressed patients treated with cognitive therapy or pharmacotherapy. *Cognitive Therapy and Research 24*, 571–584.

Rein, G., Atkinson, M., & McCraty, R. (1995). The physiological and psychological effects of compassion and anger. *Journal of Advancement in Medicine 8*, 87–105.

Roche, B., Cassidy, S., & Stewart, I. (2013). Nurturing genius: Using relational frame theory to address a foundational aim of psychology. In T. B. Kashdan & J. Ciarrochi (Eds.), *Mindfulness, acceptance, and positive psychology: The seven foundations of well-being* (pp. 267–302). Oakland, CA: New Harbinger.

Rogers, C. R. (1965). *Client-centered therapy: Its current practice, implications, and theory.* Boston: Houghton-Mifflin.

Ruiz, F. J. (2010). A review of acceptance and commitment therapy (ACT) empirical evidence: Correlational, experimental psychopathology, component, and outcome studies. *International Journal of Psychology and Psychological Therapy 10*, 125–162.

Sapolsky, R. M. (2004). *Why zebras don't get ulcers.* New York: St Martin's Press.

Schanche, E., Stiles, T. C., McCullough, L., Svartberg, M., & Nielsen, G. H. (2011). The relationship between activating affects, inhibitory affects, and self-compassion in patients with Cluster C personality disorders. *Psychotherapy 48*, 293.

Schoendorff, B., Grand, J., & Bolduc, M. F. (2011). *La thérapie d'acceptation et d'engagement: Guide clinique.* Brussels: DeBoeck.

Schoendorff, B. Purcell-Lalonde, M., & O'Connor, K. (2014). Les thérapies de troisième vague dans le traitement du trouble obsessionnel-compulsif: Application de la thérapie d'acceptation et d'engagement. *Santé mentale au Québec 38*, 153–173.

Siegel, D. J. (2012). *The developing mind: How relationships and the brain interact to shape who we are.* New York: Guilford.

Skinner, B. F. (1974). *About behaviourism.* New York: Random House.

Slavich, G. M., & Cole, S. W. (2013). The emerging field of human social genomics. *Psychological Science.* Advance online publication. doi:10.1177/2167702613478594.

Sloman, L., Gilbert, P., & Hasey, G. (2003). Evolved mechanisms in depression: The role and interaction of attachment and social rank in depression. *Journal of Affective Disorders 74*, 107–121.

Smith, J. C. (2005). *Relaxation, meditation, and mindfulness: A mental health practitioner's guide to new and traditional approaches.* New York: Springer.

Solomon, S., Greenberg, J., & Pyszczynski, T. (1991). A terror management theory of social behavior: The psychological functions of self-esteem and cultural worldviews. In M. P. Zanna (Ed.), *Advances in experimental social psychology: Vol. 24* (pp. 93–159). New York: Academic Press.

Sprecher, S., & Fehr, B. (2005). Compassionate love for close others and humanity. *Journal of Social and Personal Relationships 22*, 629–651.

Strosahl, K. D., Hayes, S. C., Wilson, K. G., & Gifford, E. V. (2004). An ACT primer. In S. C. Hayes & K. D. Strosahl (Eds.), *A practical guide to acceptance and commitment therapy* (pp. 31–58). New York: Springer.

Tirch, D. D. (2010). Mindfulness as a context for the cultivation of compassion. *International Journal of Cognitive Therapy 3*, 113–123.

Tirch, D. D. (2012). *The compassionate-mind guide to overcoming anxiety: Using compassion-focused therapy to calm worry, panic, and fear.* London: Constable and Robinson.

Tirch, D. D., & Gilbert, P. (in press). Compassion-focused therapy: An introduction to experiential interventions for cultivating compassion. In D. McKay & N. Thoma (Eds.), *Working with emotion in cognitive-behavioral therapy.* New York: Guilford.

Tierney, S., & Fox, J. R. E. (2010). Living with the anorexic voice: A thematic analysis. *Psychology and Psychotherapy: Theory, Research, and Practice 83*, 243–254.

Tomasello, M., Call, J., & Gluckman, A. (1997). Comprehension of novel communicative signs by apes and human children. *Child Development 68*, 1067–1080.

Tompkins, S. S. (1963). *Affect, imagery, consciousness: Vol. II: The negative affects.* Oxford, UK: Springer.

Tooby, J., & Cosmides, L. (1990). The past explains the present: Emotional adaptations and the structure of ancestral environments. *Ethology and Sociobiology 11*, 375–424.

Törneke, N. (2010). *Learning RFT: An introduction to relational frame theory and its clinical application.* Oakland, CA: New Harbinger.

Tsai, M., & Kohlenberg, R. J. (2012). *Functional analytic psychotherapy: Distinctive features.* New York: Routledge.

Tsai, M., Kohlenberg, R. J., Kanter, J. W., Kohlenberg, B., Follette, W. C., & Callaghan, G. M. (2008). *Functional analytic psychotherapy: A therapist's guide to using awareness, courage, love, and behaviorism.* New York: Springer.

Uvnäs Moberg, K. (2013). *The hormone of closeness: The role of oxytocin in relationships.* London: Pinter and Martin.

Van Dam, N. T., Earleywine, M., & Borders, A. (2010). Measuring mindfulness? An item response theory analysis of the mindful attention awareness scale. *Personality and Individual Differences 49*, 805–810.

Van Dam, N. T., Sheppard, S. C., Forsyth, J. C., & Earleywine, M. (2011). Self-compassion is a better predictor than mindfulness of symptom severity and quality of life in mixed anxiety and depression. *Journal of Anxiety Disorders 25*, 123–130.

Vilardaga, R. (2009). A relational frame theory account of empathy. *International Journal of Behavioral Consultation and Therapy 5*, 178–184.

Von Eckardt, B. (1995). *What is cognitive science?* Cambridge, MA: MIT Press.

Wachtel, P. L. (1967). Conceptions of broad and narrow attention. *Psychological Bulletin 68*, 417–429.

Wallace, B. A. (2009). A mindful balance. *Tricycle*, Spring, 109–111.

Wang, S. (2005). A conceptual framework for integrating research related to the physiology of compassion and the wisdom of Buddhist teachings. In P. Gilbert (Ed.), *Compassion: Conceptualisations, research, and use in psychotherapy* (pp. 75–120). New York: Routledge.

Wenzlaff, R. M., & Wegner, D. M. (2000). Thought suppression. *Annual Review of Psychology 51*, 59–91.

Whelan, R., & Schlund, M. (2013). Reframing relational frame theory research: Gaining a new perspective through the application of novel behavioral and neurophysiological methods. In S. Dymond & B. Roche (Eds.), *Advances in relational frame theory: Research and application* (pp. 73–97). Oakland, CA: New Harbinger.

Whelton, W. J., & Greenberg, L. S. (2005). Emotion in self-criticism. *Personality and Individual Differences 38*, 1583–1595.

White, R. G., Gumley, A., McTaggart, J., Rattrie, L., McConville, D., Cleare, S., et al. (2011). A feasibility study of acceptance and commitment therapy for emotional dysfunction following psychosis. *Behaviour Research and Therapy 49*, 901–907.

Wilson, D. S. (2007). *Evolution for everyone: How Darwin's theory can change the way we think about our lives.* New York: Delacorte Press.

Wilson, D. S. (2008). Social semantics: Toward a genuine pluralism in the study of social behavior. *Journal of Evolutionary Biology 21*, 368–373.

Wilson, D. S., Hayes, S. C., Biglan, A., & Embry, D. (2012). Evolving the future: Toward a science of intentional change. *Behavioral and Brain Sciences.* Advance online publication.

Wilson, K. G., & DuFrene, T. (2009). *Mindfulness for two: An acceptance and commitment therapy approach to mindfulness in psychotherapy.* Oakland, CA: New Harbinger.

Wright, J. M., & Westrup, D. (in press). *Learning ACT for group treatment.* Oakland, CA: New Harbinger.

Yadavaia, J. E. (2013). *Using acceptance and commitment therapy to decrease high-prevalence psychopathology by targeting self-compassion: A randomized controlled trial.* Doctoral dissertation, University of Nevada, Reno.

Zuroff, D. C., Santor, D., & Mongrain, M. (2005). Dependency, self-criticism, and maladjustment. In J. S. Auerbach, K. N. Levy, & C. E. Schaffer (Eds.), *Relatedness, self-definition, and mental representation: Essays in honor of Sidney J. Blatt* (pp. 75–90). New York: Routledge.

Dennis Tirch, PhD, is founder and director of The Center for Mindfulness and Compassion Focused Therapy in New York and the Compassionate Mind Foundation USA. An internationally-known expert on compassion-focused psychology, Tirch is the author of several books, including *The Compassionate-Mind Guide to Overcoming Anxiety.* Tirch is assistant clinical professor at Weill Cornell Medical College in New York, NY, and trains psychotherapists throughout the world in applied mindfulness, acceptance, and compassion.

Benjamin Schoendorff, MA, MSc, is a licensed psychologist in Quebec, Canada, and founder of the Contextual Psychology Institute. An acceptance and commitment therapy (ACT) pioneer in the French-speaking world, he has authored, coauthored, and coedited several books about ACT and functional analytic psychotherapy (FAP), including *The ACT Matrix* with coeditor Kevin Polk. A peer-reviewed ACT trainer and certified FAP trainer, Schoendorff gives training workshops across the world. He lives near Montreal in Quebec, Canada, where he works as a researcher at the Montreal Mental Health University Institute.

Laura R. Silberstein, PsyD, is a licensed psychologist in New York and New Jersey. Silberstein is the director of The Center for Mindfulness and Compassion Focused Therapy in New York and has advanced training in evidence-based therapies such as compassion-focused therapy (CFT), acceptance and commitment therapy (ACT), dialectical behavior therapy (DBT), and cognitive behavioral therapy (CBT) for adults and adolescents. Silberstein is also a clinical supervisor, CFT trainer, and coauthor of *Buddhist Psychology and Cognitive Behavioral Therapy.*

Foreword writer **Paul Gilbert, PhD,** is world-renowned for his work on depression, shame, and self-criticism. He is head of the mental health research unit at the University of Derby in the United Kingdom, founder of compassion-focused therapy (CFT), and author of several books, including *The Compassionate Mind* and *Overcoming Depression.*

Foreword writer **Steven C. Hayes, PhD,** is Nevada Foundation Professor in the department of psychology at the University of Nevada, NV. An author of thirty-four books and more than 470 scientific articles, his research focuses on how language and thought lead to human suffering. Hayes is cofounder of acceptance and commitment therapy (ACT)—a powerful therapy method that is useful in a wide variety of areas—and has served as president of several scientific societies. He has received several national awards, including the Lifetime Achievement Award from the Association for Behavioral and Cognitive Therapies.

Index

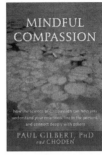

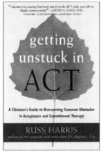

Register your **new harbinger** titles for additional benefits!

When you register your **new harbinger** title—purchased in any format, from any source—you get access to benefits like the following:

- Downloadable accessories like printable worksheets and extra content

- Instructional videos and audio files

- Information about updates, corrections, and new editions

Not every title has accessories, but we're adding new material all the time.

Access free accessories in 3 easy steps:

1. Sign in at NewHarbinger.com (or **register** to create an account).

2. Click on **register a book**. Search for your title and click the **register** button when it appears.

3. Click on the **book cover or title** to go to its details page. Click on **accessories** to view and access files.

That's all there is to it!

If you need help, visit:

NewHarbinger.com/accessories

new harbinger
CELEBRATING
40 YEARS